Local, Slow and Sustainable Fashion

"(While) we search for examples of outstanding sustainable practices, that could be amplified and applied to sustain a more gentle and efficient way of living in future, the authors (of this book) explore slow and indigenous approaches to textiles, while considering the optimal use of precious natural and renewable resources, such as wool. The chapters read as intriguing short case studies on their own, but collectively showcase a deep understanding of the threads that bind us together and how these could be strengthened to optimise natural fibre applications for future generations. Textile nerds will love it and newcomers will be inspired to learn more."

—Dalena White, *Secretary General IWTO, Brussels, Belgium*

"I have always used wool and then fell in love with woolgrowers when I visited Tasmania in 2016, so for me this book is a total must read for anyone working on sustainability and the future of our planet."

—Livia Firth, *Creative Director, Eco Age Limited, London, UK*

"Clothing is an essential part of human life, along with food and shelter. Furthermore, its culturally significant, defining who we are and where we belong. Alas, finding better solutions to the harmful ways the industry which supply our clothing operates today, is of upmost urgency. This collection of research articles offers knowledge and insights into the complex world of fiber, specifically wool, and suggests reestablishing more local value chain as part of the solution. It's a must read for those who want to be part of a much-needed change."

—Gisle Mariani Mardal, *Head of Development Norwegian Fashion & Textile Agenda, Oslo, Norway*

"Fast fashion is almost as destructive as fast food. And both embody a mindset that treats workers, consumers, livestock, and the environment like disposable commodities. Instead of having the wool pulled over eyes, through deceptive mass marketing and outright lies, we need wool back in our lives. Especially wool that's been produced locally, regeneratively, with compassion for the people and animals who make it. This important book explains how that can be done."

—Eric Schlosser, *Author, Fast Food Nation, New York, USA*

"Klepp and Tobiasson have done a remarkable job (...) and have given a comprehensive account of the successful revival of small-scale processing and marketing of local wool in some Scandinavian and Baltic countries, and set this in the context of the global wool industry and its fight to retain share in a market dominated by synthetic fibres. The authors suggest a return to the model of local consumption of local production, where profit and growth are no longer the main drivers, as a more sustainable way of clothing ourselves and our homes and reinvigorating the sheep industry in European countries. (...) Wool, with its deep roots in our European culture, our economies and our wardrobes, is ideally suited to change this."

—Lesley Prior, *Sheep Farmer, Tellenby Merino, Devon, UK*

"Such an interesting read, showing how everything is intertwined: sourcing, craftmanship, culture, economy, philosophy, physics, degrowth... A voice that should be heard in the global discussions at a time when a deep transformation is needed: the textile industry must be held accountable for its environmental and social impacts or else our planet will become the ultimate fashion victim. If clothes can tell a story, what message are we leaving for future generations?"

—Valeria Botta, *ECOS – Environmental Coalition on Standards, Brussels, Belgium*

"For the last 20 years I've been immersed in the world of fashion and textiles and it's always struck me that the list of textile features and benefits of wool read like those from a innovative new super-fibre, add the sustainable benefits of localised, small-scale wool production and you may have the most climate positive, high performing textile there is. This book outlines a solid history and case for wool as the fibre of choice for an over-burdened planet and how perhaps it's not new ideas we need in response to the climate crisis, but a rethinking of what 'good' 'better' or indeed 'best' may look like."

—Debbie Luffman, *Finisterre, ThinkCircular, Cornwall, UK*

Ingun Grimstad Klepp ·
Tone Skårdal Tobiasson
Editors

Local, Slow and Sustainable Fashion

Wool as a Fabric for Change

palgrave
macmillan

Editors
Ingun Grimstad Klepp
Consumption Research Norway (SIFO)
Oslo Metropolitan University
Oslo, Norway

Tone Skårdal Tobiasson
Nordic Initiative Clean and Ethical Fashion
Oslo, Norway

ISBN 978-3-030-88299-0 ISBN 978-3-030-88300-3 (eBook)
https://doi.org/10.1007/978-3-030-88300-3

This Palgrave Macmillan imprint is published by the registered company Springer Nature Switzerland AG
The registered company address is: Gewerbestrasse 11, 6330 Cham, Switzerland

Preface

This is a book about one fibre, wool, its role in the future of a more sustainable global textile industry, and a new approach to how we can organize how we use local resources in a better way. As a reader, you may wonder why this is important. As the latest report published in August 2021 by the Intergovernmental Panel on Climate Change so clearly states, we must act now. In the clothing and textile sector, several decennials have been wasted on chasing new technology—most hardly suited for reducing the environmental impact at the scale needed—along with a hopelessly unproductive discussion around which fibres are 'greener' than others. We have no more time to waste. Not because this industry is the largest or the worst, but because of the overload and pressure on land, oil reserves, chemicals, water and more for producing clothes that are thrown away after too few uses, or not used at all—must stop. A sector with such a gross over-production and over-consumption of finite resources has an enormous potential to improve its footprint. We have chosen the lens of wool, as it is the fibre we know the best and which is Indigenous to our home country, Norway.

This book was written on the initiative of the publisher, Palgrave Macmillan, on the basis of a final report from a research project on wool. KRUS—enhancing value chains in Norway, sought to take better care of the Norwegian wool and discuss what local clothes are or can be. As KRUS ended, we saw new projects emerging in the international landscape, some in cooperation with the 'team' that had been forged through the aforementioned project. WOOLUME is such a project, and continues the work with local wool and value chains; however, transferred to Polish mountain sheep and their fleeces. With both the projects and with this book, we want to contribute to sustainable development and a good place to live for all who walk the Earth, on two or four legs, or with wings and fins for that matter. We want positive change to happen faster, dig deeper and galvanize more effect than what politics and business have so far been willing to. We also want people to feel at home in their clothes, feel beautiful, warm and partake in all settings—be they social or in lone communion with nature—with the freedom of being well-dressed. We believe that living within the planetary boundaries does not have to make our lives poorer, nor less filled with fun or colour.

KRUS was mainly a Norwegian project, but sheep, and other animals that have those much-coveted fibres, are found all over the globe. In many places, we find clothes, textiles, use patterns, techniques and production modes that have been adapted and developed over thousands of years. However, cultural diversity, heritage and richness of variation are threatened by the globalized industrial development and are currently poorly safeguarded. We hear reports from around the world that the cost of shearing sheep has surpassed the economic gain—though the animals must be shorn, for animal welfare reasons, and wool is a valuable and versatile fibre. So, something must be wrong. We will seek to provide insight into exactly what ails the system and a way out of this conundrum through the infinite abundance of examples of value chains for wool, current and historical, and how they have evolved and changed—and in many ways remained the same. In other words, our goal is neither to write a book about Norwegian nor Polish wool but to provide insight into better care-taking of both wool and other natural fibres, through learning from history and looking towards a more sustainable future.

Textile production is one of the world's most globalized industries, where not only does the production involve a massive transfer of raw materials and processed goods through a long and complicated supply chain, but where the second-hand clothing market is also massive, global and problematic. In other words, each garment has travelled more than most people in the world travel in a lifetime. It is as if this global aspect of clothes is so obvious that the word 'local clothes' gets stuck in the mouth. The same giant apparel chains are found in every city around the world, and to be blunt—they don't necessarily bring more diversity or beauty into our lives.

At the same time, clothing is also one of the things that actually characterizes local cultures. In Norway, the bunad (national costume) indicates which valley you or your closest relatives come from (at least that is one of the features), and most Indigenous peoples are recognized and create community precisely through clothing, often with a long history and advanced craft techniques. These have been developed based on locally available raw materials or those imported, perhaps also decorated with imported valuables.

The editors of this book have their professional roots in consumer research and textile sustainability. We are specialists mainly in the use of clothing but have studied fashion, tailoring, crafts, ethnology and sociology. At the same time, KRUS was a project with an emphasis on the *collaboration* that happened and happens in the value chain. This means that it was important for us to see production and consumption in context. Sheep farmers (or wool growers as they are called in other parts of the world), carders, spinners, knitting factories, weaving mills and designers have something in common with you and me—we are all part of the value chain—also sometimes called the textile 'sector'. We believe that it is through closer cooperation in these localized value chains that the greatest environmentally positive results can be achieved. This is a radical thought. Closer cooperation can be achieved, among other things, through production and consumption taking place closer to where we are, linked to our territories—or *terroir*. This book attempts to bring forward this connection between consumption and production, two processes in which it is just as fruitless to discuss what is the cause and what is the effect, as debating about which came first, the chicken or the egg.

However, the place for wool fibres in the wardrobe and in markets of the future also depends on a variety of political decisions and economic processes. No man is an island. We believe that the wicked problem, that a majority of the raw wool in the EU is thrown away before it is even used, is now a crisis of magnitude. The crisis has been augmented by the Covid-19 pandemic, but this does not excuse that any fibre causes serious environmental problems, alongside animal and human suffering, nor that this is the result of the same economic system where profit is the goal and competition is the means. That is why we have included a discussion about economic models which is part of the 'green growth' debate. Is growth crucial, or is it even part of the future our Earth demands? Is a paradigm shift with continuous growth, however 'green', possible?

How the discussion about sustainability develops is also important for the future. What are the premises for the debate? Who owns the truth and, not least, what should count when we measure? We not only need to contribute to wool being availed and used more sustainably, we also need to contribute to the debate so that we do not become helpless observers as wool is removed from the list of fibres with eco-credentials. It may sound incredible to those who have not followed the ongoing debate, but this is a very real outcome of today's discussions around sustainability, whether it be climate change, biodiversity, environmental footprint and even animal welfare. Let this book enlighten you to the seemingly counter-intuitive greenwashing of non-renewable fibres.

Wool is close to our hearts, and the book is written to spread knowledge about how wool can contribute to sustainable development. Whether wool and products from animals are generally better or not, opinions are divided. We have a growing vegan movement that does not in any way or form accept products from animals, be it honey, eggs or—wool. We want to contribute with perspectives related to this debate, so that you, the reader, can think this through. In this discussion, we draw on other natural fibres and their status against the alternative: synthetic fibres. Don't misunderstand us, synthetics have their place in some products, where their properties are unsurpassed. However, their cheap price and exponential growth in the market offers concern when they displace more expensive and better-suited fibres for a given use. Especially if this is based on industry tools that give a green light for their eco-credentials.

While the environmental debate has been about what we CANNOT continue to do, less has offered a way forward. We have tried to make the centre of gravity as forward-leaning as possible. We want to show what is possible if we want to make the change. We must set the stage for a world where we can be well-dressed without ruining the access to resources for future generations. That was the essence of Norway's former Prime Minister, Gro Harlem Brundtland's, definition of sustainability. An equilibrium. This may be too late, but it is high time to roll up our sleeves and get started.

The book consists of 7 chapters. They can be read as separate articles, or as a complete volume. We think the latter will be most useful. We also have a glossary that explains difficult words and those pesky acronyms. All in all, we hope that language and acronyms will not be what stands in the way of better collaboration, vibrant communities and beautiful textiles—with provenance and value for us all.

We would like to thank: The Norwegian Research Council, The National Centre for Research and Development, EEA Norway Grants and the Norwegian Agricultural and Food Industry Research Funds. We are also thankful to anonymous peer reviewers and those in our professional networks who have participated and will cooperate in this important work going forward. Our most profound thanks, however, goes to Vilde Haugrønning, Lisbeth Løvbak Berg and the rest of the clothing research team at SIFO, OsloMet[1] for their invaluable help in getting everything in order during the very last inning of this book-marathon and because they, together with all those engaged young people out there, are our true hope for the future.

Oslo, Norway

Ingun Grimstad Klepp
Tone Skårdal Tobiasson

[1] https://clothingresearch.oslomet.no/about-us/

Contents

Notes on Contributors

Jan Broda works as a Professor at the University of Bielsko-Biala, Faculty of Materials, Civil and Environmental Engineering. He completed his master' degree in textile engineering (1982) and then obtained a Ph.D. in textile engineering from the Technical University of Lodz (1991). He combines research and teaching on technical textiles, fibres science and high-performance fibres. His research interests include the structure and properties of natural and man-made fibres, formation and modification of polypropylene fibres and functionalization of textiles. Broda is the project leader of the WOOLUME project.

Rebecca Burgess, M.ed is Executive Director of Fibershed 2010–2020, an international member organization that develops regional and regenerative fibre systems based in California. Her many roles and capabilities include non-profit executive level management, expository writing, public speaking, fundraising, textile and ecology focused curricula development and delivery (private and public universities), community organizer and coordinator, agricultural cooperative organizer, in-field design and implementation capabilities specific to regenerative agriculture demonstration, advanced textile weaving (mechanical and handloom), natural dye recipe developer, farm-to-skin textile product development and management, published author (Workman & Chelsea Green publishing houses). She is currently involved in the Amazing Grazing project, which we describe in this book.

Maria Ehrnström-Fuentes is an assistant professor at the Department of Management and Organization at Hanken School of Economics in Finland. Her research focuses on the interaction of people, places and nonhuman beings in the organizing of sustainability in the local sphere. She has also an extensive record of critical examination of the politics of CSR in natural resource-based industries, Indigenous ways of knowing and organizing around issues of sustaining land-based practices. Her current Finnish Academy Project focuses on the organizational aspects of grassroots movements engaged in building alternatives from below, through regenerative land practices, and how these place-based organizations contribute to beneficial outcomes for the climate and the ecology in different parts of the world.

Ingvild Svorkmo Espelien CEO of Selbu spinneri in Norway, is a biologist (Cand sci.). Selbu Spinning Mill is a wool mill, currently employing four. A passion for wool, quality and caring for the local natural resources is a great driver for both her and the mill she started, aiming from the start to increase the demand and price of pigmented wool from the old, indigenous Norwegian sheep breeds. Developing and disseminating knowledge about the different properties of wool and traditional crafts is also important. The spinning mill cooperates with a number of other local/national businesses in the wool value chain. Espelien is one of the active partners in WOOLUME, and is also part of Amazing Grazing and hiWOOL projects; besides having a vital role in KRUS.

Sophia E. Hagolani-Albov, M.Sc. is a doctoral researcher in the Interdisciplinary Environmental Studies Programme (DENVI) at the University of Helsinki. She is a student affiliate of the Helsinki Institute of Sustainability Science (HELSUS) and the Program Coordinator of the

Global Extractivisms and Alternatives Initiative (EXALT). Her research is rooted in sustainable food systems, specifically the concept of Agroecological Symbiosis (AES) and the localization of food production, processing and consumption in the Finnish countryside. She is originally from California.

Vilde Haugrønning is a Ph.D. Candidate in the research project CHANGE at Consumption Research Norway (SIFO). She holds a master's degree from the Centre for Environment and Development (SUM) at the University of Oslo and a bachelor's degree in Social Anthropology and Visual Culture from NTNU. She has previously researched food consumption in Norwegian households, and her current research area is consumer research on clothing consumption and sustainability. Her Ph.D. project is about the use of clothing in everyday life from a practice oriented perspective, investigating the underlying drivers of growth and the dynamics and complexities behind women's and men's clothing consumption.

Kjellaug Isaksen is a Sámi duojár and scholar, and works as head of the Museum Department at the Davvi álbmogiid guovddáš/Centre for Northern peoples in Norway, and situates her approach within contemporary Sámi reality. She is educated in duodji, Sámi culture and art history, and builds her work on multicultural experiences and rootedness in Sámi culture and identity. Her main focus is on research and working practice with traditional Indigenous knowledge within the Sámi art and craft field. Her work includes how research can be conducted and how institutions engage and disseminate Indigenous perspectives by sharing strategies relating to the value, the transmission and representation of Indigenous knowledge from within.

Ingun Grimstad Klepp is a Professor in Clothing and Sustainability at Consumption Research Norway (SIFO), at Oslo Metropolitan University. She has led a number of research projects on wool, including KRUS, and has been central in all the projects from which this book springs. She currently leads two research projects on clothing and sustainability, CHANGE and Wasted Textiles. The relationship between clothes, social and physical characteristics and how these are woven together is at the core of her interest. She hates waste and loves to spin threads and words together into texts and textiles as well as to share the joy of developing knowledge. She has written several books and articles about sustainable textile, wool, knitting, laundry and clothing together with good colleagues and uses a lot of time on popular dissimilation and discussions. Klepp wrote her M.A. and Ph.D. in Ethnology on leisure time and outdoor life at the University of Oslo. She combines historical perspectives with knowledge of the textile's technical properties and social aspects.

Katarzyna Kobiela-Mendrek works as an Assistant Professor at the Faculty of Materials, Civil and Environmental Engineering of the University of Bielsko-Biala, Poland. She is a graduate of the Lodz University of Technology, Branch in Bielsko-Biala. She received Ph.D. in textile engineering from the University of Bielsko-Biala in 2006. Her scientific interests have evolved from issues related to aesthetic properties through the hygienic properties of textiles to fatigue research of composites based on textiles. In recent years, she has participated in international projects on the application of geotextiles and wool waste fibres for soil reinforcement and erosion control on slopes and embankments. She is an active partner in the WOOLUME project.

Kirsi Laitala, Ph.D. is a Senior Researcher at Consumption Research Norway (SIFO), Oslo Metropolitan University. Her main research area is sustainability and clothing consumption, and she has researched and published on areas related to clothing quality, maintenance, safety, environmental issues, design, as well as fit and size issues. Her current interests include sufficiency connected to standard of living. She uses interdisciplinary research methods based on her educational background in textile engineering (M.Sc.), Ph.D. in Product Design and long experience working with social science research methods. She currently heads the LASTING project.

Lorrie Miller (settler) is an artist, educator and writer. She weaves her passion for textile art forms with her interest in slow and Indigenous pedagogies. She holds a Ph.D. and an M.A. from the University of British Columbia and a B.Ed. from the University of Regina. She teaches

Textile Design and Pedagogical Approaches: Art Education for the Department of Curriculum Studies at the University of British Columbia and has worked in teacher education for much of this past decade. As the Associate Director for the Institute for Veterans Transition, at UBC, she works towards making the university a more welcoming place for veterans who are transitioning from active military service into civilian life by way of the academy.

Mafalda Pacheco is a Ph.D., Architect by the IST/University of Lisbon (2018) and a research fellow at CHAM—Centre for the Humanities of the FCSH/NOVA University. In 2015 she founded the project and the association Salva a Lã Portuguesa (Save the Portuguese wool), being the president since then. She is part of the scientific committee of DTex International Textile Design Conference. Her research focuses on the history of traditional architecture, construction and textiles with several works published on these subjects.

Jane Philbrick is the artist founder of the farm-specific wool initiative TILL: bioFASHIONtech in New London, Connecticut. In 2021, the name changed to Wear Wool New London, and the initiative is anchored by an environmentally sensitive wool scouring system providing the flexibility to serve the rich diversity of breeds of the small (compared to the American West) sheep industry in the Northeast. She also was instrumental in launching the local UCRF Connecticut Chapter on March 7, 2020.

Monika Rom is an Assistant Professor at the University of Bielsko-Biala, Faculty of Materials, Civil and Environmental Engineering in Poland, where she has been since 2003. She received M.S. from Lodz University of Technology in 2001, and a Ph.D. in Textile Engineering from the University of Bielsko-Biala in 2008. Her research interest lies in the broad areas of textile engineering and materials from bioresources. Specifically, her research focuses on the following areas: (1) structure and properties of wood-based cellulosic fibres from enzymatically biotransformed pulps, (2) structure and biodegradation of polymers from bioresources, (3) biodegradation of wool and valorization of low-quality wool by nonstandard applications. She is an active partner in the WOOLUME project.

Anna Schytte Sigaard holds a master's degree from the Centre for Development and the Environment (SUM) and a bachelor's degree in Sociology, both from the University of Oslo. She has previously researched cotton production in India and is currently a Ph.D. Candidate in the project Wasted Textiles at Consumption Research Norway (SIFO). The topic of her Ph.D. project is synthetic textile waste in Norwegian households.

Tone Smith is a researcher in the fields of ecological economics, social-ecological transformation and degrowth. Originally a human geographer, she recently completed a doctoral degree in ecological economics at the WU Wien.After a career in the field of sustainability indicators, environmental performance assessment and environmental statistics (with Statistics Norway and the OECD), her doctoral thesis was a critical examination of the role of numbers in environmental politics. Since 2019, she is an independent researcher and freelance writer. She is also head of the advisory board of Rethinking Economics Norway and is active in the international degrowth movement. She is originally from Norway.

Tone Skårdal Tobiasson journalist and author, went from managing editor of fashion magazines in Norway to become a founder of NICE (Nordic Initiative Clean & Ethical) Fashion, originally a platform for sustainable development within the Nordic Fashion Association. Currently, she is responsible for the dissemination of several major research projects in Norway, related to wool, localism, sustainable, slow and regenerative fashion, and has been involved in all the projects mentioned in the book. One of these, Amazing Grazing, also involves food. She has co-written 'Pure Wool', the history of Norwegian knitting, 'Knit with Norwegian wool', and three books on apparel care, sustainable apparel and repairing clothes together with Klepp. She is a contributor to EcoTextile News, Wool2Yarn and other international publications, and is a Board member of the Union of Concerned Researchers in Fashion.

Abbreviations

AWI	Australian Wool Innovation
ELRP	Earth Logic Research Plan
GND	Green New Deal
GWP	Global Warming Potential
IWTO	International Wool Textile Organisation
LCA	Life Cycle Assessment
NIBIO	Norwegian Institute of Bioeconomy Research
NRC	Norwegian Research Council
NSG	Norwegian Association of Sheep and Goat Breeders
NSRS	Norwegian National Sheep Recording System
PDO	Protected Designation of Origin
PEF	Product Environmental Footprint
PGI	Protected Geographical Indication
SAC	Sustainable Apparel Coalition
SDG	Sustainable Development Goals (as defined by the United Nations)
SIFO	Consumption Research Norway
SPT	Social Practice Theory
TBL	Triple Bottom Line

List of Figures

1

KRUSing into the Future: Restoring a Local Value Chain Through Cooperation

Ingun Grimstad Klepp, Vilde Haugrønning, and Tone Skårdal Tobiasson

KRUS, which means crimp in Norwegian and refers to the exceptional good crimp in the Norwegian crossbred wool, is also the title of an extensive 4-year research project Enhancing local value chains in Norway. It was financed by the Norwegian Research Council (NRC) and led by Professor Ingun Grimstad Klepp at SIFO/Oslo Metropolitan University, with Tone Skårdal Tobiasson as responsible for dissemination. Though KRUS officially concluded in 2019, ripples from the project

I. G. Klepp · V. Haugrønning (✉)
Consumption Research Norway (SIFO), Oslo Metropolitan University, Oslo, Norway
e-mail: vildeh@oslomet.no

I. G. Klepp
e-mail: ingunk@oslomet.no

T. S. Tobiasson
Nordic Initiative Clean & Ethical Fashion, Oslo, Norway

I. G. Klepp and T. S. Tobiasson (eds.), *Local, Slow and Sustainable Fashion*,
https://doi.org/10.1007/978-3-030-88300-3_1

have extended into new networks, research projects, international attention and additional emergent opportunities. One of these opportunities is the creation of this volume, and most of the following chapters have threads that weave back to KRUS. In the process of crafting this volume, authors have considered the subjects and themes in other chapters. With this weave, we find the pattern for systemic change (Fletcher, 2010), which we explore on multiple levels throughout this book, then in the last chapter shape this as a regenerative vision for a fibre and fashion future within the boundaries of the planet.

In order to understand the impact of KRUS, and how a research project can create change, we first need to understand the reason why the project was initiated, how it was structured, what the anticipated outcomes were, the emergent outcomes and some failures along the way. To do that, we need to look back at the preceding wool valuation projects in Norway.[1] KRUS has specifically looked into problems that surfaced during Valuing Norwegian Wool, which related to issues in the value chain for wool: there was no public or political attention or understanding of local production as an opportunity within sustainability and business development. There was also a lack of cooperation, product development, transparency and coherent labelling. Additionally, there were challenges with the older sheep breeds, specifically those with links back to Viking times, which had galvanised the KreaNord project VikingGold. In KRUS, this translated into combining research with development work on several levels within the value chain. When we combined biology, service and technology surrounding important questions related to breeding and improved wool quality, new business models, marketing and the important issue of labels of origin—the ultimate aim emerged: To increase the use of Norwegian wool in the Norwegian market so that it does not disappear into a global market with low value creation and close to zero transparency.

We wanted Norwegian sheep on the red carpet and designers and users of wool in the sheep barns, and planned to redefine what sustainable fashion could look like, through uniting ideas and working methods,

[1] (1) Valuing Norwegian Wool (2010–2012) and (2) KreaNord project VikingGold (2013–2015).

activities and people who seldom interact (Engeström, 2001). We wanted people to experience and gain knowledge of where clothes come from and understand the local systems of clothing production and consumption. The cross fertilisation of disciplines and institutions was 'food for thought' and increasingly stood out as a vital ingredient in any work towards economically and ecologically sustainable development.

For the reader who is unfamiliar with wool in Norway, here are some basic facts. Most of the wool is collected by two major actors, the farmers' cooperative Norilia, and the privately owned slaughterhouse company Fatland, through the wool stations that are spread throughout Norway. Almost all the wool is sent to Bradford in the United Kingdom, where the wool is scoured, after which somewhere around 20% or more returns to Norway to the spinning mills, and also to a major weaving mill (Gudbrandsdalens Ullvarefabrikk AS), where the wool is processed into yarns, *mostly* for hand-knitting. Some companies who use Norwegian wool in their products rely on a different value chain, such as international spinners elsewhere, f. ex. Dale of Norway, who buy their yarns from Schoeller, and some of the spinners scour some wool themselves to avoid the costs and complexities of transporting it in and out of the EU.

There are several reasons why Norway still has an intact production or value chain, and we have earlier in our writings pointed to the popularity of the wool-based national costumes—the *bunad*—and to the importance of hand-knitting as a wide-spread hobby, which increased even more during the lockdown in the Covid-19 pandemic (Klepp & Laitala, 2018; Klepp & Tobiasson, 2013). Norway also has its own wool classification system, The Norwegian Wool Standard, which is controlled by Animalia/Wool Advisory Office and the Agricultural Directorate. It differs from wool classification systems in other countries by not focusing on the breeds, but rather on when the wool is sheared (fall or spring), micron, whiteness/pigmentation, vegetable matter, fibre length and crimp. Norway thereby has a wide variation in wool qualities from various breeds, that may fall into the same class. There is, however, a distinction between the dual-coated and the uniform length wool.

New income opportunities for agriculture in Norway and Europe have been studied by many (Almås, 2002; Bessière, 1998; Marsden, 1998), as well as niche products, alongside alternative marketing and channels for sale (Rye, 2011; Vittersø, 2012). These opportunities and the way they have been studied are very much based on the current economic, market-based system, which we will discuss in more detail in Chapter 6. We will already here establish that we are not enamoured by the ongoing push for 'green growth' or 'circular fashion', which we will return to in almost all the following chapters. However, in this chapter, we will shy away from the major and important discussion, except related to two points: Volume and local. But before we go into this minefield, let's discuss labelling.

The role of labelling schemes tied to local provenance has also surfaced as a means for adding value (Morgan et al., 2008). However, most of these studies have centred on food and not on textiles, or leather and fur for that matter, as agriculture tends to be synonymous with food. This is the case even if the same animal and thus the same farm can contribute to both food and fibre. 'Local' and 'slow' food have received a lot of attention; and while 'slow fashion' has begun to permeate the public debate as the anti-thesis of 'fast fashion', 'local fashion' had yet to reach the same noise level as the KRUS project embarked on its four-year hiatus.

Even before KRUS was launched, we had seen sheep farmers and micro-/small-sized businesses start to promote local wool in yarns and woven products. However, there was no systematic marketing of these products and, even if we had explored labelling schemes in Valuing Norwegian Wool—authorities and the value chain from wool collecting to spinning mills and other commercial actors—agreed neither on the scope nor the premises for such a scheme. This, in spite of the fact that knitting yarns made from local Norwegian wool lack transparency in the supply chain, and yarns with Norwegian flags or other national symbols are spun in far-off places like China and made from unidentifiable wool still gained local credibility. Unfortunately, the more the Norwegian flag were used, the less likely it was that the product was made of Norwegian wool (Hebrok et al., 2012; Klepp et al., 2014).

A Brief History of Wool Labelling

Labels of origin, or labels that in other ways signal an added value for the consumer, are considered practical and in many ways vital for products in a competitive market. These could be eco-credentials, such as the Nordic Swan or the EU Eco-Label. For wool, Woolmark is the label most often associated with the fibre itself; however, even if many consumers think this is an eco-label—the label does first and foremost reflect the percentage of wool content. AWI (Australian Wool Innovation), who acquired ownership to the almost 70-year-old label in 2001, test products that carry the label on quality aspects (Hebrok et al., 2012) and this is also what most consumers associate with Woolmark: Quality wool.

In some countries (not in Norway), a 'made in' label is required, but this will usually refer to the last or most important process in the production and says nothing about where the raw materials come from. To distinguish wool products in the market, labelling tied to origin is an emerging trend. This is inspired by the slow and local food movement on the one hand and animal welfare on the other. In the case of wool, it would be possible to tie a labelling scheme to the animal as such—the sheep—and have the same origin-label include both the meat and the wool, as well as other products from the ruminant. This was explored both in Valuing Norwegian Wool and KRUS, as Norway has several such labelling schemes for food. The Work Package 'Marketing and Transparency' in KRUS studied this in depth and explored policies tied to this in Norway. A separate study also looked at origin labels tied specifically to wool, most of which are privately owned labels (Vittersø et al., 2017). This is explored further in a project called Amazing Grazing, which began in April 2021, funded by the Norwegian Agriculture and Food Industry Research Funds. The project aims to provide new knowledge on how sheep rangeland grazing can be part of sustainable food and fibre (textile) systems, and how stakeholders in the value chain can enhance value creation in a wide sense.

Some labels of origin for wool are: SwissWool, British Wool, Icelandic Wool, American Wool and Wools of New Zealand. There are also labels for South African and Dutch wool; however, these are less known. When it comes to wool-related labels tied to animal welfare and/or ecological claims; the third-party label ZQ[2] originated in New Zealand—but wool from anywhere in the world can join the scheme. This is also the case with the SustainaWOOL scheme (based in Australia). The Responsible Wool Standard is owned and operated by the international NGO Textile Exchange, and has no geographical ties. The only exception of a third party approved label for wool we have found, was the EU-approved label of origin for organic Shetland wool under the system of protected designations (Protected Designation of Origin) (Vittersø et al., 2017). We come back to this discussion in Chapter 3.

As a result of KRUS, even though the project itself was not able to galvanise a process resulting in a Norwegian wool label, over a year after the project ended, Animalia (Norway's ruminant and poultry research and development office/Wool Advisory Office) initiated a dialogue with the two wool-collection organisations in Norway, Norilia and Fatland. The aim was to undertake the creation of a Norwegian label of origin.

There is, however, an internationally used label for Norwegian wool, *Viking Wool from Norway* (Fig. 1.1), owned and marketed by Curtis Wool Direct. It appears in wool trade publications alongside other private labels developed by the same company, also a Real Shetland wool label, which has nothing to do with the aforementioned PDO for organic Shetland wool. On the Norwegian market, Rauma Yarns and Røros Tweed (owned by the same company and family) developed their own private label for 100% Norwegian wool used to market knitting yarns, wool sweaters and woven wool throws. Vingtor, a company producing Norwegian Viking-inspired throws and outerwear in Norwegian wool, has developed their own label as well, *Norwegian Wool* (Fig. 1.2), with a pictogram of a sheep with woven 'threads' on the body. Flokk furniture has also developed a label for Norwegian Wool, in a simple, Nordic aesthetic, together with the weaving mill, Gudbrandsdalens Ullvarefabrikk (Fig. 1.3). They were very early in developing furniture textiles in Norwegian wool from crossbred sheep.

Rauma Yarns and Røros Tweed, as mentioned, have their own label; which they are currently updating to better reflect its purpose. They also

[2] ZQ has since we wrote the report morphed into ZQRX, which is for wool in regenerative agricultural systems.

Fig. 1.1 Curtis Wool Direct's label: *Viking Wool from Norway* (*Photo credit* Tone Skårdal Tobiasson)

describe that this wool has the Nordic Swan label and Cradle 2 Cradle status on their websites. The products, on the other hand, do not use the Swan label or C2C status—as the downstream production of the yarns and the products after the wool has left Haworth Wool Scouring Mill in the UK have not undergone the stringent scrutiny of the claims that need to be met for these schemes. Thus, it is the wool as such, and not the products, that can claim the Nordic Swan or Cradle 2 Cradle approval.

All along, the reasoning behind the label developed by Curtis Wool Direct for Norwegian Wool, was its eco-credentials. Because of the colder climate in Norway, so-called 'dipping' of sheep is not normal practice. This refers to the application of chemicals in a 'bath' so that sheep are not attacked by invasive insects. This means that Norwegian wool has fewer problematic chemicals that need to be removed during scouring and that there are fewer chemicals used in sheep husbandry than in many other countries. However, the *Viking Wool of Norway* was, despite several

Fig. 1.2 Vingtor label and trademark: *Norwegian Wool*—a line of throws and clothing (*Photo credit* Tone Skårdal Tobiasson)

attempts, never adopted for the Norwegian market. There are many reasons for this; but Nortura—the main stakeholder in Curtis Wool Direct and Norilia were opposed to the adoption, based on an already established trademark in Norway: Viking Yarn. This is a cheap line of yarns produced in China with unknown wool origin, and the confusion would be detrimental for Norwegian wool (Hebrok et al., 2012). In addition, to display Vikings on labels in Norway is associated with cheap souvenirs for tourists, and not quality products (Vittersø et al., 2017). The labels developed by Norwegian companies have all chosen a more clean, minimalist style compatible with that associated with Nordic design and good taste.

There are, of course, other ways to 'localise' wool or rather to signal provenance, and as such tie it to a smaller geographical area. Spinning mills in Norway, such as Selbu spinning mill, Lista Yarns and Oslo Micro Spinning Mill; but also, Rauma, Røros Tweed, Sandnes and Hillesvåg, all

Fig. 1.3 Flokk furniture and their label for *Norwegian Wool* (*Photo credit* Tone Skårdal Tobiasson)

have named their companies after the township, village or area where they belong. For Selbu, they can also profit from the heritage of the famous Selbu-pattern, which gives the name of the company an extra 'knitting' dimension. Lofoten Wool (Fig. 1.4), on the other hand, base their business model on wool from only this geographical area (spun at the Hillesvåg Woolen Mill, where the wool and yarn travels back and forth to the Bergen area on the famed coastal steamer *Hurtigruten*) and has exploited another trademark: Lofotlam (Lofoten Lambs meat) with the tagline 'world-class lamb'. The owner of Lofoten Wool, Ragnhild Lie, sources the wool from the same slaughterhouse as Lofotlam 's lambs-meat, Fatland (Klepp & Tobiasson, 2017).

Fig. 1.4 Ragnhild Lie, the owner of Lofoten wool. The yarns are from the Lofoten sheep (*Photo credit* Leander Berg Fredriksen)

The development of regional or international systems for labelling related to environmental and animal welfare issues or origin can also have negative consequences. In Chapter 2, we enter into a deeper discussion on the problems surrounding the most commonly used comparison tool for textiles' environmental impacts today and show how this, and the planned labelling scheme(s) based on it, affect natural fibre producers, consumers and ultimately also the climate and the environment. Origin labelling is not an easy exercise, as we will discuss in Chapter 3, based on work in this area. Tailoring is f. ex. needed to develop criteria for regenerative farming practices, where forms of operation must be adapted to natural and local conditions, culture, etc. (Glover, 2021).

Textile History and Product Development

Even though the label Viking Wool of Norway never launched on the Norwegian market, the push-and-pull between Haworth Wool Direct,

Norilia and the ongoing work in Valuing Norwegian Wool did have a very concrete outcome: the VikingGold project. The Nordic Council of Ministers funded cultural collaborations under the funding scheme called KreaNord, and the Norwegian Fashion Institute, The Norwegian Museum of Cultural History, the Icelandic Fashion Council and SIFO secured a two-year project looking at the woollen textiles from our Nordic Viking heritage, tying this to both archaeological knowledge and modern production and design. There was a certain irony in that the idea for the project stemmed from the Viking Wool of Norway label, or rather a need to prove that our Nordic Viking heritage included superb craftmanship and global trade routes, which brought the old Norse sheep breeds far and wide (Coulthard, 2020).

The Vikings' textiles were actually technically superior, alongside beautiful and functional. They decorated residences, ships and people, and kept them warm and dry—in open ships—sailing as far as Constantinople and North America (Vedeler, 2006). The tightly woven sails in wool brought them across the seas and enabled cultural exchange and trade; also, of textiles. In graves like Oseberg, textile production tools and textiles held a central place and are found in a plethora of techniques and functions, such as advanced weaving, embroidery, decorative interior textiles, carpets and linens (Vedeler, 2014). Despite this, there has been little research on the Vikings' textiles and little available literature or other dissemination platforms. The typical rendition of Vikings as trolls, with horn-decorated helmets, has dominated the tourist market and is probably as far from the original as the local renditions of the textiles as felted, bulky and non-aesthetic sack-like clothing. The VikingGold project sought to counter this idea by using the older textile tradition as inspiration in new products, based on our Indigenous sheep breeds, which closely resemble the sheep kept by the Vikings. By using the capabilities of our modern, local Norwegian textile industry, the project was able to develop a refined fabric which captured attention both nationally in Norway and internationally.

In the VikingGold project, five Norwegian and two Icelandic designers were invited to design modern fashion interpretations, three of which were invited to produce the designs based on a diamond-twill pattern from one of the oldest known whole Norwegian garment (a tunic which melted out of the Lend glacier from around year 300). In addition, these designs were crafted from 200 m of wool fabric, using the Old Norse sheep breeds' dual-coated white and pigmented wool. The resultant sketched designs were exhibited in the Museum of Cultural History in Oslo and the actual resultant garments were exhibited in the Coastal Museum in Florø (Fig. 1.5). The project led to the weaving mill (Krivi Vev) starting up production of the textile and further interest from fashion and interior designers.

What the VikingGold project showcased, besides a hitherto little studied rich textile heritage, were industrial constraints surrounding the wool from these old Norse breeds, both the wool from the 'Wild sheep' (Old Norse sheep) and from the Norwegian Old Spæl breed, both breeds that had been close to extinction. A third problem and near-extinct breed was identified, the Grey Trønder Sheep. The Norwegian White Spæl breed had a slightly different challenge, we had found through VNW: Increased kemp and medullation, which poses a problem for yarn dyeing. The wool from this breed has been the basis of a vibrant weaving tradition of tapestries in Norway since Medieval times, with its lustrous coat, and the resulting colour-fastness that has held up throughout centuries

Fig. 1.5 Exhibition at Florø Coastal museum (*Photo credit* Tone Skårdal Tobiasson)

(Klepp & Tobiasson, 2013). An important and old art form was therefore in danger of disappearing.

There is a lot that remains unexplored in the use of history in the development of good clothes today. The idea of fashion as something constantly 'new' has stood in the way of finding the deeper roots of clothing. As so often, food is at the forefront with an emphasis on local traditions in marketing and labelling (Fletcher & Vittersø, 2018). In Norway, the same people, including Indigenous peoples, and sheep have inhabited the same territory for thousands of years, which of course has led to the development of specific cultural manifestations in language, art and clothing. This is an unexplored landscape, although it is to some extent highlighted in identity work, not least for the world's Indigenous peoples, because clothing makes them recognisable. We will discuss this in more detail in Chapter 4 and then with a specific look at Indigenous textiles and heritage.

Other 'Black Sheep' in the Wool Industry

In the process of identifying problem areas for KRUS to address, these three breeds came into focus: The Old Norse breed, the White Spæl and the Grey Trønder (a cross-breed between Old Norse breed and the now extinct Tautra breed, thought to be a relative to Merino-sheep) (Klepp et al., 2019). Even though all activities in KRUS looked for practical solutions to specific challenges related to evaluating, collecting, classifying and pricing, the development work was divided into three, with a focus on different breeds and in different areas in Norway. Thus, various problems were addressed. Choosing different geographical locations, issues, breeds and research questions made it easier to focus and to galvanise the necessary change and deliver results.

Taking a cue from how local branding and value chains for food products has resulted in value creation, the development work also sought to explore how the current underuse of the wool could change through user-driven innovation and adaptation of similar strategies, including storytelling and unique positioning. There was, after all, already some precedence for wool yarns using the beforementioned 'problem' of pigmentation to their advantage, in creating heathered yarns with exceptional lustre, at higher price points.

The research related to the Norwegian White Spæl Sheep and its diminishing quality was perhaps the most important for the spinning industry as a whole and was led by the Norwegian Institute of Bioeconomy Research (NIBIO). A key factor here was the involvement of the Norwegian Association of Sheep and Goat Breeders (NSG). Up until 2014, wool had not factored into the Total Merit Index for dual-coated breeds, which was what decided which rams were picked out in the Estimated Breeding Value (EBV) matrix. The renewed interest in wool from NSG represented a milestone for the wool industry in Norway.

The Spæl Sheep represent under 10% of the sheep population in Norway, with around 30.000 breeding ewes registered in the National Sheep Recording System (NSRS), its unique dual-coated and lustrous wool has held an important place in Norwegian handicraft tradition (Koppen, 2006). We have already mentioned the tapestries, which have survived for centuries because of the tenacity of the fibres; however, the wool is also the raw material for embroidery yarns for the 'bunad' and for weavers in general. The colour selection for these yarns has traditionally been much wider than for knitting yarns, but as weavers dwindled in numbers and the quality of the wool decreased, there were major and increasing concerns from the spinning mills and The Norwegian Folk Art and Craft Association, that they would lose access to this important resource (Klepp & Tobiasson, 2017).

Investigating approaches to ensure the desired wool quality, several means were implemented. One was closer monitoring of the wool from given rams; analysing the samples by two different OFDA machines. Another was extensive tutorials and workshops. In addition, actors in KRUS decided early on to produce an instructional video and a simple kit for looking at the wool against a black background under a small pocket-sized microscope that any farmer could purchase cheaply and easily use. The kit also included scissors and a ruler, all neatly fitting into a small box (Fig. 1.6). This quickly identified both kemp and medullation.

In 2018, 70 tonnes of the White Spæl Sheep wool were classified as F1 (the best) and 105 tonnes as F2 (the lower) grade. During the

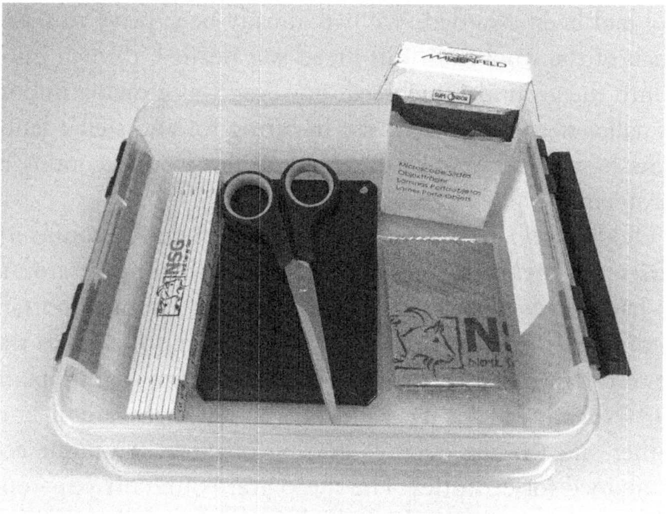

Fig. 1.6 Wool evaluation kit (*Photo credit* Ingun Grimstad Klepp)

KRUS project, there were detected slight improvements. However, it was accepted that a marked and statistically significant improvement would take more time. The project developed the basis for a common understanding of the desirable wool quality traits. This was important for the ram judges alongside farmers and other interested parties, such as employees in the spinning mills, in order to safeguard these traits, and was one of the most important results which will impact this work in the long term.

Old Norse Sheep—The 'Wildest' Wool

The research activity related to the pigmented Old Norse Sheep was led by the Lygra Heathland Centre in close cooperation with the Hillesvåg spinning mill. The work conducted in this package was both extremely challenging and at the same time rewarding. This 'Wild Sheep' wool was a true 'wild card' in the project, as their wool was one of the lowest grades in the Norwegian Wool Standard and during the very start of the project, the Agricultural Directorate even cut out the meagre subsidy that the wool had been awarded. We had already been privy to information that much of the wool from this breed was burned, thrown into the sea or dug into the ground. The breed, however, was growing in popularity, for its smaller size, tasty meat, ease in caring for and stellar landscaping ability. So, how could we turn the trend on this wool becoming a serious waste problem?

The Old Norse Sheep was saved from extinction around 1960, by enthusiasts on the West coast of Norway, where only around 1000 animals had survived. In earlier times, it had been an important breed that dominated the Norwegian coastline and contributed to the maintenance of the heathlands that covered the coastline of Europe from the North of Norway to Portugal and Spain. Through careful burning of the heather and the regenerative grazing practices, a unique ecosystem was maintained for centuries. The sheep graze outdoors year-round, and in addition to the meat and wool, the sheep contribute with nature's own fertiliser to the soil. The Lygra Heathland Centre was established to maintain this tradition, and their flock is now part of the 60.000 winter-fed Old Norse Sheep found along the over 100 thousand kilometres long Norwegian coastline, the world's second longest, thanks to the many fjords.

There was no quality wool standard for the Old Norse Sheep. The quality of the wool varies a lot and the fleece can contain guard hairs that sieve off the rain, the soft underwool, some kemp and beard. The big variation is because the Old Norse Sheep is not really a breed, it is a primaeval sheep with a gene pool that can be bred into any sheep. This means one cannot breed out characteristics just because they do not fit a commercial purpose today. Kemp in this wool turned out to not be much of a problem though, while medullation was. In 2016, it was therefore decided to develop a breeding standard for Old Norse Sheep, also on wool.

Another feature of this primaeval sheep is how the fleece naturally sheds at a certain time of the year (which is called moulting), and the wool can be 'rooed'. This means that the fleece more or less peels off in one piece. This happens sometime between May and early July. Shearing, rooing, or doing both in combination, and the timing, is extremely important for how the wool can be used; and since the actual moulting varies greatly within a flock and between flocks. This work has to be timed precisely to avoid that the wool felts, or that the new wool growing out becomes entangled in last year's wool. If this happens, it is more or less impossible to spin the wool into yarn. Better utilisation of the wool thus has to do with the timing of the shearing. It also turned out to be much easier to utilise lambswool, because it has a more even quality.

This was maybe the most practical part of the whole KRUS project, as a hands-on approach to solve rather pressing problems for this specific wool also turned out to give the best results. For those selecting rams to breed with, the workshops quickly showed the farmers what to look for, and how the wool was to be sorted. Two years down the line, there were clear improvements in the quality of the wool which created optimism about continued improvements. In the workshops, both the intangible cultural heritage surrounding the wool and sheep breed and the tacit knowledge, passed on from generation to generation of sheep farmers, were important. During these workshops, a questionnaire was distributed to get a better understanding of barriers in the value chain, what type of products or uses the wool hitherto had ended up in, and to what degree the wool had been disposed of.

The responses to the questionnaire have become an important baseline for the continued work with the Old Norse Breed, which also forged a stronger cooperation between the Heathland Centre, Hillesvåg, local museums, the Wool Week Festival, the Nordhordland Biosphere project and the local chapter of Norwegian Folk Art and Craft Association and the North Atlantic Sheep & Wool Conference. Together they have created a Wool Forum and VisitBergen, the tourism organisation for the region, launched a Wool Heritage Route. This takes travellers to Hillesvåg, the Heathland Centre—where the results and products from this subdivision of the Work Package have found a permanent home—and to other local wool-based industries, such as the companies Oleana, Dale of Norway and Norlender, along with the museums. Along the way, those following the route can observe the sheep dotting the hillsides along the fjords.

The Old Norse Sheep is not the largest wool producer, by far. If each sheep produces one kilogram of wool, the total population of winter-fed sheep should deliver 60 tonnes. Hillesvåg spun 5000 kilos of hand-knitting yarnin 2018, some of which was dyed in three heathered shades and some of which was sold with the natural grey hue, which is the shade of pigmented wool they have found the easiest to work with. Unlike the grey wool, the brown fibres are brittle and harder to work with. Smaller quantities have been spun by Selbu spinning mill, and some are returned to local farmers as part of the commission spinning system; but the fate of the rest of the wool is not accounted for, except for a very special project with lambswool.

When KRUS started, there was no industrial experience using the Old Norse Sheep's wool on a large scale or for commercial garment production. One could say that there was a certain disbelief if this was at all possible. The sports brand Ulvang, named for the cross country ski champion Vegard Ulvang who championed wool socks and underwear in the 1990s and changed the dress habits of Norwegians for outdoor activity, decided to test lambswool from the Old Norse Sheep (Klepp & Tobiasson, 2018). Working closely with Hillesvåg, they launched the Ulvang Feral sweater in the fall of 2018, with a total of 500 pieces and a high price point. The lambswool proved to be possible to spin fine enough for industrial knitting machines. In January 2019, the Feral sweater was nominated for the Scandinavian Outdoor Award at the world's largest sports fair, ISPO, based on 'functionality, quality, innovation, design and sustainability' (Fig. 1.7).

The weaving mill, Krivi Vev, carried out experiments with the Old Norse Sheep yarns, as a continuation of the VikingGold project, with a focus on interior and furniture fabrics. This was done with both established office interior companies and a small furniture start-up; and the plan is to further explore how these products can be marketed through the Amazing Grazing project. At the Lygra Heathland Centre, the new curtains for shielding sunlight in the auditorium were woven by Krivi from the industrial-strength, finer yarn.

Developing new products and yarns from the older breeds has been important. The slightly chunkier, but airy and light hand-knitting yarn,

Fig. 1.7 Ulvang sweaters in Norwegian wool, the Feral sweater to the far left (*Photo credit* Tone Skårdal Tobiasson)

found its way into new knitting patterns tested out at the Lygra Heathland Centre, and one of these patterns appeared in the hand-knitting book *Knit with Norwegian Wool* (Klepp & Tobiasson, 2017). Sweaters and caps made from this yarn are extremely warm; they start out as slightly prickly and stiff—but through wear the stiffer fibres shed and the clothing becomes softer. The book also featured Old Norse Sheep wool that had been carded at Kåfjorddalen Wool Carding Mill and some also spun at Selbu Spinning Mill, which for example was knitted into traditional 'sea mittens', garments that have been used actively for centuries. These mittens were used at sea, for instance in the important winter fishing in the North Sea and were a main reason for the survival of the dual-coated breeds. Immersing the mittens (which are knitted several sizes too large) into the seawater and then rowing out to the fishing grounds, ensured that the mittens felted and that they were warm, as air was trapped effectively inside the wool. This is one of the properties of wool that is unknown, except in local lore, along the coastline of Norway (Klepp & Tobiasson, 2017). In other words, there is a connection between usability and preservation of the older breeds. Learning from this, we can find good use for this wool today. The focus on softness as synonymous with quality makes this work more difficult, but not impossible. We will discuss this 'obsession' with softness in Chapter 3.

All the actual results from the work with the older breeds, including the permanent exhibit at Lygra Heathland Centre and the Heritage Wool Route, alongside the finished products and better sorting and handling of the wool, does not mean all problems are solved for this unique wool. Far from it. During the KRUS project, it was identified that farmers with the larger flocks (more than 50 winter-fed sheep), were significantly more prone to dig down, burn or throw their wool into the sea. Turning the tide on this should be the focus for further research and projects, finding new and better uses for this wool. The WOOLUME project (see Chapter 3) will explore this based on Polish sheep farmers that have even more challenges with utilising their wool. We also explore this in a smaller project, hiWOOL, with Portuguese partners. Results will also inspire new opportunities in Norway.

New Warps and Wefts Weave a Future

The last part of the breed related activities in KRUS, developed several new sub-projects during the period and we were able to access funding through other sources in order to achieve more than the promised results. This highlighted the need for projects to be more dynamic than they usually are designed for, to allow for following up opportunities along the way. The work that centred around Selbu Spinning Mill was closely tied to the founder of the mill, Ingvild Svorkmo Espelien, and her unique knowledge and understanding of breeds, biology, spinning and wool. In the WOOLUME project, Espelien also has a central role in transferring knowledge. She was also pivotal in developing the fabric in VikingGold, and she is very much involved in Amazing Grazing and hiWOOL.

Unexpected emergent outcomes from the KRUS project included: a permanent exhibit in Selbu and a bestselling pattern book for knitted mittens. To understand how this came about, one needs to have some background knowledge of the Norwegian knitting history and how certain patterns are tied to geographical areas. Selbu is one of these geographical areas with a strong tradition that emerged when economic hardship hit the area during the second half of the nineteenth century. A standardised pattern, called the *Selbu rose* (Fig. 1.8), has decorated millions of mittens produced in this village; but many variations over this pattern also surfaced, and over 400 were collected by Anne Bårds-gård, who then developed the patterns for the book *Selbuvotter* (Selbu

Fig. 1.8 Mittens knitted in the Selbu rose pattern (*Photo credit* Ingun Grimstad Klepp)

mittens) (Bårdsgård, 2016; Klepp & Tobiasson, 2017). The book was truly a treasure trove for documenting a local heritage. Selbu Spinning Mill developed thinner yarns, using the naturally pigmented wool to create the two coloured patterns; the thinner yarns facilitated the very detailed patterns.

Another project stemmed from the rather alarming finding that 50–60% of the wool from the fleeces delivered to Selbu Spinning Mill ended up as waste. This could be because the wool had felted or contained too many coarse hairs. As previously mentioned, the older breeds have very varying wool quality and although some is suitable for knitting yarn, there is also much that is not. To alleviate this problem, the spinning mill experimented with an unspun yarn, which is popular for rugs and in so-called 'big knit'. In the pattern book *Knit with Norwegian Wool*, a crocheted basket in varied sizes using this non-spun yarn was introduced alongside a description of how this 'big knit' yarn had come about (see Fig. 3.2 in Chapter 3) (Klepp & Tobiasson, 2017).

Updating Breed Standards for Wool

Alongside these product developments, which had highly successful outcomes, Selbu Spinning Mill also delved into some very technical issues related to wool and breeds. This is important work that will be valuable for other actors who want to understand the specific properties of different breeds' wool. While we know there has been breed specific research looking at VOC-absorption rate in the UK (Mansour et al., 2016), a lot of academic research around wool tends to bunch wool together when it comes to the fibre's attributes, neither relating to breeds nor processing methods (Mansour et al., 2016). The potential differences between breeds and type of wool related to different properties were part of what Selbu Spinning Mill wished to study and document for future breeding and use of the wool. This included colour-fastness of pigmented wool, lustre in colour, gloss, fibre tension (resistance to stretching/change of crimp) and flammability—which has been added to the classification descriptions of the wool types that were studied (mainly the older, dual-coated breeds and the Grey Trønder sheep) (Espelien, Unpublished).

To further advance knowledge on these wool types, the following things were examined:

- Durability of a standardised yarn spun from wool from the breed that maintains spin quality, in some cases sorted in lambswool and adult wool.
- Washing characteristics of standardised knitting samples knitted from the standardised yarn of each sheep breed.
- Felting qualities in wool from adult sheep, primarily wool sheared in spring.
- A description of wool properties and suggested uses, sheep breed by sheep breed.

This characterisation is an important addition to the breed standards, as they have also focused on lambs', rams' and ewes' wool. Based on the results of the characterisation, it is possible to set new breeding goals in order to change the wool quality relative to the breed-type properties of the wool, or one can preserve the qualities as they are today. All this information and samples of yarns and textiles, have been collected into a permanent exhibit housed in the spinning mill itself but can be loaned out to anyone who asks. This is an important testament of the research, and constitutes a valuable and vibrant library for further study, adding much more detailed information related to sheep health, age, geographical differences and a more textured view of the breeds. In preindustrial societies, many different nuances in raw material qualities were utilised to optimise usability and durability (Coulthard, 2020). In the work of re-establishing textiles as lasting and worthy, we need research that recovers knowledge about nuances in the raw material qualities.

Projections and Failure

In the KRUS proposal, we had envisioned that the search for viable business or entrepreneurial models would lead us into the landscape of customer co-creation for these to reach a scale that could deliver value to customers (and other stakeholders), and be potentially economically sustainable. This was based on the assumption that value can be increased by engaging the consumers more actively in the value creation process. Co-creation can encompass a specific creation process of a joint product or service, as well as focus on creating a relationship with the customer to maximise the experiential aspects of the consumption itself ('value in use') (Payne et al., 2008). Incorporating the consumers actively as part of the business or entrepreneurial model and value proposition has been a growing trend, relevant for both agriculture and sustainable development within textiles. The co-creation perspective, often called 'prosumption' (Ritzer & Jurgenson, 2010), has been highly relevant for a commodity such as handicraft yarns and home production, which we will discuss more in Chapter 5.

Since the establishment of the textile industry in Norway and up until today, there has been extensive collaboration between home production and industry. This has happened through systems such as commission spinning, where you receive your own wool back as spun yarn, which is also done today. The carding-mills early took over the heaviest part of the work with the raw wool, even when it was still spun at home. Today, many hand spinners also spin using the carded, un-washed wool, where Kåfjorddalen carding mill, which is described in Chapter 4, plays an important role. How important, will be explored in depth there. The most important item from the other Norwegian spinning mills today is, however, knitting yarn, which together with colourful weaving yarns are produced for the hand-knitting market. The spinning mills have been important in developing patterns for home production and these are developed and shared both privately and through commercial actors, for free or at a cost. Several spinning mills also actively contribute with courses, lectures and other activities both online and in connection with factory visits where home production is promoted. Good yarn and a constant stream of new patterns have maintained the interest in hand-knitting (Klepp & Tobiasson, 2017, 2018).

In KRUS, what we saw as a very clear effect, was more cooperation and local anchoring than actual prosumption. The cooperation happened on several levels, as described in Viktorija Vičiūnaitė's PhD thesis and in Alana Lennon's Master's thesis. Lennon's study centred on the Selbu Spinning Mill and found that the interaction with the local community—both the public sector and private citizens—particularly galvanised a more resilient business model for the mini-mill. Local enthusiasts bought shares through a Facebook page, the mill was able to move to larger facilities and the ties to the community became closer and more pronounced. These new network-forms are called 'mesh-works' in Chapter 6, and are an important glue in an economy based on other values than growth.

Lennon detailed this process in her thesis *Natural Regional Resilience Determining the Sustainable Value of Local Wool Industry through Actor-Network Theory*. Actor-Network Theory is a theoretical framework and methodology which offers a holistic approach to researching complex relational activity. This makes it possible to understand the collaboration and relationships stretching across space and time. Lennon postulated that the local wool industry has a deeper focus on ecological sustainability, super-ceding the capitalist focus on competition and economic interests. Thus, the local focus is more on sustainable regional resilience rather than regional 'development'—which is what mainstream media has promoted as the catch-all for success (Lennon, 2017).

Lennon identified the delicate balance when value creation based on resources on the verge of being defined as waste is at the core; as this can be tied to an idea of hyper-local products. This could be commission-spun yarns tied to a tourist market, where connecting the wool to a specific region, grazing system or farm, is paramount. This dynamic between the larger and smaller-scale systems is something that is well known from the food sector, e.g. within Protected Designation of Origin (PDO). This has also been important for the actor Lofoten Wool, as mentioned, and has been an important factor, as with the Selbu mittens and the locally sourced and spun naturally pigmented wool. The Amazing Grazing project will be researching this further, also related to a new upstart, Tingvoll Wool[3]. 'Cultural history and animals steeped in

[3] Tingvoll is currently very well known for an internationally award-winning cheese and also houses Krivi Weaving Mill.

traditions, and the forms of operations surrounding them, are resources that bear much more potential to be utilised' (Klepp et al., 2019, p. 83).

Serendipitous Cooperation

These smaller start-ups tied to geographical areas that resonate with local patrons and tourists, could signal stronger competition between actors. However, one of the more serendipitous effects of KRUS has been the increase in cooperation between industry actors. This was specifically addressed in Vičiūnaitė's PhD thesis *Moving towards sustainability: business models and entrepreneurship in the Norwegian wool industry* (Vičiūnaitė, 2020).

The collaborations that VikingGold and KRUS forced on actors, who had earlier only communicated very superficially and often in a guarded manner in order not to divulge IP or other business-related secrets, made something happen. New spontaneous ideas and platforms for further cooperation arose as unexpected bonuses—often in loose discussions about something quite different. Collaboration is a little studied and underestimated field in business development and we will elaborate more on in Chapters 5 and 6. Extensive media attention focused on increased use of Norwegian wool coupled with the power of storytelling if the wool stemmed from sheep that were endangered in some way; captured new actors who wanted to be part of the ongoing resurgence of better use of local resources. Some of the very concrete epiphanies have been captured in Vičiūnaitė's PhD, and they reflect an air of positive surprise with quotes such as: 'I had never even thought of that as a possible market', or 'it was just a whole different way of looking at it, it was just "WOW"'; 'suddenly you realize, this is fantastic, we can use this for something', and 'you never know what relations will be useful, that's the point',. All the quotes reflect results from conversations with other actors in the network, and with invisible exclamation marks (Vičiūnaitė, 2020).

The two books KRUS produced for the popular market were also a result of a serendipitous event. One of the books had been part of the project plan from the outset; however, it was proving impossible to find a publishing house. The idea was to show-case the different wool types and yarns from the variety of Norwegian breeds and mills, and present patterns to match each wool type. However, how this came about is worth describing, as it shows how 'blind spots' develop in certain fields of study.

Handicraft yarns and knitting is an area that has been largely ignored by most serious research, with a few exceptions. Partly to address this gap in the literature, we wrote an op-ed highlighting this fact. Our op-ed was a response to a celebrated Norwegian (male) commentator on social issues who had written a scathing review of knitting pattern books, claiming that if you knew how to knit you did not need this type of literature (Søbye, 2015). As we had been able to glean from the little available research, that Norwegian women knit twice as much as British, Swedish and American women—and Norwegian spinning mills were experiencing an economic boom—his depreciation of knitters was an affront to women all over Norway. In addition to this, the field was glaringly under-researched, as the last time someone had described the history of Norwegian knitting in print, had been 30 years prior.

Shortly after the op-ed was published, Klepp received a call from a small publisher on the West coast of Norway, asking if she could write the history of Norwegian knitting. The publisher had read the op-ed and found it intriguing that such a popular hobby and artisanal expression received so little attention and offered a book deal. Klepp, however, suggested that if the publishing house first published a knitting recipe book with Norwegian wool yarns, she and Tobiasson would also write the history book. The publisher accepted. This is a good example of possibilities that can emerge, as long as there is the capacity to adjust and an aspect that seldom is highlighted in project proposals or calls.

In line with what Rebecca Burgess highlighted in her book, *Fibershed*, the pattern book aimed to describe and elevate 'the voices and faces of farming, ranching, and artisan community by bringing together their stories into the public eye' (Burgess & White, 2019, p. 223). In addition, the book aimed to go beyond presenting 'only' patterns, but also wanted to be a 'cook book', where the ingredients were described for their specific properties, in order to elevate the result to a 'gourmet' level. The book highlights how the entire spectrum of Norwegian wool can be used in ways where the individual breeds, yarn types and more are utilised.

The patterns have been carefully selected to demonstrate the diversity of the ingredients and how they can be used in hand-knitted (and a few crocheted) homemade products. Bringing this knowledge forwards was of utmost importance to this project, through concretely show-casing that quality is not one specific thing, but a spectre, as we will discuss more in Chapter 3, related to Merino wool's position as 'quality wool'.

When writing both books, describing the value chain and specifically the spinning mills in Norway, was an important task and the patterns used yarns from all the mills, while also offering suggestions on how to exchange one yarn with another. The fact that Norway did have three large spinning-mills for wool yarns, and two mini-mills at the time (there are now even more), is unique in a European context and does tie back to the knitting- and handicraft interest that we pointed to in the mentioned op-ed. The interest of local sheep farmers to commission-spin their own wool was (and is) clearly also growing, in line with the predictions in the KRUS application—following the trajectory of the local food movement and the increase in local fairs. This meant that the waiting time for commission spinning was increasing. However, as the KRUS final report went to print, Espelien informed the KRUS-team that as many as five new mini- or micro-mills were planning to open up. So far, we've seen two make their presence known on social media: Lista Yarns and Oslo Micro Spinning mill.

Local Clothing

One of KRUS's two main goals was to change the discussion about sustainable fashion. We wanted to ascertain that the use phase of clothing was included in the discussion and that the knowledge of local clothing production as an environmental strategy was increased. To achieve these goals, we needed to develop concepts, methods, knowledge and arguments.

Much of the work on new methods for studying local clothing in KRUS was not completed in the form of an overall presentation. SIFO and Professor Kate Fletcher, from University of the Arts London, had been working on method development for a long time (Fletcher, 2018;

Fletcher & Klepp, 2018). Klepp and Fletcher wanted to start further development with an overview of the knowledge that had already been put forward and published the method book *Opening up the Wardrobe*: '... the most comprehensive result of the work within this type of method development so far. The book presents 50 methods for exploring actions, relationships and the material content of wardrobes. Organised as a practical guide to gathering information about people and their clothing beyond the point of purchase'. Methods for studying the consumption of clothing are absolutely crucial in order to gain an understanding of the growth in quantities and of the environmental impacts from the use phase. SIFO's work on these issues has also taken a more quantitative direction in collaboration with Australian Wool Innovation (AWI), work that is important both for criticising (Laitala et al., 2017, 2018) and improving LCA tools (Klepp et al., 2020; Laitala & Klepp, 2020; Wiedemann et al., 2020, 2021).

The more radical ideas around understanding local textiles and fashion, in the context of the local and slow movement, did pose a challenge. One outcome was a Special Issue of the *Journal of Fashion Practice*, which explored frameworks, dynamics and practice of localism as a route to radical sustainability change. Fletcher and Klepp took on the role of being guest editors, and it was a start, but possibly a bit premature, to publish such an issue.

The issue set out to explore localism as a process that prioritises communities over economic gains, through safeguarding a region's natural factors and by what ensures long-term prosperity. Being small scale, shaped by traditions, necessity, climate and other factors, as opposed to the forces of globalisation and the highly decentralised textile and clothing systems, localism offers community empowerment, heterogeneous products, local stories, a myriad dress practices and fewer goods. Here the wish was to explore how a transformation of the sector's underlying organising and infrastructures could catalyse new knowledge about products and their production for consumers, through their proximity to sites of manufacture. This again could change the understanding and respect for goods. Here is an excerpt from the Special Issue, that highlights that localism in relation to textiles and sustainability, has not been a focus:

> It is at least somewhat true that 'local' is part of the contemporary textiles and clothing vernacular; consider for example heritage fibres, traditional cloth construction techniques, the highly skilled techniques of hand-finishing only possible at small scales. Further, clothing manufacturing activity is increasingly moving 'home', that is relocating production near high value markets to reduce lead times and cut costs. Indeed, all of these features can be seen to be have been adopted within fashion brands in various configurations and at different scales as part of conventional business practices. Yet as a coherent conceptual framework and explicit set of practices for sustainability change, localism is little explored in the fashion context. (Fletcher & Klepp, 2018, pp. 134–135)

In Norway, local clothing is—to a certain degree—understood. This is linked to a distinctive clothing habit in Norway; the use of national costumes (*bunad*) where each costume is tied to a specific area in Norway, including the Sámi traditional dress. In addition, home-knitted sweaters, mittens, socks and caps with distinctive patterns with names from the area they have been used, is part of this understanding of 'local'. An added layer to this is a complicated system of the necessary connection to place and who has the 'right' to use the garments, especially the bunads, although this is normally not an issue with the knitted garments. As already described, this has kept a local value chain in the form of spinning and weaving mills, as well as knitting factories (Klepp & Laitala, 2018; Klepp & Tobiasson, 2013). Understood, most of Norway's textile industry had, as in the rest of Europe, been closed down. But due partially to a revitalisation of artisan- and craft-based activity, as well as an increased interest in owning a bunad, the wool-based textile industry was positioned to 're-shore' or 'on-shore', depending on what best captures the opposite of the globalised 'off-shoring' trend.

However, this was not what Fletcher and Klepp wanted to explore as the main focus within this conceptual framework of KRUS. During the project period, the understanding of what local textiles or clothes mean to Norwegians and Brits was explored in ongoing conversations. Their main aim was to address how clothing can support improved ecological practices for land use and rich and unique cultural expression; framing fashion localism as a restorative force for the environment, animals and people. This was a novel and daring approach. A better understanding of this was however difficult to frame and has been one of Fletcher's further explorations, which can be called 'work in progress'.

Through several publications, things evolved organically; and again, we can claim that serendipity played a role. The focus on the textile industry's overproduction and overconsumption grew alongside voices such as that of Greta Thunberg and once the pandemic hit in 2020, the noise became deafening. Fletcher initiated the Union of Concerned Researchers in Fashion and co-authored the Earth Logic document with Mathilda Tham, where 'local' was one of the clear trajectories (Fletcher & Tham, 2019). We can observe a more distinct and polarised debate where the industry, and unfortunately also governments and research funding institutions, dream about 'new technology' and recycling as the answer to the conundrum, while research institutions address overconsumption, poor utilisation of resources and the use phase of clothing. These are important topics we think we didn't deliver on in KRUS, although it was what we worked on the most, especially in the form of articles, op-eds and lectures. With this book, we take the discussion further, in the form of a critique of the focus on 'sustainable fibres' in Chapter 2, the economic background for the ideology behind new technology and recycling, through green growth as the ideal, in Chapter 6, and last but not least the need for a discussion quantity, which is repeated throughout the book, but is discussed most in its breadth in Chapter 7.

Several circumstances in Norway caused KRUS to have the effect we have described. There was a value chain, even though it was poorly connected and even less visible or known. There was interest in local clothes in the form of national costumes and home production, and there are probably many countries where it is far more difficult to create an impact in the media on this topic. Still, we set many goals, and reached some of them, as well as saw some new ones surfacing. KRUS resulted in bigger change than we had dared to believe. Maybe the timing was right, but above all, we think it was collaboration that did the trick. We have taken this belief with us and it characterises our work with wool following KRUS, and which we will of course explain in more in detail in the next chapters.

References

Almås, R. (2002). *Norges landbrukshistorie: Frå bondesamfunn til bioindustri: 1920–2000. IV*. Samlaget.

Bårdsgård, A. (2016). *Selbuvotter*. Museumsforlaget.

Bessière, J. J. S. r. (1998). Local development and heritage: Traditional food and cuisine as tourist attractions in rural areas. *Sociologia Ruralis, 38*(1), 21–34.

Burgess, R., & White, C. (2019). *Fibershed: Growing a movement of farmers, fashion activists, and makers for a new textile economy*. Chelsea Green Publishing.

Coulthard, S. (2020). *A short history of the world according to sheep*. Apollo.

Engeström, Y. (2001). Expansive learning at work: Toward an activity theoretical reconceptualization. *Journal of Education and Work, 14*(1), 133–156.

Espelien, I. (Unpublished). *Karakterisering av ull fra norske saueraser. Rapport fra prosjekt ved Selbu spinneri 2014–2017*.

Fletcher, K. (2010). Slow fashion: An invitation for systems change. *Fashion Practice : The Journal of Design, Creative Process & the Fashion Industry, 2*(2), 259–266. https://doi.org/10.2752/175693810X12774625387594.

Fletcher, K. (2018). The fashion land ethic: Localism, clothing activity, and macclesfield. *Fashion Practice: The Journal of Design, Creative Process & the Fashion Industry, 10*(2), 139–159.

Fletcher, K., & Klepp, I. G. (2018). A note from the editors of fashion practice. *Fashion Practice: The Journal of Design, Creative Process & the Fashion Industry, 10*(2), 133–138. https://doi.org/10.1080/17569370.2018.1458500.

Fletcher, K., & Klepp, I. G. (Eds.). (2017). *Opening up the Wardrobe: A methods book*. Novus.

Fletcher, K., & Tham, M. (2019). *Earth logic: Fashion action research plan*. JJ Charitable Trust.

Fletcher, K., & Vittersø, G. (2018). Local food initiatives and fashion change: Comparing food and clothes to better understand fashion localism. *Fashion Practice: The Journal of Design, Creative Process & the Fashion Industry, 10*(2), 160–170. https://doi.org/10.1080/17569370.2018.1458496.

Glover, S. (2021). The regeneration game. *Ecotextile News(102)*, 53.

Hebrok, M., Klepp, I. G., Tobiasson, T. S., Laitala, K., Vestvik, M., & Buck, M. (2012). *Valuing Norwegian Wool*. Retrieved from Oslo http://www.sifo.no/files/file78335_fagrapport_5-2012web.pdf.

Klepp, I. G., & Laitala, K. (2018). Nisseluelandet—The impact of local clothes for the survival of a textile industry in Norway. *Fashion Practice: The Journal of Design, Creative Process & the Fashion Industry, 10*(2), 171–195. https://doi.org/10.1080/17569370.2018.1458497.

Klepp, I. G., Laitala, K., & Wiedmann, S. (2020). Clothing lifespans: What should be measured and how. *Sustainability, 12*(15).

Klepp, I. G., & Tobiasson, T. (2017). *Strikk med norsk ull*. Vormedal forlag.

Klepp, I. G., Tobiasson, T. S., Haugrønning, V., Vittersø, G., Grøva, L., Kvingedal, T., Espelien, I., & Kubberød, E. (2019). *KRUS final report: Enhancing local value chains in Norway*.

Klepp, I. G., & Tobiasson, T. S. (2013). *Ren ull*. Aschehoug.

Klepp, I. G., & Tobiasson, T. S. (2018). *Norsk strikkehistorie*. Vormedal.

Klepp, I. G., Vramo, L., & Laitala, K. (2014). Too old: Clothes and value in Norwegian and Indian wardrobes. In M.-L. Nosch, Z. Feng, & L. Varadrajan (Eds.), *Global textile encounters* (Vol. 20, pp. 237–244). Oxbow Books.

Koppen, M. B. (2006). *Norwegian tapestry weaving*. Eikeskog Press.

Laitala, K., Klepp, I., & Henry, B. (2018). Does use matter? Comparison of environmental impacts of clothing based on fiber type. *Sustainability, 10*(7). doi:https://doi.org/10.3390/su10072524.

Laitala, K., & Klepp, I. G. (2020). What affects garment lifespans? International clothing practices based on a Wardrobe survey in China, Germany, Japan, the UK, and the USA. *Sustainability, 12*(21), 9151. https://www.mdpi.com/2071-1050/12/21/9151.

Laitala, K., Klepp, I. G., & Henry, B. (2017, November 9). *Use phase of wool apparel: a literature review for improving LCA*. Paper presented at the Product Lifetimes And The Environment—PLATE 2017, Delft.

Lennon, A. (2017). *Natural regional resilience: Determining the sustainable value of a local wool industry through actor-network theory*. NTNU.

Mansour, E., Curling, S., Stéphan, A., & Ormondroyd, G. (2016). Absorption of volatile organic compounds by different wool types. *Green Materials, 4*(1), 1–7. https://doi.org/10.1680/jgrma.15.00031.

Marsden, T. (1998). New rural territories: Regulating the differentiated rural spaces. *Journal of Rural Studies, 14*(1), 107–117.

Morgan, K., Marsden, T., & Murdoch, J. (2008). *Worlds of food: Place, power, and provenance in the food chain*. Oxford University Press on Demand.

Payne, A. F., Storbacka, K., & Frow, P. J. (2008). Managing the co-creation of value. *Journal of the Academy of Marketing Science, 36*(1), 83–96.

Ritzer, G., & Jurgenson, N. (2010). Production, consumption, prosumption. *Journal of Consumer Culture, 10*(1), 13–36. https://doi.org/10.1177/1469540509354673.

Rye, J. F. (2011). Conflicts and contestations. Rural populations' perspectives on the second homes phenomenon. *Journal of rural studies, 27*(3), 263–274.

Søbye, E. (2015). Mellom rett og vrangt. *Morgenbladet*.

Vedeler, M. (2006). *Klær og formspråk i norsk middelalder*. Universitet i Oslo.

Vedeler, M. (2014). The textile interior in the Oseberg burial chamber. In S. Bergerbrant & S. H. Fossøy (Eds.), *A stitch in time: Essays in honour of lise bender Jørgensen* (pp. 281–300). Gothenburg University.

Vičiūnaitė, V. (2020). *Moving towards sustainability: business models and entrepreneurship in the Norwegian wool industry* (PhD Thesis). NMBU, https://hdl.handle.net/11250/2676452.

Vittersø, G. (2012). *Ren idyll? Forbrukets betydning for bygdeutvikling med utgangspunkt i lokal mat og hytteliv.* (PhD). Universitet i Oslo.

Vittersø, G., Klepp, I. G., Tobiasson, T. S., & Kviseth, K. (2017). *Opprinnelsesmerking av norsk ull*. www.hioa.no/content/download/139130/3967899/file/OR5%20-2017%20-%20opprinnelsesmerking%20av%20norsk%20ull.pdf.

Wiedemann, S. G., Biggs, L., Nebel, B., Bauch, K., Laitala, K., Klepp, I. G., Swan, P. G., & Watson, K. (2020). Environmental impacts associated with the production, use, and end-of-life of a woollen garment. *The International Journal of Life Cycle Assessment, 25*, 1486–1499.

Wiedemann, S. G., Biggs, L., Nguyen, Q. V., Clarke, S. J., Laitala, K., & Klepp, I. G. (2021). Reducing environmental impacts from garments through best practice garment use and care, using the example of a Merino wool sweater. *The International Journal of Life Cycle Assessment*. https://doi.org/10.1007/s11367-021-01909-x.

2

The Fate of Natural Fibres in Environmental Evaluations: A Question of Volume

Ingun Grimstad Klepp, Kirsi Laitala, Vilde Haugrønning, Anna Schytte Sigaard, and Tone Skårdal Tobiasson

Attention related to the large environmental impact from the clothing and textile industry is growing rapidly and the need for knowledge on these issues is accordingly increasing. One area that has received a lot of attention, is what is defined as 'sustainable materials' and especially understood as which fibres are 'best'. At the same time, a review of the methods and tools that are used to measure environmental sustainability show large weaknesses when they are compared. Very few complex and full Life cycle assessments (LCAs) have been executed (Luo et al.,

I. G. Klepp · K. Laitala · V. Haugrønning (✉) · A. S. Sigaard
Consumption Research Norway (SIFO), Oslo Metropolitan University, Oslo, Norway
e-mail: vildeh@oslomet.no

I. G. Klepp
e-mail: ingunk@oslomet.no

T. S. Tobiasson
Nordic Initiative Clean & Ethical Fashion, Oslo, Norway

I. G. Klepp and T. S. Tobiasson (eds.), *Local, Slow and Sustainable Fashion*,
https://doi.org/10.1007/978-3-030-88300-3_2

2021). Evaluating environmental sustainability for textile products has been difficult because of the complexity both in the production and consumption processes, combined with few and deficient analyses (Luo et al., 2021). The fashion and textile industries are also faced with socio-ecological issues of a scale that require interdisciplinary analytical concepts and perspectives (Takedomi Karlsson & Ramasar, 2020).

Despite this lack of solid data, the industry's inclination to point to 'sustainable fibres' prevails. Policymakers follow suit, in line with their belief that consumers must be better informed in order to make environmentally correct choices (Heidenstrøm et al., 2021). Thus, there has been an increasing demand for comparison tools, integrity and labelling schemes, and evaluations of environmental impacts. Online solutions and books have been and are being developed and authored on how we (the consumers)—or companies—can reduce the environmental footprint through the right choice of fibres. Some have started to question how these rankings favour synthetic over natural fibres (Kassatly, 2020a; Kassatly & Baumann-Pauly, Forthcoming; Kviseth & Tobiasson, 2011). How did this come to be? We will look at the evaluations and tools being used in these rankings and the actors who advocate them.

The Focus on Fibres

The main issue when discussing environmental impacts related to clothing and other textiles is that fibre is the main focus (Textile Exchange, 2020a; Wolfe, 2018). It is taken for granted that 'sustainable materials' are equivalent to particular fibres, excluding other stages of the production such as dyeing and finishing. This is alarming, considering that an overview of impacts in different phases of garment production shows that fibre production only accounts for 15% of climate impacts from clothing, while dyeing and finishing account for the highest impacts (36%), followed by yarn preparation (28%) (Quantis, 2018). The comparable numbers for Swedish clothing consumption are estimated by Mistra (see Fig. 2.1) to be 16% for fibre and 23% for dyeing and finishing, while yarn preparation is 10% (Östlund et al., 2020).

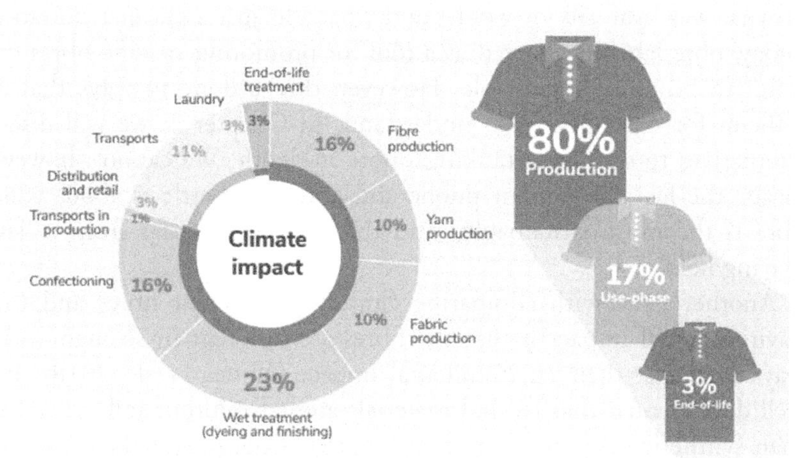

Fig. 2.1 Climate impact of Swedish clothing consumption. Illustration: ECOS (*Source* Mistra)

The details are not the most important here. What is important; however, is that these reports all agree that the fibre production is such a small part of the environmental footprint, e.g. measured in the climate impact of apparel. Changing from one fibre to another will thus not have much potential to reduce the environmental impact, even if it should be the case that the difference between them was large. The fibre content is likely in focus, not because of its relative importance, but due to the current labelling requirements and what information is easily available on any given garment. The lack of requirements for information on the dyeing and finishing chemicals makes these invisible, although finishes such as the colour are obviously visible, while other finishes such as water- and windproof membranes are tactile.

Many countries, including Norway, imposed fibre labelling on clothing as a result of new manmade fibres (first viscose and later synthetics) being produced as imitations of natural fibres, making it difficult for consumers to know what they were buying, in the middle of the 1900s. All other components present in clothing, such as chemicals, laminates, finishes, etc., are outside the realm of requirements for labelling. Thus, fibre labelling has its roots in making consumers aware of what was 'real' silk or wool—and what was just a cheaper imitation. Today, fibre labelling is used as a tool for promoting specific fibres that claim to be more sustainable. However, this is done in ways that are difficult for most people to understand. In Chapter 3, we will discuss alternatives to simplistic rankings more in-depth. We cannot, however, escape the fact the current public and academic battle is about which fibre is the most 'sustainable', and this battlefield is far from a 'level playing field'.

Another issue with comparing clothes in different fibres and their environmental impact is that the fibres are different in so many other ways than just their environmental impact (Laitala et al., 2018). It is well documented that natural materials are less odorous following wear than synthetic ones. It is a proven fact that wool retains the least smell and polyester the most (McQueen & Vaezafshar, 2019). This means that closefitting garments in polyester are laundered more often, and antibacterial chemicals and compounds are therefore often added to synthetics to achieve some of the same properties that come naturally to wool. However, despite the applied odour control technologies, synthetics still smell more than wool and cotton after use (Klepp et al., 2016). The differences between fibre properties also apply to flammability, where wool does not easily ignite, while many other fibres do, specifically acrylic, a fibre that often replaces wool (Sinclair, 2015). Materials that burn easily or are dangerous because they melt and drip, must be treated with flame retardant chemicals that in themselves have a negative environmental impact (Nazare, 2009), to achieve the same level of flame resistance as wool naturally has. On the other hand, wool has properties that provide a need for finishing that is not needed on other fibres. Some types of wool shrink easily when laundered. Therefore, anti-shrink treatment is used on wool that requires frequent washing, such as underwear and socks. This is a problematic chemical finish that only lately has found alternative methods by major actors. Also, moths are big fans of wool, and the chemicals earlier used for mothproofing are now illegal (Klepp & Tobiasson, 2020).

The above are examples of different efforts to produce similar properties, but in many cases, there are no alternatives. Wool will offer more warmth than cotton and polyester under otherwise equal conditions.

Comparing fibres is thus not fruitful because it would be better to source the fibre best suited for different uses and purposes. This applies both in comparison between synthetic, animal and cellulose-based fibres, but it also applies when comparing wool fibres with different properties, which we will discuss more in Chapter 3.

Evaluations and Comparisons

Since Made-By introduced their tool based on global averages (Wolfe, 2018), the method of comparing fibres has more and more often involved evaluations and rankings (Kviseth & Tobiasson, 2011). The Higg Index is in the process of positioning itself as the most important tool developed by the Sustainable Apparel Coalition (SAC, 2020). According to them, the Higg Index is a suite of tools that enables brands, retailers and others 'to accurately measure and score a company or product's sustainability performance. The Higg Index delivers a holistic overview that empowers businesses to make meaningful improvements that protect the well-being of factory workers, local communities, and the environment' (SAC, 2020). Through the development of the Higg Index, SAC, which is an association of the largest fast fashion, apparel and sports brands, is attempting to gain control over what is marketed as sustainable. Some companies have started using the data accumulated by SAC for products sold online, with a Higg Index 'material seal', which shows the products 'sustainability level' compared to a conventional product, based on global averages.The Higg Index is now privately owned and their tools and datasets are behind a paywall. For those who have access, their data or methods still appear opaque (Kassatly, 2020a).

Scientific analysis of the Higg Index and other basic LCAs for textiles have pointed to some fundamental problems (Luo et al., 2021; Watson & Wiedemann, 2019): 'First, the production and consumption process of the textiles and apparel products are typically long and unstandardised, which can make data collection highly difficult for quantitative methods such as LCA' (Luo et al., 2021). Strictly speaking most LCAs for textiles, including the basis for the Higg Material Science Index which rates the fibres, are so-called 'cradle-to-gate' evaluations, and with very different boundaries and scopes for each fibre. The international standard for LCAs states: 'Generally, the information developed in an LCA or LCI study can be used as part of a much more comprehensive decision process. Comparing the results of different LCA or LCI studies is only possible if the assumptions and context of each study are equivalent'(ISO 14040, 2006). When adding into the mix that global averages do not at all capture local, place-specific variables in fibre production, it is clear that the basis for the general comparison of fibres is very weak. This becomes even more clear when the same global averages are applied to specific products, which we will shortly turn our attention to.

Another problem is that this way of measuring environmental impacts does not reflect the volume of any given fibre—and when wool is only 1% of the total fibre market, the impact from wool will of course be significantly less than the impact from e.g. polyester, which is more than half of the total fibre market (Textile Exchange, 2020a). We will address this later in this chapter.

Several key players are now adopting the Higg Index MSI, such as the Textile Exchange, which use it as its 'baseline' in its work on 'preferred fibres', and the whole basis for how clothing is to be evaluated and how to achieve climate goals (Textile Exchange, 2020b). In this system, recycled materials are by definition better (less environmentally damaging) than virgin fibres without this being necessarily examined empirically. Shen et al. (2012) show that not all recycled fibres necessarily have a lower environmental impact. We know that many materials are weakened in these processes and in an LCA analysis, where, for example, wool is compared to recycled wool, the comparison does not include actual lifespan.

According to Östlund et al. (2015) under certain circumstances, there is a risk that textile recycling increases several environmental impacts. In their case studies, it was shown that climate impact can increase if recycling processes are powered by fossil energy and/or if virgin cotton as a consequence is assumed to be replaced, as cotton is a fibre associated with relatively low climate impact. That certain environmental impacts can increase, while others decrease, was also shown by Shen et al. (2010) and Schmidt et al. (2016) for textile recycling, and by Bodin (2016) for textile reuse. The impacts of recycled products are strongly influenced by the choice of the allocation method applied to open-loop recycling (Shen et al., 2012). This will be further explored within the framework of the circular economy in Chapter 6, but already here we see how the love affair between the idea of a circular economy and recycling are blurring real empirical comparisons.

The EU is currently developing a consumer-facing product labelling, based on a system called the European Union Product Environmental Footprint (PEF). In this work, the Higg Index and the Sustainable Apparel Coalition have actively participated in the process and provided some of the baseline data, but more importantly the methodology for using the data. It is a paradox that data sets that are behind a paywall will partially be the base for assessing environmental impacts of products sold 'openly' on the European market, no matter if this takes a form as mandatory or voluntary labelling or is the basis for what green claims companies can use for their products.

In late May 2021, two companies, Swedish H&M and Norwegian Norrøna, introduced consumer-facing 'sustainability profiles', the Higg Material Seal,[1] on two selected products. The products' materials are said to 'show the following reduction in impact when compared to conventional versions of the same materials' with impacts measured for global warming, fossil fuels, water use and water pollution. The comparison is between organic and conventional cotton for the two products. In both these cases, the biggest impact to achieve a better score for the organic product was water savings. However, as rainwater-fed or irrigated cotton, varies from region to region, from year to year—and is not dependant on the cotton being organic or not; this is obviously misleading for a single product (Ferrignos, 2021). All in all using global averages on single, constantly changing products, will never reflect the impact of a given product. Higg Co has also added the following disclaimer: 'The Higg Sustainability Profile and Higg Index Materials seal confirm compliance of the materials used in the product with the criteria set by the Higg Index. It does not certify compliance of the material with the applicable legislation, if any, in the jurisdiction where the product is placed on the market'.

[1] https://profiles.higg.com/profile/PZV6339P gives an example of a organic cotton t-shirt.

Both the development of PEF in the EU and SAC's Higg Index MSI have been the subject of criticism, in research, in media and in the form of EU consultations (Klepp et al., 2021; Kassatly, 2020a, 2020b; Laitala et al., 2018; Watson & Wiedemann, 2019) and have also been subject to much activity on social media platforms. The Executive Director of SAC, Amina Razvi, has responded to parts of this criticism by emphasising that the Higg Index MSI 'is not intended to compare different materials to each other, such as trying to compare cotton to polyester, and it is not a comprehensive roster of "good" or "bad" materials' (Razvi, 2021). The problem is that this is exactly the way the tool is used, and if one accesses the overview of the fibres on the Higg platform, it clearly shows that alpaca, silk and wool have a much higher impact than synthetic fibres[2]. In August 2021, Higg Co added several new materials to the MSI, some of which are patented by members of SAC, and are not based on global averages, but the members' own LCAs. Thus, the current MSI has even less of an 'even playground'. In the following, we will quote and refer to some main points in this critique.

Plastic as a Blessing

In 2019, polyester, polyamide and other synthetic fibres represented about 63% of annual global fibre production, comprising about 66.6 million metric tons of plastic fibre consumption (Textile Exchange, 2020a). In their input to the EU on PEF, the Australian Wool Innovation emphasises the need to distinguish between renewable and non-renewable raw materials. They argue that 'Comparisons between textiles comprised of synthetic and natural fibres are compromised by the way the system fails to account for renewability. This results in an implicit bias against renewable raw materials' (AWI, 2020). We can add that in other product groups that use LCAs for comparison, it is highly improbable that fossil based and natural materials are compared, or used within

[2] For example presented at the webinar 'Higg Index Onboarding' on 15.04.2021, available here: https://howtohigg.org/events-resources/general-webinar-recordings/.

the same data sets or tools. We have tried to come up with other examples where this is the norm, and have failed.

This fundamental system boundary difference exists because the calculated environmental impact of fibres produced from petroleum does not include the biological processes required to generate the feedstock (because these processes occurred millions of years ago). Rather, the supply chains begin with the extraction of the raw material from the ground (or ocean beds), with a relatively low environmental footprint. The obvious limitation, is that these materials are non-renewable and from a fundamental perspective, this means supply is finite and the material use is therefore unsustainable. However, the means to quantify this is currently not reflected in LCAs. In contrast, assessment of renewable, natural fibres includes all the environmental impacts associated with growing feedstock like cotton and wool fibre on farms (i.e. the plant and animal processes involved, and the agricultural system required to support these). Typically, LCAs for renewable agricultural production show high impacts for land use (i.e. the farm), nutrient addition to the soil, water consumption and GHG emissions, whereas sourcing fossil fuel involves minimal land use (i.e. land for the oil drilling rig), water consumption and GHG emissions. However, recent observations from satellites have identified major methane leaks from oil and gas extraction, as well as along the pipelines transporting the fuel.[3] This inherent bias should be a source of investigation in the Impact Assessment process and indicates the system is not ready for mandatory adoption.

Microplastics

Synthetics and fossil fashion are problematic for several reasons and extra problematic when they enter nature. Clothing made from synthetic materials are the type of plastic that sheds and leak microplastics into the environment through both washing and daily use (De Falco et al., 2020). Laundering of textiles is an important contributor to microplastic pollution of the sea (Browne et al., 2011; Henry et al., 2019; Ross et al.,

[3] https://e360.yale.edu/features/in-push-to-find-methane-leaks-satellites-gear-up-for-the-hunt.

2021). Daily clothing and textile use release fibres into the air at a rate that is equal to or potentially greater than the release of microfibres through washing (De Falco et al., 2020). Airborne microfibres are deposited onto land and into water systems from routes outside of laundering, and therefore filtration is an insufficient solution to addressing microplastic and microfibre pollution.

The knowledge about microplastics from clothing has developed in parallel with the development of both LCA and PEF methodology for textiles and at alarming rates, but without so far having consequences for the said methods. Microplastics are not considered in the 16 environmental indicators for PEF (which are climate change, human toxicity, eutrophication, resource depletion, acidification, eco-toxicity, land use, etc.), and they are not included in the Higg Index MSI or Product Module. As of 2021, no LCAs, integrity or labelling schemes for textiles address this problem.

The Variation in Materials

Synthetic materials are based on a relatively uniform raw material source, which is extracted by the petroleum industry. Wool and the other natural fibres, on the other hand, have a history starting 10–8000 BC and has evolved through various local adaptations across the globe. Wool has been collected from wild and later domesticated animals, also plucked or shorn from animals such as dogs, cats, yak, alpaca, camels, goats, rabbits, musk ox, vicuñas and sheep that have been kept for many different purposes and in different cultures. Even today, the production and use of sheep and other wool animals vary a lot. In Norway, the sheep (and goats) graze in open landscapes such as forests and mountains during summer, and because lambs are born in the spring, grazing is utilised to the maximum in the season where plants germinate and grow. This is part of the natural carbon cycle. The main product is, however, meat (in the case of goats, milk), and wool is a by-product. In Poland, which we will look closer at in Chapter 3, on the other hand, the main products for mountain sheep are meat and milk, but there is still a focus on grazing in open landscapes, so-called 'rangeland grazing' and the use of this wool is nearly non-existent.

In the largest producing countries today, such as Australia, wool is the main product, and meat is a by-product; thus, the production is not about the number of lambs, but growing as much wool as possible on each animal. The sheep farmers also call themselves 'wool-growers'. The LCA evaluations for these different production systems will vary, but the figures entered in the current evaluations are based on Australian Merino. Overall, it is very complicated to claim what are the environmental impacts of wool, because it depends on the form of operation and the allocation of the impact on the different products, something we will return to in the discussion of regenerative agriculture and climate-positive wool.

The problem when it comes to silk and how it has received such a poor score in the MSI probably relates to how the information was obtained. China is the world's largest silk producer and has the optimal natural conditions for producing this fibre with lower environmental impact, but does not openly share details about its production. Lack of openness has led to figures from India being used—particularly a study that was not intended to be used in this way but rather to show-case the lack of naturally optimal conditions, and which is therefore not suitable for giving a good picture of global silk production (Kassatly, 2020b). Decisive for the low environmental impact scores of polyester, is that LCA data from Europe is used as a basis, and not data from the large (and more polluting) petroleum-based industry in the Far East (Kassatly, 2020a). As Luo et al. (2021) state, 'Due to the large technical differences in different regions, the data of developing and developed countries are not necessarily interchangeable'.

For the further processing of fibres into yarns and knitted and woven garments, very different environmental impacts and the lack of data from China, also cause problems. Most of the LCA databases, especially the ones used by Higg, 'were developed for the European countries. Data from developing countries, where a majority of the textiles and apparel production occur, are very limited' (Luo et al., 2021). This leads to major scope and parameter problems, as described more in detail by Kassatly (2020a, 2020b, 2021b). Her criticism of the Higg Index MSI for their use of nonrelevant data, and especially for using this data to expand to global averages, using marginal studies, showcases how this became highly problematic.

Natural Material's Significance for Biological and Cultural Diversity

LCA and comparison tools that calculate environmental impacts, do so by quantifying only negative factors. Human activity over many thousands of years has obviously affected our planet in many ways that are negative, but this activity can also be positive. An example of the positive is the great diversity of species in the cultural landscape and the grazed landscape (Muri et al., 2020) and the development of biodiversity within livestock and for all other species (Leroy et al., 2018). In Chapter 4 we will discuss some of the other positive aspects, such as cultural heritage and historic factors.

Loss of biodiversity is considered one of the major environmental threats and the second largest factor when addressing the planetary boundaries (Steffen et al., 2015), but in order to maintain biodiversity, a number of traditional ways of utilising nature, e.g. grazing animals, need to be maintained. In the same way, UNESCO focuses on crafts and the preservation of Indigenous cultures. The long cultural history and the diverse handicraft techniques underpinning the processing of natural fibres are cultural troves in the same way as biodiversity. This great cultural and biological diversity is not considered as positive in an LCA context or in the tools that build on these datasets. This deficiency becomes particularly conspicuous when we see the consequences for Indigenous peoples, as cultural preservation for them is a critical priority, but this vital aspect of sustainability goes unaddressed (Kassatly, 2021b). This will be further discussed in chapter 4.

The Use Phase

The methodology for LCAs and also for PEF includes the use phase as one of the stages in the life cycle of clothing. However, not many LCAs of clothes have been carried out where the use phase is included in detail (Laitala & Klepp, 2020). In the few that have been done, all show that use, both in terms of lifespan and in the number of laundry cycles, is of great importance for the final result (Klepp et al., 2020). In an LCA of a wool sweater, the results showed that the 'garment use phase was a significant contributor to fossil fuel (30.4%), global warming (13.4%), and water stress (37.1%). Consumer transport and the retail of garments in stores contributed to 12.6% fossil fuel, across the value chain' (Wiedemann et al., 2020). In the analysis of the said sweater, an average number of wears and frequency of use was calculated. This amounted to 109 times of use (divided between two users) and with an average of 5.2 times of use between laundering. Therefore differences in laundry and use habits are very important for the totality, and the use phase thus becomes relatively more important the longer the garments are used (Wiedemann et al., 2021).

An important question is whether this varies with fibre? That is, if clothes made from different fibres are used and laundered differently, used longer or more often, and if they are used by several people. The answer here is 'yes' (Laitala et al., 2020), but because clothes not only vary in which fibre they are made from but also for example whether they are underwear or a coat, this is a highly complex matter.

In the development of PEF, there is agreement that use should be included in the evaluation, but so far, the 'how' is elusive. There is an important difference in the discussion[4] between basing use on the properties of the clothes, or on empirical knowledge of how similar garments are used. An example of this is longevity. One school of thought bases lifespans on strength, which is a complex, yet measurable, phenomenon for clothing. Strength can be measured as pilling, tear strength, abrasion resistance and more, and can be done in textile laboratories and

[4] Information about PEF is from the IWTO's TAG group, which includes Laitala and Klepp, and which supports the IWTO's representative in PEF with professional advice.

thereby provide verifiable answers. Synthetic fibres are far stronger than natural ones, especially finer wools and silk. Nevertheless, wool and silk are used longer than synthetics, and synthetic clothes are reused less often than clothes in natural fibres (Laitala & Klepp, 2020). This shows that there is no accordance between technical and social lifespans for synthetic garments (Klepp et al., 2020).

Basing the 'longevity' of clothing on strength will further improve synthetics' environmental status in the PEF accounts. If, on the other hand, we look at use, the picture is different. Wool and the other natural fibres are overrepresented among clothes with several users. Natural fibres are 'weaker' in comparison with polyester, but do not have a shorter lifespan. In Norway, the national costume, *bunad*, and knitted sweaters in wool are, on average, the oldest garments in the wardrobe (Laitala et al., 2018). Another way to discuss this is to look at the reasons for disposing of clothes (Laitala, 2014), which show that wear and tear is an important reason, but not the only reason. Approximately 1/3 of clothes are disposed of for this reason, as clothes must also suit the body and the occasion, and be liked by the owner, in order to stay in active use (Laitala, 2014).

In the development of the EU's PEF for clothing, there have been many good suggestions for indicators of longevity, ranging from price and number of collections a year, to questions that have to do with clothing design. The logic behind frequent collections is that they increase the speed of turn-around, and on the one hand, this makes it harder for quality assurance and development of collections, and on the other hand, it contributes to an increase in consumption, with a steady stream of 'new' products.

There is widespread agreement that repair extends garment lifespan. But which clothes are 'repairable'? And what is deliberately made to have a short lifespan and how, in other words, how is 'planned obsolescence' part of clothing design? There are obvious examples of non-repairable clothing, such as built-in batteries and flashing elements placed on garments, or event logos that clearly tie a piece of clothing to a given and short use (so-called 'merch') (Klepp et al., 2021). But can an extra button attached to the shirt actually lead to the missing button being replaced? Or will it contribute to actual higher environmental impacts because these buttons are most often not used? Those who have a habit of sewing on a button, do so regardless of whether there is such a spare button attached or not. These are some of many empirical inquires that have not been investigated, but need to be if the spare button' is to be used as an indication of a more repairable garment. This illustrates that the legitimate wish to label apparel with their environmental footprint is at an immature stage, as knowledge and methodologies for the use phase are lacking.

Who Has the Credibility to Talk About Fibres?

Industries have played an active role in undermining research and facts that harm their business and bottom line. This is well known from the tobacco, sugar and pesticide industries (Givel, 2006; Jansen, 2017; McHenry, 2018; Norum, 2005). Could it be that the greenwashing of synthetics is a similar case, in other words, a strategy to increase profits from synthetic fibres by claiming that they are 'greener' than the more expensive natural fibres?

Several claims on this have been made and Kassatly (2020a, 2020b, 2021a) is the one who has addressed this the most profoundly, painstakingly tracing the origin of the 'facts' about cotton and synthetic fibres back to an obscure blog from the polyester sector in 2009. She shows how the undocumented claims live their own life and are constantly referred to by various sources and re-referenced. The origin itself is a company that stood to gain economically from an increase in sales of synthetic fibres as the company itself produced dyes that could not be used on natural fibres at all. Kassatley's work is convincing and is supported by a report from Transformers Foundation (2021) about the widespread misinformation and myths surrounding cotton's environmental impact. At the same time it is somewhat paradoxical that the non-scientific aspect of such sources is criticised by publications that are neither academic nor peer reviewed. In other words, it is difficult to thoroughly document such claims. What is easier to document, however, is the lack of scientific documentation of the natural fibres' large environmental footprint, and also the actual circumstances surrounding the relationship between the plastic industry and the advent and growth of fast fashion. As already mentioned, irrigated vs. rainfed cotton, whether organic or conventional, will vary from region to region and from year to year (Transformers Foundation, 2021).

Several studies have thus shown that the environmental footprint from natural fibres have quite different impacts and offer better results. Studies of wool have shown that the production has lower environmental impacts than the production of synthetic materials (Asdrubali et al., 2012). The energy required to process wool as a raw material is lower compared to that required for synthetic materials (Borlea Mureşan et al., 2020). Hassan and Carr (2019) found that processing 1 m^3 of sheep wool insulation produces only about 5.4 kg of CO^2 whereas the same quantity of mineral wool produces 135 kg of CO^2. Parlato and Porto (2020) argue for an additional environmental advantage of wool related to transport, as wool can be compressed allowing for big reductions in volume, and thereby for more wool to be transported at a time. It is, in other words, clear that different studies rank wool against synthetic fibres in varying ways and with very different results.

Kassatly has, as we have written, followed up on the 'facts' that compare cotton and synthetic fibres back to an obscure blog from the polyester sector in 2009, the same year the Made-By assessment first appeared (Kviseth & Tobiasson, 2011). However, the competition between natural and synthetic fibres is much older. The synthetic fibres were invented in the 1930s and their use increased in the 1980s by replacing many essential garments in wool, such as thermal underwear and thicker woollen garments, with mid-layers in acrylic, or polyester fleece (named after the wool fleece as the structure imitates what is shorn off the sheep), outerwear and Gore-Tex clothing. Even the most important garments in cotton, the casual t-shirt and jeans, were increasingly blended with elastane, and in the formal attire, wool was challenged by polyester, not only as cheaper raw material, but also as easier to produce, because the moulding of wool through the time-consuming tailor-technique with heat and pressing, and sewing, has been replaced by the synthetics being cast permanently with only heat. Since the 1980s, the use of synthetic fibres has exploded, and it is mainly the production of synthetic fibres that has increased, as the natural fibres have been fairly constant on the market, and wool has even decreased slightly. We can therefore claim that fast fashion was made possible through the easily and cheaply available fossil-based synthetics and would not be possible without these. Central to this argument is that the increase in demand has not led to higher prices (Kassatly, 2020a; Schor, 2005).

The dominant business model for 'fast' or 'fossil fashion', including the sports/athleisure industry, is based on large volumes, fast turnover, low quality, inadequate control systems and insufficient product information. Overproduction is thus a systemic problem (Fletcher, 2009). According to the industry's own 'state of fashion' report, there has been a doubling of clothing production and consumption levels in the past 20 years (referenced in the industry as the rise of fast fashion). The average consumer purchases 60% more clothing than they did 15 years ago and wears each item for half as long (BOF & McKinsey Company, 2019). It is difficult to envisage a similar continued growth based on natural fibres. Although volume is an issue that none of the evaluation tools discussed actually address, it is nevertheless the most important issue in this chapter. Designating the synthetic fibres as a green solution will enable the global sports and fast fashion industry to improve their environmental footprints based on the tools described, all the while increasing their production. Because the volumes of natural fibres, except for cotton, are so small, they are easy to both phase out and replace. Continued volume growth may be the result of an environmental strategy that is unwilling to address volume, which in trade forums is often called 'the elephant in room'. For large and small producers of natural fibres around the world, such a strategy will be catastrophic, and specifically so for smallholders and farmers in the mountain and marginal rural areas who make a small living by selling wool from grazing animals.

So far, it is clear that the biggest Fast Fashion and sports brands do not take microplastics and plastic pollution seriously (Kassatly, 2020a). The Higg Index's failure to address these issues is a good example. The issue is seen as a technical one that needs to be further studied before they include the shedding as an environmental problem. However, we and other researchers argue for a radical, systemic change instead, which puts the planet and the health of all species, including humans, before industry and business' need for profit, thus opposing an economic growth logic, expressed as the *Earth Logic Research Plan* (ELRP) (Fletcher & Tham, 2019). The ELRP presents a perspective including reduction in production and consumption of textiles, and where synthetics are sourced out and replaced by natural, biodegradable fibres (Biomimicry Institute, 2020; Patel et al., 2020). Synthetic textiles are seen as highly problematic, as synthetic textiles in the way of all plastics cannot be isolated in separate closed loops from natural materials, as they inevitably 'leak', especially during use and laundering. A consequence of this is the standpoint that 'any material in use must not pollute when it inevitably escapes' and 'there is no alternative to the phasing out of non-compostable materials like polyester' (Biomimicry Institute, 2020, p. 9–10). This position is in clear contrast to the idea of recycling plastic as a way to solve the problem, as is often promoted by the textile industry itself (McKinsey & GFA, 2020). This is also a theme in Chapter 6.

A Question of Volume or Quality

If one sees the environmental problems in the textile industry as one of volume, where too much is produced, acquired, laundered and disposed of, then it is urgent to find solutions and regulations that reach the core of this problem. In finding solutions to ease environmental impacts, replacing one product with another product (with actual or alleged lower environmental impact) is a strategy with lower potential, compared to strategies where fewer products enter into circulation, whether through a reorganisation of consumption or through less consumption (Stø et al., 2017). The same problem applies to ecolabels more generally, because they are based on a comparison between products and the quantity/service life aspect is therefore poorly addressed, if at all. So far, neither PEF, the Higg Index MSI, nor ecolabels possess the tools that are suitable for systemic change. As we have seen, they are hardly suitable to compare one garment against another, as the data is of too poor quality and too old, and the value chains are too global and complex. As Luo et al. (2021) state, the Higg Index has 'certain limitations. In particular, difficulty in data acquisition and unidimensionality are main problems'.

When facing branding schemes and comparison tools, information campaigns, etc., we believe that some important questions should be asked:

- Are they suitable for tackling the big problems: volume and overproduction?
- Are they based on open sources and transparent data and assumptions?
- Who makes a profit from the claims put forward, and are these the same actors that are responsible for the development and/or management of the systems?
- Who stands to be hurt by the results and consequences of following the advice?

Documenting and comparing environmental impacts of different products, such as clothing, is necessary for the work towards sustainability. Nevertheless, the desire to launch such tools quickly, must not come at the expense of quality and credibility. So far, the tools available to compare environmental impacts from textiles are at best immature, at worst unreliable or even corrupt. They use deficient and opaque sources, and the 'winners' in the system are also seemingly the ones who mostly control the underpinning truths on which the tools themselves are based. When facing this conundrum, it is therefore probably best to point out their weaknesses while continuing to work for better tools. It is even more important, however, to work for both climate and environmental improvements in all parts of the value chains. Finally, the discussion needs to shift to the quantity being produced, to quality, longevity and functionality, and it should be acknowledged that all production growing rapidly and uncontrolled is in itself a threat to the planetary boundaries. This discussion will continue in the chapters that follow, looking at how the global textile industry and its push for cheap labour and raw materials has relied on growth and increasing margins, rather than safe-guarding humans, animals, our land, waterways and fresh air—everything we rely on to protect our biosphere.

References

Asdrubali, F., Schiavoni, S., & Horoshenkov, K. V. (2012). A review of sustainable materials for acoustic applications. *Building Acoustics, 19*(4), 283–311. https://doi.org/10.1260/1351-010X.19.4.283

AWI. (2020). *Feedback from Australian wool innovation Ltd to EU initiative "Environmental performance of products & businesses—Substantiating Claims"*. Brussels

Biomimicry Institute. (2020). *The nature of fashion: Moving towards a regenerative system.* https://bioplasticsnews.com/wp-content/uploads/2020/07/The-Nature-of-Fashion.pdf

Bodin, R. (2016). *To reuse or to incinerate?: A case study of the environmental impacts of two alternative waste management strategies for household textile waste in nine municipalities in northern Stockholm.*

BOF & McKinsey Company. (2019). *The state of fashion 2019.* https://www.mckinsey.com/~/media/mckinsey/industries/retail/our%20insights/the%20state%20of%20fashion%202019%20a%20year%20of%20awakening/the-state-of-fashion-2019-final.ashx

Borlea Mureşan, S. I., Tiuc, A.-E., Nemeş, O., Vermeşan, H., & Vasile, O. (2020). Innovative use of sheep wool for obtaining materials with improved sound-absorbing properties. *Materials (basel), 13*(3), 694. https://doi.org/10.3390/ma13030694

Browne, M. A., Crump, P., Niven, S. J., Teuten, E., Tonkin, A., Galloway, T., & Thompson, R. (2011). Accumulation of microplastic on shorelines woldwide: Sources and sinks. *Environmental Science & Technology, 45*(21), 9175–9179. https://doi.org/10.1021/es201811s

De Falco, F., Cocca, M., Avella, M., & Thompson, R. C. (2020). Microfiber release to water, via laundering, and to air, via everyday use: A comparison between polyester clothing with differing textile parameters. *Environmental Science & Technology, 54*(6), 3288–3296. https://doi.org/10.1021/acs.est.9b06892

Ferrignos, S. (2021.)Breakouts from Bremen. *Ecotextile News, 103*, 58.

Fletcher, K. (2009). Systems change for sustainability in textiles. In R. S. Blackburn (Ed.), *Sustainable textiles: Life cycle and environmental impact* (pp. 369–380). The Textile Institute: Woodhead Publishing.

Fletcher, K., & Tham, M. (2019). *Earth logic: Fashion action research plan.* JJ Charitable Trust.

Givel, M. (2006). Punctuated equilibrium in Limbo: The tobacco lobby and U.S. state policymaking from 1990 to 2003. *Policy Studies Journal, 34*(3), 405–418. doi:https://doi.org/10.1111/j.1541-0072.2006.00179.x

Hassan, M. M., & Carr, C. M. (2019). A review of the sustainable methods in imparting shrink resistance to wool fabrics. *Journal of Advanced Research, 18*, 39–60. https://doi.org/10.1016/j.jare.2019.01.014

Heidenstrøm, N., Strandbakken, P., Haugrønning, V., & Laitala, K. (2021). *The status of product lifetime in environmental policy.*

Henry, B., Laitala, K., & Klepp, I. G. (2019). Microfibres from apparel and home textiles: Prospects for including microplastics in environmental sustainability assessment. *Science of the Total Environment, 652*, 483–494. https://doi.org/10.1016/j.scitotenv.2018.10.166

ISO 14040. (2006). *Environmental management—Life cycle assessment—Principles and framework.* International Organization for Standardization.

Jansen, K. (2017). Business conflict and risk regulation: Understanding the influence of the pesticide industry. *Global Environmental Politics, 17*(4), 48–66.

Kassatly, V. B. (2020a). Was it polyester all along? *Apparel Insider (14).* https://www.veronicabateskassatly.com/read/was-it-polyester-all-along

Kassatly, V. B. (2020b). Silk revisited. *Apparel Insider(14).* https://www.veronicabateskassatly.com/read/silk-revisited

Kassatly, V. B. (2021a). Natural versus plastic: How the truth got twisted. *Apparel Insider.* https://apparelinsider.com/natural-versus-plastic-how-the-truth-became-twisted/

Kassatly, V. B. (2021b). *Why questioning the sustainability of wool is misguided.* https://fibershed.org/2021/11/17/why-questioning-sustainability-of-wool-is-misguided/?utm_medium=email&utm_source=newsletter&utm_campaign=newsletter_feature&utm_content=content.

Kassatly, V. B., & Baumann-Pauly, D. (Forthcoming). *The great green washing machine part 2: The use and misuse of sustainability metrics in fashion.* Eco Age.

Klepp, I. G., Buck, M., Laitala, K., & Kjeldsberg, M. (2016). What's the problem? Odor-control and the smell of sweat in sportswear. *Fashion Practice: The Journal of Design, Creative Process & the Fashion Industry, 8*(2), 296–317. https://doi.org/10.1080/17569370.2016.1215117

Klepp, I. G., Laitala, K., & Wiedemann, S. (2020). Clothing lifetimes: What should be measured and how. *Sustainability, 12*(6219), 21. https://doi.org/10.3390/su12156219

Klepp, I. G., & Tobiasson, T. S. (2020). *Lettkledd. Velkledd med lite miljøbelastning*. Solumbokvennen.

Klepp, I. G., Tobiasson, T., & Haugsrud, I. (2021). The COP26 plastic uniforms are a disaster for the environment. *Science Norway*. https://sciencenorway.no/clothing-opinion-plastic/the-cop26-plastic-uniforms-are-a-disaster-for-the-environment/1931507

Kviseth, K., & Tobiasson, T. S. (2011, April 26–27). *Pulling wool over our eyes: The dirty business of LCAs*. Paper presented at the KEA Conference Towards sustainability in Textiles and Fashion industry, Copenhagen.

Laitala, K. (2014). Consumers' clothing disposal behaviour—A synthesis of research results. *International Journal of Consumer Studies, 38*(5), 444–457. https://doi.org/10.1111/ijcs.12088

Laitala, K., & Klepp, I. G. (2020). What affects garment lifespans? International clothing practices based on wardrobe survey in China, Germany, Japan, the UK and the USA. *Sustainability, 12*(21). doi:https://doi.org/10.3390/su12219151

Laitala, K., Klepp, I. G., & Henry, B. (2018). Does use matter? Comparison of environmental impacts of clothing based on fiber type. *Sustainability, 10*(7), 2524. https://doi.org/10.3390/su10072524

Laitala, K., Klepp, I. G., Kettlewell, R., & Wiedemann, S. (2020). Laundry care regimes: Do the practices of keeping clothes clean have different environmental impacts based on the fibre content? *Sustainability, 12*(18), 7537. https://doi.org/10.3390/su12187537

Leroy, G., Hoffmann, I., From, T., Hiemstra, S. J., & Gandini, G. (2018). Perception of livestock ecosystem services in grazing areas. *Animal, 12*(12), 2627–2638. https://doi.org/10.1017/S1751731118001027

Luo, Y., Song, K., Ding, X., & Wu, X. (2021). Environmental sustainability of textiles and apparel: A review of evaluation methods. *Environmental Impact Assessment Review, 86*,. https://doi.org/10.1016/j.eiar.2020.106497

McHenry, L. B. (2018). The Monsanto papers: Poisoning the scientific well. *International Journal of Risk & Safety in Medicine, 29*, 193–205. https://doi.org/10.3233/JRS-180028

McKinsey & GFA. (2020). *Fashion on climate*. https://www.mckinsey.com/~/media/mckinsey/industries/retail/our%20insights/fashion%20on%20climate/fashion-on-climate-full-report.pdf

McQueen, R., & Vaezafshar, S. (2019). Odor in textiles: A review of evaluation methods, fabric characteristics, and odor control technologies. *Textile Research Journal*. https://doi.org/10.1177/0040517519883952

Muri, K., Tufte, P. A., Coleman, G., & Moe, R. O. (2020). Exploring work-related characteristics as predictors of Norwegian sheep farmers' affective job satisfaction. *Sociologia Ruralis, 60*(3), 574–595.

Nazare, S. (2009). Environmentally friendly flame-retardant textiles. In R. Blackburn (Ed.), *Sustainable textiles* (pp. 339–368). Elsevier.

Norum, K. R. (2005). World health organization's global strategy on diet, physical activity and health: The process behind the scenes. *Scandinavian Journal of Nutrition, 49*(2), 83–88. https://doi.org/10.1080/11026480510037147

Östlund, Å., Roos, S., Sweet, S., & Sjöström, E. (2020). *Investor brief: Sustainability in textiles and fashion.* https://www.mistra.org/wp-content/uploads/2020/09/mistradialogue_rapport_investor_brief_textiles_final.pdf

Östlund, Å., Wedin, H., Bolin, L., Berlin, J., Jönsson, C., Posner, S., Smuk, L., Eriksson, M., & Sandin, G. (2015). *Textilåtervinning: Tekniska möjligheter och utmaningar*. Naturvårdsverket.

Parlato, M. C. M., & Porto, S. M. C. (2020). Organized framework of main possible applications of sheep wool fibers in building components. *Sustainability (basel, Switzerland), 12*(3), 761. https://doi.org/10.3390/su12030761

Patel, D., Moon, D., Tangri, N., & Wilson, M. (2020). *All talk and no recycling: An investigation of the U.S "chemical recycling" industry*. https://www.no-burn.org/chemical-recycling-us/

Quantis. (2018). *Measuring fashion. Environmental impact of the global apparel and footwear industries study*. Retrieved from Lausanne, Switzerland https://quantis-intl.com/wp-content/uploads/2018/03/measuringfashion_globalimpactstudy_full-report_quantis_cwf_2018a.pdf

Razvi, A. (2021). *The purpose and power of the Higg MSI*. https://www.linkedin.com/pulse/purpose-power-higg-msi-amina-razvi/

Ross, P. S., Chastain, S., Vassilenko, E., Etemadifar, A., Zimmermann, S., Quesnel, S.-A., Eert, J., Solomon, E., Patankar, S., Posacka, A. M., & Williams, B. (2021). Pervasive distribution of polyester fibres in the Arctic Ocean is driven by Atlantic inputs. *Nature Communications, 12*(1), 106. https://doi.org/10.1038/s41467-020-20347-1

SAC. (2020). *The Higg index*. https://apparelcoalition.org/the-higg-index/

Schmidt, A., Watson, D., Roos, S., Askham, C., & Poulsen, P. B. (2016). *Gaining benefits from discarded textiles: LCA of different treatment pathways*. Retrieved from Copenhagen: http://norden.diva-portal.org/smash/get/diva2:957517/FULLTEXT02.pdf

Schor, J. B. (2005). Prices and quantities: Unsustainable consumption and the global economy. *Ecological Economics, 55*(3), 309–320. https://doi.org/10.1016/j.ecolecon.2005.07.030

Shen, L., Worrell, E., & Patel, M. K. (2010). Open-loop recycling: A LCA case study of PET bottle-to-fibre recycling. *Resources, Conservation and Recycling, 55*(1), 34–52. https://doi.org/10.1016/j.resconrec.2010.06.014

Shen, L., Worrell, E., & Patel, M. K. (2012). Comparing life cycle energy and GHG emissions of bio-based PET, recycled PET, PLA, and man-made cellulosics. *Biofuels, Bioproducts and Biorefining, 6*(6), 625–639.

Sinclair, R. (2015). *Textiles and fashion: Materials, design and technology* (Vol. 126).

Steffen, W., Richardson, K., Rockström, J., Cornell, S. E., Fetzer, I., Bennett, E. M., Biggs, R., Carpenter, S. R., de Vries, W., de Wit, C. A., Folke, C., Gerten, D., Heinke, J., Mace, G., & M., Persson, L. M., Ramanathan, V., Reyers, B., & Sörlin, S. (2015). Planetary boundaries: Guiding human development on a changing planet. *Science, 347*(6223), 1259855. https://doi.org/10.1126/science.1259855

Stø, E., Throne-Holst, H., Strandbakken, P., & Vittersø, G. (2017). Review: A multi-dimensional approach to the study of consumption in modern societies and the potential for radical sustainable changes. In *System Innovation for Sustainability 1* (pp. 244–264) Routledge.

Takedomi Karlsson, M., & Ramasar, V. (2020). Selling women the green dream: The paradox of feminism and sustainability in fashion marketing. *Journal of Political Ecology, 27*(1), 335–359. https://doi.org/10.2458/v27i1.23584

Textile Exchange. (2020a). *Preferred fiber & materials market report 2020.* https://textileexchange.org/wp-content/uploads/2020/06/Textile-Exchange_Preferred-Fiber-Material-Market-Report_2020.pdf

Textile Exchange. (2020b). *Preferred fiber and material matrix. Draft methodology summary for public consultation.* https://textileexchange.org/wp-content/uploads/2020/12/PFM-Matrix-Public-Consultation-Final.pdf

Transformers Foundation. (2021). *Cotton: A case study in misinformation.* https://www.worldcottonday.com/location/cotton-a-case-study-in-misinformation/

Watson, K. J., & Wiedemann, S. G. (2019). review of methodological choices in LCA-based textile and apparel rating tools: Key issues and recommendations relating to assessment of fabrics made from natural fibre types. *Sustainability, 11*(14), 3846. https://doi.org/10.3390/su11143846

Wiedemann, S. G., Biggs, L., Nebel, B., Bauch, K., Laitala, K., Klepp, I. G., Swan, P. G., & Watson, K. (2020). Environmental impacts associated with the production, use, and end-of-life of a woollen garment. *The International Journal of Life Cycle Assessment, 25*(8), 1486–1499. https://doi.org/10.1007/s11367-020-01766-0

Wiedemann, S. G., Biggs, L., Nguyen, Q. V., Clarke, S. J., Laitala, K., & Klepp, I. G. (2021). Reducing environmental impacts from garments through best practice garment use and care, using the example of a Merino wool sweater. *The International Journal of Life Cycle Assessment*. https://doi.org/10.1007/s11367-021-01909-x

Wolfe, I. (2018). Made-by environmental benchmark for fibres. *Good on you.* https://goodonyou.eco/made-by-environmental-benchmark-for-fibres/

3

Upping the WOOLUME: Waste Prevention Based on Optimal Use of Materials

Vilde Haugrønning, Jan Broda, Ingvild Svorkmo Espelien, Ingun Grimstad Klepp, Katarzyna Kobiela-Mendrek, Monika Rom, Anna Schytte Sigaard, and Tone Skårdal Tobiasson

A well-known folk song in Norway tells the story of a hunter who shoots a crow and all the end-uses and resources he is able to derive from the dead bird. The results are meat, long ropes and manure grips, to name

The original version of this chapter was revised: The figure credits of this chapter (Figs. 3.2 and 3.3) were inadvertently switched. The correction to this chapter is available at https://doi.org/10.1007/978-3-030-88300-3_8

V. Haugrønning (✉) · I. G. Klepp · A. S. Sigaard
Consumption Research Norway (SIFO), Oslo Metropolitan University, Oslo, Norway
e-mail: vildeh@oslomet.no

I. G. Klepp
e-mail: ingunk@oslomet.no

J. Broda · K. Kobiela-Mendrek · M. Rom
University of Bielsko-Biala, Bielsko-Biala, Poland

I. S. Espelien
Selbu spinneri, Klæbu, Norway

T. S. Tobiasson
Nordic Initiative Clean & Ethical Fashion, Oslo, Norway

I. G. Klepp and T. S. Tobiasson (eds.), *Local, Slow and Sustainable Fashion*, https://doi.org/10.1007/978-3-030-88300-3_3

a few of the outcomes. The last verse ends thus: 'he who is not able to use a crow in this way, is not worthy of a crow at all'. Making good use of materials and resources once they are harvested, was the very melody in most pre-industrial economies and one had great respect for what one did harvest. Nothing was wasted, and a variety of resources was utilised in the best way possible. Industrialisation has led to many local and even surprising resources, such as wool, being exchanged for cheaper ones. Since wool in Europe is mostly a by-product of sheep meat or milk production, it is also a 'fly in the ointment' in an economy that tends to have a one-eyed, mono-cultural view of agriculture and other production systems. In this chapter, we will take a deep dive into the sad fate of wool in Europe. Based on the experiences from sheep farming in Poland and the WOOLUME project, we will look into the different uses of wool. As a resource, wool has much potential that today is not optimised. This is partly due to the fact that wool lacks a clear definition in EU regulations, and this ambiguity around the definition of wool in Europe is one factor that hinders optimal utilisation.

The Proud History of Polish Wool

Sheep farming belongs to the oldest known human activities and its history coincides with the history of mankind. For many centuries, sheep determined the wealth and prosperity of great civilisations. The earliest records of sheep farming on Polish territory are dated back to the thirteenth century, when Wallachians, settlers from the Balkans, obtained areas in the Carpathian Mountains and introduced pastoral management (Wistuba et al., 2018). This brought about significant changes in the Polish mountains, as shepherds adopted the traditions and economic system of the Wallachians. Transhumant pastoralism was introduced almost everywhere, and new settlements cropped up as groups of shepherds moved between pastures. Wallachians quickly assimilated with the local population, and in all the areas they settled, they introduced this new way of farming. They grazed sheep that produced wool and cheese, which allowed for economic development based on the mountain resources. Today, similar grazing methods are prevalent in the entire

Carpathians and even in old rituals common to Carpathian shepherds, such as leading the sheep to the mountain pastures on April 23rd St. Wojciech Day, after mass.

At the beginning of the nineteenth century, the sheep population was over 12 million. During this time, the Habsburgs, who ruled the area, decided that pastoralism was an obstacle to the effective harvesting of wood and banned transhuman sheep grazing and activity, depriving highlanders of the right to use meadows, pastures and forests. In the second half of the nineteenth century, afforestation of the highest lands in the mountains began as a means to industrialise timber harvesting. Following this, sheep herding lost its importance.

For centuries, it was clear that sheep farming did have great economic importance. Sheep products—meat, milk, skins and wool—were all commonly used and provided a livelihood for many rural families (Gruszecki et al., 2017). For a long time, wool was the most precious sheep product and what generated the most income for farmers. The production of wool significantly contributed to the Polish textile industry's development, which used to be one of the most important industries in the Polish economy. However, the wool textile industry and traditional sustainable wool processing connected with farming activities in mountain regions were two different stories. In 1548, the Polish guild of weavers/clothiers took steps to protect their craft against competition from the mountain artisans. Historically, farming activities, including breeding and taking care of sheep up to the shearing of wool, scouring and combing were men's duties. Further processing, such as spinning, was reserved for women and was an important part of social life. According to Kamiński 'Women, when men are away for trade, govern households; they spin flax, wool, produce linen or cloth; they are considerate not to waste any of the acquired goods' and this tradition continued until the Second World War (Kamiński, 1992).

In mountain areas, in the period of the subsistence farming economy before industrialisation, wool was used, among other things, to produce uniform fabrics or blankets, all woven in plain weave and all in the natural colours of the white or pigmented wool; different shades were obtained by mixing wool. The typical woven fabrics for outer coats were fulled or felted, making them wear-resistant, heat-insulating and impermeable. The other possibility for creating garments was knitting, and the main products made in this technique were socks and sweaters. Today, traces of the tradition of both weaving and knitting, and manufacturing clothes, is still partially present in folk costumes. The industrial processing of wool developed in parallel. The application of local Polish wool was possible only in lower quality woollen fabrics and in technical fabrics. For the production of high-quality worsted fabrics, wool imported from England and Australia was used.

In conjunction with the political and economic upheaval at the end of the twentieth century, the wool industry collapsed alongside other industries, and the demand for wool in Poland dramatically decreased. Consequently, the hitherto well-organised wool market disappeared. After the Second World War, the number of sheep had reached its highest level in the middle of the 1980s. Later the sheep population decreased dramatically from 5 million in 1986 to less than 1 million in 1994. By the beginning of the new millennium, sheep numbers dropped to approximately 0.2 million and today remain at this level (Fig. 3.1).

The WOOLUME project has its *terroir* in the Beskids mountains, in a region with long sheep farming traditions. After the collapse of

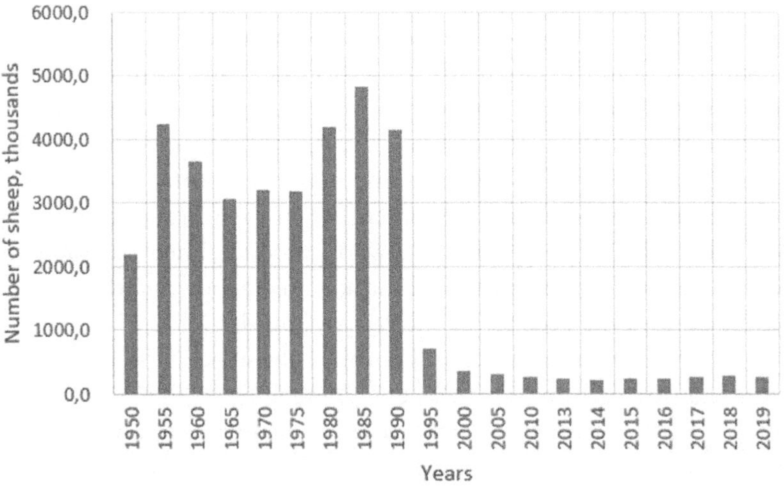

Fig. 3.1 Sheep farming in Poland from 1950 to 2019 (*Illustration* Jan Broda)

the traditional farming practice at the turn of the twenty-first century and a period of deep crisis, the regional project Owca Plus was implemented, aiming to revive grazing activity. The programme has so far mainly supported a renewed interest in cultural identity associated with pastoralism, transhumance, fostering the tradition of folk culture, developing crafts and processing sheep and goat products. This is something we will discuss more in Chapter 6. As a result of this, new farming centres opened, and herd sizes were considerably increased. During the implementation of the programme, meat and cheese became sought-after products. Simultaneously, even though there were measures taken to use wool and sheepskins, and promoting regional products made from these, the situation for wool was not improved. The wool, which previously had determined the wealth of sheep farmers, had lost its economic value, and shearing could not cover the cost of bringing the wool to market. As a result of the textile industry's lack of interest, the wool is sheared, but not sorted, resulting in the quality of wool decreasing even further. The wool has become a waste product.

WOOLUME—The Best Use of Raw Materials

Materials have different qualities and applications, and adding the sustainable lens relates to how materials are used. The WOOLUME project's ambition is to develop solutions for the utilisation of wool from Polish mountain wool, which currently constitutes a waste problem, has the potential to replace the usage of other virgin materials, and as such contribute to local economic development. In particular doing this through collaboration to find good and new uses, that are economically viable instead of being wasted, with, among others, Selbu Spinning Mill, SIFO at Oslo Metropolitan University and the University of Bielsko-Biala in Poland. Selbu Spinning Mill has for a long time developed products that provide opportunities to utilise all wool, and thus avoiding waste. As part of the work in the KRUS project, presented in Chapter 1, Selbu Spinning Mill worked with minimising waste in a process of becoming more sustainable, as 50–60% of the wool from the fleeces delivered are not suited for spinning into knitting yarn. This could be because the wool had felted or contained too many coarse hairs, kemp or medullation. In order to alleviate this problem, the spinning mill experimented with unspun yarn, which is popular for rugs and in so-called 'big knit'. In the book *Knit with Norwegian Wool*, a crocheted basket (Fig. 3.2) in varied sizes using this unspun yarn was introduced alongside a description of how this 'big knit' yarn had come about (Klepp & Tobiasson, 2017).

There are many opportunities to utilise coarser wool such as for path groundings, soil improvement (e.g. fertiliser pellets), insulation, etc. Common to these is that they do not capture a high price on the market. To accelerate or at least revive the wool industry in Poland, it is necessary that products can be sold at a higher price and thus carry as much as possible of the infrastructure and systems that must be in place to ensure the processing of the raw material. We see that new uses that can capture this higher value are being and have already been developed, such as using sheep wool as a material for acoustic and sound absorbing products. These products are used for acoustic attenuation in spaces such as open-office landscapes, museums, libraries, schools and lobbies. Several

Fig. 3.2 Kittens in a 'big knit' crocheted basket (*Photo credit* Tone Skårdal Tobiasson)

studies of the qualities of wool as a sound absorber have concluded that the material holds good acoustic properties and may be used as a substitute for or even compete with market-leading, manmade materials like mineral wool and polyurethane foam (see for example Allafi et al., 2020; Arnesen, 2015; Corscadden et al., 2014; Sigaard & Haugrønning, 2021) (Fig. 3.3).

Using wool instead of manmade materials means creating products where customers are willing to pay a little more because of the aesthetic, emotional satisfaction or other properties delivered. Other properties of wool include natural anti-inflammatory abilities, self-extinguishing effects, allergy-friendliness and biodegradability. These make wool an attractive material for interior products as it is more pleasant to work with during production and has positive effects on the indoor climate where the products are used.

Today, many acoustic wool products are made using Merino wool and other high-quality wool types, mainly due to availability in the market along with concerns for quality factors related to processing, dyeing, etc. Only very fine wool allows for the production of felt with

Fig. 3.3 This type of yarn is one of the things that is now being tried out with Polish wool, among other things to see if they are suitable for tufting (*Photo credit* Jan Broda)

a smooth and even surface. However, even if Merino wool is of high quality in terms of fineness and softness, using Merino for acoustic products may not entail the best application of this wool. If the same level of sound absorption can be achieved using coarser wool, then this will lead to better utilisation of materials, as Merino may instead be used for clothes or other products where softness is an important factor. Accordingly, coarse wool may be most applicable for products where touch or next-to-skin feel is not essential to the user. This includes acoustic installations such as space dividers, screens, carpets, curtains and panels for ceiling and wall, but also other interior products like seat pads, coasters and decorations.

More unconventional products which may be produced from coarse wool include thermal insulation packaging and even funeral urns and coffins. Common to these products is that the end-user is not concerned with the coarseness of the material. For some products, like carpets and rugs, coarser wool may even be preferred, due to durability. In addition, wool is often chosen over man-made materials due to its natural aesthetics. Using a coarser wool will provide a raw and more rustic look and more variety for naturally pigmented wool for the product, which some may prefer (Sigaard & Haugrønning, 2021). Ironically, nonwovens are not reliant on 'softness' in the same way—the wool when unspun is soft—and a New Zealand company[1] has developed diapers, menstrual and cosmetic pads from unspun wool.

Breeds Vary as Product-Focus Differ

The sheep breeds found in Europe are a result of a long history with varying emphasis on different qualities of wool, meat or milk. The older breeds generally have a short tail, as these sheep, like the Old Norse sheep, have a dual-layer coat consisting of an inner layer of short, fine wool fibres (undercoat) and an outer layer of long, coarse wool fibres (guard hairs), which has been described in Chapter 1. Crossbred is a term for sheep with equally long wool fibres in the coat and a long tail, which

[1] https://woolchemy.com/.

we also described in Chapter 1. They have medium-coarse to coarse fibres and were bred to suit the textile industry's requirements for good, strong and easy-to-process wool.

Crossbred sheep were originally introduced to Norway and other countries due to these specific, industrial wool properties, but have since been bred for meat as the populations grew in towns and cities and the need for food increased. At the same time, imported textile fibres became more available, such as cotton. Native breeds of sheep in the Polish Carpathians (such as Polish Mountain Sheep, Zackel, Coloured Mountain Sheep) were bred based on the Wallachian Zackel and were brought there by the Wallachians. A characteristic feature of Mountain sheep is their exceptional resilience when it comes to climatic conditions and diseases. They are strong, undemanding and suitable for long treks and as well as enclosures. Due to the high density of their wool coat, composed of thin down underfibres and much thicker medium and guard hairs, they are excellently protected against prolonged rain (Kawecka & Krupinski, 2014; Kosiek et al., 2012).

Fine-fibred wool has a long history in England and the Iberian Peninsula, where Merino sheep from Spain and Portugal developed the soft and fine wool we now all embrace. It is this breed that has been further honed in South Africa, South America, New Zealand and Australia, which became the 'wool colony'. Today, the Australian Merino wool industry, led by Australian Wool Innovation (AWI), fronts the marketing of wool worldwide with the Woolmark label, and its important research. An influential slogan has been 'no finer feeling' with emphasis on the exceptional softness of said wool. Both the marketing as an 'itch-free' fibre, and a general increase in people's skin sensitivity and focus on physical discomfort/comfort, has made Merino synonymous with 'quality'. Making Merino softer, while marketing itch-free wool as an undeniable positive, has led to new usage of wool in underwear, sports clothes, baby apparel and bedding. This represents markets that for a long time was dominated by cotton and synthetic fibres, though going back 40 years or more this was not necessarily the case (Klepp et al., 2016). It is beneficial that new good products have been developed and that new users have adopted clothes that enable them to exercise and have a good life outdoors in all kinds of weather. However, the one-sided focus on softness is at the same time also problematic. Coarser wool has lost its value and some products are produced in too fine wool, where coarser wool would have been a better choice. In the discussion of wool, expressions such as fine versus less fine/coarse wool are often used, but another expression for coarse wool can also be 'strong wool' (NZ expression), which indicates that the coarser wool has properties that the fine wool does not have.

The one-sided focus on a single property also contributes to others being overlooked and thus not made relevant. For many years, whiteness was such a crucial characteristic, and as a result, the potential for making heathered yarns from pigmented wool was overlooked. Today, as was pointed to in Chapter 1, these yarns have a potential for great market value and uptake. In the same way, the focus on softness has contributed to coarser wool losing market value also in products where this coveted property does not make a difference. As with pigmentation, something is lost along the way. Other wool may have greater strength, elasticity, lustre, etc., or it may have a lower price. Unlike much else that is emphasised in the knowledge base of the circular economy, this aspect of using the best available raw material for products, and not those that are 'too good', is a 'no-go' topic.

Waste Prevention in a New Light

There is no data on the amount of greasy wool being disposed of as waste. On an EU scale, it is hard to estimate exactly how much as this has not been studied. In connection with an overview of the Nordic region, the following statistics emerged: 'Back in 2010, a study was published by the Textile College in Borås stating that "up until three years ago, without wool collection stations at the point of slaughter-house, 80% of the Swedish 1100-ton wool-clip was burned or thrown away as waste". (…) Most of the wool shorn in Denmark, ended up as waste until recently. (…) Of the around 572 tons estimated wool produced, the national Finnish Natural Resource Center believe that somewhere between 70 and 90% of all wool is waste' (Tobiasson, 2020). During the Baltic Wool Conference in the fall of 2020, Professor Ave Matsin from Tartu Cultural Academy, claimed that somewhere between 85 and 90% of Estonian wool is destroyed or wasted, based on figures from the 'Wool Industry Development Plan 2016–2036' written in 2015 made by a voluntary working group at the Estonian Sheep and Goat Breeders Association.[2] If one extrapolates these findings to the rest of the EU, it is highly probable that the numbers are similar. This has been the basis for both the WOOLUME project with Poland and the hiWool project with Portugal.

Three countries that are not part of the EU, on the other hand, have well-functioning wool value chains: the United Kingdom, Iceland and Norway. Here, most of the wool is collected, scoured and sold on both the local and global markets. During Covid-19, though, there have been reports that the price of wool dropped below the price of shearing.[3] Norway's share of wool waste is small; however, some wool is also wasted here. In a survey from the KRUS project among farmers with the Old Norse sheep breed, 50% of the farmers with larger herds, between 50 and 190 sheep, replied that they throw away the wool. Wool from older sheep breeds such as these has meagre prices and also lack industrial uptake, which means that it is often burned, thrown into the sea, dug down in the soil or disposed of in other manners. Some artisans have used wool for felting for many years, and on a smaller scale, wool has been used for spinning yarns for knitwear and fabrics. Hillesvåg Spinning Mill has for several years received Old Norse sheep wool from some farmers for commission spinning and has found that the wool quality varies widely from flock to flock. Research has shown that if large volumes of Old Norse sheep wool are to be collected in the long term, more active efforts must be made towards this specific segment, especially related to quality, shearing time and delivery/finances (Klepp et al., 2019).

Some of the experiences from working with the Old Norse sheep farmers in Norway can be helpful to ameliorate the situation for the Polish mountain sheep and their wool. The amount of wool wasted is particularly high in Poland. During the last 15 years, the average share of

---

[2] https://lammas.ee/uus/wp-content/uploads/2019/03/Villa-ja-villat%C3%B6%C3%B6stuse-kava_ELaS.pdf.

[3] https://news.sky.com/story/covid-19-farmers-forced-to-compost-wool-as-prices-plummet-during-coronavirus-pandemic-12144149.

wool output was about 33%, which means that on average 67% of greasy sheep wool is lost, perhaps more as this can be under-reported. Wool has thus become a problematic by-product of Polish sheep farming, treated mainly as waste. For years, only a small portion of the wool was sold to the owner of the scouring facility in Poland, a monopolist enterprise. At the moment, the price offered for sheep wool does not cover the cost of shearing. The price also fluctuates greatly, which entails an unpredictable income for sheep farmers. For the very coarse wool from the mountain sheep, the problem with finding a market and good end-products will be similar to such wool anywhere (Fig. 3.4).

Due to the lack of profitability, a significant portion of the wool is stored without being scoured or deposited in local, not always legal, landfills. However, interest in the processing of wool is increasing in Poland. In 2018, one of the companies operating on the wool processing market invested in a competitive scouring line, which gives sheep owners new opportunities. Apart from selling greasy wool, scouring and carding wool is now possible at competitive prices. Scouring and carding wool provides new possibilities for using wool, even the coarse types from sheep of mountain breeds. Nevertheless, it is important to popularise

Fig. 3.4 A lamb with spots from the Beskids mountains in Poland (*Photo credit* Jan Broda)

such possibilities and group together sheep owners so that they can meet the current minimum amount of 1000 kg. At present, the system in Poland does not support the creation of producer cooperatives. A barrier is low social trust and the ageing generation of sheep farmers, who do not take into account the changes and patterns that flow from other cultures through social and more conventional media. We know from Norway that the interest in the wool is higher among female farmers, and this may also be the case in Poland. If so, both age and sex may be factors to take into account.

Waste prevention and efficient use of resources is a clear strategy in the EU, but wool is not included in said strategy or in any policy documents as far as we know. The definition of wool in the EU regulations is not straightforward, as it is referred to both as an agricultural product, a waste product and an animal by-product. The latter indicates that the material is not consumed by people. However, there is no doubt that too much wool is wasted within the EU, and that it is not included in official waste statistics. The amount of wool wasted on sheep farms is a clear example of insufficient use of raw materials. This is not the case in all industries, where there are policies in place for utilising also by-products. An example of this is the EU ban from 2019 on throwing overboard unwanted fish and other catch, such as sea turtles and dolphins, known as 'bycatch' (Stokstad, 2019). The situation in the food production sector is also relevant, concerning, among other things, wheat, maize and rice. Even one of the main by-products from wool scouring, lanolin, has found good uses in the cosmetic industry and as chassis treatment for cars to prevent rust. But to do this, someone must see the economic benefit alongside the ecological and obvious outcomes of thinking like the crow hunter. There seems to be a logical shortcoming in the circular economy thinking, where only some waste or by-products are put forward as solutions, while others remain in the blind zone.

But let us return to the harsh realities surrounding European wool. Meagre raw material prices and lack of downstream systems are the main reasons why wool is disposed of. As described in detail in Chapter 2, with the current position wool holds in the many comparison tools based on LCAs and similar databases, this could result in even more wool being lost, as prices decrease even further. This would then be a downward spiral with dire consequences. The LCA calculations do not address these side effects. Using something that is already produced (such as Polish wool) for a purpose for which the material is applicable and highly suitable, is better for the environment than producing virgin materials to fulfil that same purpose. Leaving wool to rot or burning the wool also has adverse climate impacts. The current political landscape contributes to an error in logic, in that it assumes that production takes place in order to procure the raw materials in question, which of course is not the case when they are by-products.

A circular economic strategy and the sustainable development that this is based on, demands that natural resources are used in the most efficient way (European Commission, 2021). Several influential policy documents published by the EU Commission from 2011 to 2015, focus on resource efficiency and waste prevention as essential strategies. Though policies in practice have largely been focused on recycling and reuse of waste, a political desire to increase the utilisation of waste as a resource does exist. The work of the International Resource Panel (IRP) has specifically looked at resource efficiency but from a green growth perspective. Resource efficiency is here a way of using resources more efficiently over their life cycle, e.g. by product substitution (UNEP, 2017). Therefore, the political gaze is concentrated on using what we have several times but not on what we use and how we use it. However, resource utilisation is mentioned in the context of food production as a way of intensifying production that could involve the utilisation of underused resources (UNEP, 2017). The latter is what is at stake for wool as a resource, and prosperous use of resources should involve by-products and side-streams, whether it is fish skin, chicken feet or the fur of dead animals—or wool.

Making Better Use of Wool

Poor material utilisation can be said to be a negative effect of industrialism and standardised mass production. The utilisation of resources and materials is often specialised and concerted (Mehlum, 1994), which is not sustainable for the ecosystem within which they are located. Greenberg (2006) calls this the tragedy of commodification, which occurs when natural resources are not handled as integral parts of a specific ecosystem but are only considered as resources for human consumption. Nature is transformed into commodities, and the rationality that governs the capitalist market is very different from that which governs biological conditions. This tragedy is also about how countries exercise policies and regulations for natural resources, where the processes are the result of political and economic goals that do not necessarily take into account the ecological conditions that this policy affects (Greenberg, 2006). The commodification of nature has led to raw materials found in nature being extracted as if there were inexhaustible quantities, but this is not the case, though some may be regenerative in nature, which means they are biological resources that are renewed at the same or higher rate than they are extracted. In all cases, it is, however, important to limit the use of virgin raw materials and utilise the materials that have already been extracted from nature, in the best possible way. In many crafts and in artisanal production, this is an obvious part of the knowledge transfer and a type of knowledge that seems to have entered into the shadows when the industrial form of production has taken over. So far, it does not seem that broad material utilisation as a method for less waste is a developed or systemic approach in the circular economy.

In a push towards utilising more European wool, we have so far seen little overarching policy-backing or labelling schemes that work (Vittersø et al., 2017), or even major industry drivers; rather, what we have seen are small-scale local initiatives and enthusiasts. They have worked to increase collaboration and develop products, as we describe in more detail in Chapter 5. In the work to develop products are two prominent strategies: (1) to improve or change the wool itself, and (2) to find good utilisation for the existing raw material. Of course, these two strategies are not mutually exclusive, but they are still two different ways of thinking.

An example of the first strategy is work conducted in Sweden to introduce Merino sheep and also to breed Merino-genes into the Jämtland sheep, in order to produce finer wool. The former was done by the Swedish Poll Merino Association and has a clear focus on softer, and what they would define as better wool. The second initiative resulted in the investment in a so-called OFDA, an advanced measurement instrument that measures the micron of the wool fibre. All in the name of breeding 'better' wool. Even in Norway, there has been a small import of Merino sheep, as part of the idea that the 'problem' lies in the wrong wool (Klepp & Tobiasson, 2017).

In KRUS, we worked with improvements based on the sheep indigenous to Norway, through better wool classifying, but also weighting wool more in the breeding. This specifically related to the Modern Spæl sheep, where the wool was increasingly found to contain kemp and medullation, which was problematic in dyeing. We see that we can either aim to breed on specific wool traits or choose a strategy based on raw materials as they are, and work with better processing and product development. A 'take it or leave it' strategy, per se. If we are to utilise the resources we have available, variations must be considered both in the raw materials and in the possible needs that are to be met. What is a valued trait for some products, will be unimportant, or even a flaw, for other products.

Labelling as a Strategy

In order to promote the wool that is locally available, albeit through more complicated value chains, it will necessitate knowledge transfer, infrastructure and better cooperation; alongside better communication of what environmental benefits this leverages. The latter could easily be achieved through adopting labelling schemes that cover the aspects one is looking for. However, it may not be as simple as this. Wool has ended up in the firing line as we have described in Chapter 2, alongside also being targeted by animal rights organisations such as PETA.[4] This has resulted in several (competing) animal welfare schemes, such as the Responsible Wool Standard, SustainaWOOL, Authentico and ZQ. The latter has morphed into ZQRX, which includes regenerative farming principles in the standard. When it comes to regenerative labelling schemes, there is another set of standards to look at and evaluate, including Land to

[4] People for the Ethical Treatment of Animals.

Market (Savory Institute), Regenerative Organic Certified, Fibershed's Climate Beneficial Wool and the aforementioned ZQRX.

The definition of wool in EU regulations impacts how wool as a product could end up being labelled. The sheep producing wool initially 'belongs' to a place, and the localities within that place may have shaped both the breeds and the traditions for managing this wool. This way of thinking is the baseline for origin-designation labels that are highly connected to EU agricultural policies. In order to 'protect and promote quality products with a focus on traditional products and products from a designated origin' (Bureau & Vaiceschini, 2003, p. 71), the EU founded a programme in 1992 to support and register certain food and agricultural products. The most relevant labels are Protected Designation of Origin (PDO) and Protected Geographical Indication (PGI), which in theory can be applied to all agricultural products but are mainly found on food products. The way of attaching a product to something local has the potential to give the product a special value and is reflected in the French term *terroir*, which refers to 'an era or terrain, usually rather small, whose soil and microclimate impart distinctive qualities to products' (Barham, 2003, p. 131). In other words, it indicates a balanced utilisation of the available soil and nature in a particular place, which is also produced over a long period of time.

Today, Shetland wool is the only product that has obtained such a standard in our sector. Within the wool community, it is obvious that many more products could be eligible to receive a PDO or PGI, but complications arise in the definition, in addition to the complex value chains that involve a number of different locations, not within the *terroir*, which is the case with Norwegian wool, which is scoured in the UK before it is spun into yarns in Norway. The situation is not improved by private schemes, which can claim wool to be country-specific, such as SwissWool, Wools of Holland, Icewool, etc., but these are not an indication of quality or a guarantee for geographical indication (Vittersø et al., 2017).

The sheer volume of labelling schemes is problematic, in addition to the lack of an overarching and EU-certified quality label for wool—or any other fibre for that matter (linen, flax, hemp, viscose, fish or other meat-related skins). If one goes back in history, it is interesting to note that the need for different schemes addressing different aspects of fibres, is closely tied to the increased global trade, and the long and opaque value chains starting with the raw materials being global commodities that are sold at auctions. During an International Wool Textile Organisation Congress in Venice in 2019, one of the 'old-timers' lamented how in the 'good old days' the fibre knowledge was in the 'fingers' of the traders. They would also know and trust those wool farmers they bought the clip from. In an industrialised, commodified market, this is no longer possible. Developing a standard for the quality of the clip had been a long and painful process, we were told; and now that standards for animal welfare and environmental aspects were competing for a position, many remembered the turbulent years before one quality standard finally was agreed upon. Such historically traumatic stories are more often than not neither chronicled nor talked about; but for us it was an interesting glimpse into the power-struggles that emerge when there is a lot at stake: Money, defining power and market shares. Today, the story is not on the standard or micron-understanding of the wool, but about the eco-credentials; and the power-struggle is even more intense. Who owns the truth?

In the rather new discussion around regenerative farming and grazing as a part of a more environmental friendly agricultural system, which we will discuss further in Chapters 5 and 6, the question about inappropriate labelling schemes is made apparent. Schemes related to regenerative agriculture have received criticism (Glover, 2021), related to a misconception of regenerative practices. Regenerative agriculture is all about promoting a healthy soil, which can be measured by a number of factors such as carbon content, water retention, level of organic matter and biodiversity increase. However, this measurement is not necessarily what defines a labelling scheme for regenerative farming. The schemes do not always account for the landscape, the *terroir*, but rather the farm level of the product (Glover, 2021). Therefore, such certifications do not account for an essential problem that affects many areas, which is the overexploitation of land. This problem needs to be addressed if we are to solve our mismatched use of resources. If knowledge can be reintroduced at the local community level so that it once again is 'in the fingers' and not prescribed by global organisations with little knowledge on the *terroir*-level; perhaps we can see some real change and ultimately better products that take into account both a love for the animals, the landscapes and the people that benefit from using them. This is why labelling schemes based on long traditions such as the PGI and PDO are important, while those who try to put a global straight-jacket on local-specific issues, are not.

Worthy Wool

Focusing attention on the qualities of the materials is absolutely crucial in order to improve the quality and increase the longevity of the resulting products. Following this, it is essential to understand quality as a characteristic of something that makes the material suitable for specific products. Thus, 'qualities' would be a more proper term. The fact that we have variations in materials means that we have the opportunity to utilise different resources for different functions. Variety in species and breeds will make us more equipped in the future when new requirements and needs arise. There will not always be a complete correlation between what we have and what we need. This necessitates a responsibility for finding the best adaptations. We must use what we have, and we must develop good products based on the raw materials available, and simultaneously look at opportunities over time for developing these materials. In developing knowledge about *terroir* and craftsmanship, the potential in developing industrial symbiosis based on by-products and side-streams, as well as regenerative resources, will be important in value creation. How these can then replace the extraction of virgin materials, including the fossil-based ones, is important in creating a future with less plastic. Wool seems to be a suitable example through which we can explore this future scenario. The reasons for this are both the many different technical properties of wool, many of them are little studied, such as acoustic properties. The second reason is the long cultural history, and thus the great variety there is both in the wool itself and in the associated techniques and ways of using it. In this chapter, Poland is used as an example, but the EU and the rest of the world are full of similar sad stories where both natural and cultural resources are wasted; our recent work with Portugal shows the same.

The moral that emerged in the song about the crow hunter refers to a time when using the whole animal, all by-products and side-streams, was the norm. This moral code still exists in an ingrained reluctance many people feel by throwing away usable things and edible food. In sharp contrast to this morality, waste and even throwing a lot away, is part of today's economic system. This applies not only to the raw materials that we have discussed here but in all stages of production and consumption and is particularly visible in the production of clothing. At the other end of the clothing value chain, the large quantities of returned e-commerce goods and their destruction, could be banned or prevented. For clothing, 25% of all items, increasing to 40–50% for high fashion items bought online, have been returned (Cullinane et al., 2019). Knowledge about this part of the value chain is also lacking and needs to be understood, also for wool, to prevent this waste to proliferate.

The circular economy seeks to remedy this by applying a bandage principle to a situation more akin to cancer. In the circular economy, resource efficiency and sustainable resource utilisation are the main ideas, especially using waste to generate resources. Capitalist market economics, which we will discuss more in Chapter 6, has made Europe and the rest of the global North rich, but has at the same time made it unnecessary to safeguard raw materials and other resources, and has contributed to increasing waste production. The poor utilisation of wool in Poland, as in many other countries, is the result of an economic system, at the same time it is precisely the possibilities within this system that we are currently exploring to solve the problem and utilise the wool better. The inherent paradox will become clearer as we discuss this further in the book.

References

Allafi, F., Hossain, M. S., Lalung, J., Shaah, M., Salehabadi, A., Ahmad, M. I., & Shadi, A. (2020). Advancements in applications of natural wool fiber:

Review. *Journal of Natural Fibers, 1–16*. https://doi.org/10.1080/15440478.2020.1745128

Arnesen, K. (2015). *Naturlig ull som lydabsorbentmateriale*. NTNU.

Barham, E. (2003). Translating terroir: The global challenge of French AOC labeling. *Journal of Rural Studies, 19*(1) 127–138. https://doi.org/10.1016/S0743-0167(02)00052-9.

Bureau, J.-C., & Valceschini, E. (2003). European food-labeling policy: Successes and limitations. *Journal of Food Distribution Research, 34*(3), 70–76.

Corscadden, K. W., Biggs, J. N., & Stiles, D. K. (2014). Sheep's wool insulation: A sustainable alternative use for a renewable resource? *Resources, Conservation and Recycling, 86*, 9–15. https://doi.org/10.1016/j.resconrec.2014.01.004.

Cullinane, S., Browne, M., Karlsson, E., & Wang, Y. (2019). Retail clothing returns: A review of key issues. In P. Wells (Ed.), *Contemporary operations and logistics: Achieving excellence in turbulent times* (pp. 301–322). Springer International Publishing.

European Commission. (2021). *Raw materials*. https://ec.europa.eu/environment/green-growth/raw-materials/index_en.htm.

Glover, S. (2021). The regeneration game. *Ecotextile news(102)*, 53.

Greenberg, J. B. (2006). The political ecology of fisheries in the upper Gulf of California. In A. Biersack & J. B. Greenberg (Eds.), *Reimagining political ecology* (pp. 121–148). Duke University Press.

Gruszecki, T. M., Warda M., Kulik, M., Jankuszew, A., Patkowski K., Bojar, W., Tomczuk, K., Greguła- Kania, M., Dudko, P., Bielińska E.J., Drozd, L., Szczepaniak, K., Szymanowska, A., Szymanowski, M., Wiercińska, K., & Krupiński J. (2017). *Wiadomości Zootechniczne*, 177–184.

Kamiński, L. (1992). *O mieszkańcach gór tatrzańskich*. Kraków.

Kamiński, L. O. (1992). *Mieszkańcach gór tatrzańskich*. Kraków.

Kawecka, A., & Krupinski, J. (2014). Sheep in the polish Carpathians: Genetic resources conservation of the Podhale Zackel and Coloured Mountain Sheep. *Geomatics, Landmanagement and Landscape, 1*, 35–45.

Klepp, I. G., Laitala, K., & Tobiasson, T. S. (2016). *Woolbed—Sweet dreams in merino*. Retrieved from Oslo: http://sifo.no/files/file80443_oppdragsrapport_no_2_2016_-_woolbed_final.pdf.

Klepp, I. G., & Tobiasson, T. (2017). *Strikk med norsk ull*. Vormedal forlag.

Klepp, I. G., Tobiasson, T., Haugrønning, V., Vittersø, G., Grøva, L., Kvingedal, T., . . . Kubberød, E. (2019). KRUS final report: Enhancing local value chains in Norway.

Kosiek, A., Sikora, J., & Kawecka, A. (2012). Characteristics of wool from Podhale Zackel sheep. *Acta Scientiarum Polonorum, Zootechnica, 11*, 35–40.
Mehlum, M. H. (1994). *Garving. Bearbeiding av huger og skinn*. Arbeidsproesser og redskaper: Teknologisk forlag.
Sigaaard, A. S., & Haugrønning, V. (2021). *WOOLUME: Mapping the market for acoustic and sound absorbing products made of wool*.
Stokstad, E. (2019, January 4). Controversial European policy bans ships from throwing unwanted fish overboard. *Science*. https://www.sciencemag.org/news/2019/01/controversial-european-policy-bans-ships-throwing-unwanted-fish-overboard.
Tobiasson, T. (2020). Wool, yarn & beyond. *Wool2Yarn Global*. https://issuu.com/ely12155/docs/wool_2_yarn_global_2020.
UNEP. (2017). *Resrouce efficiency: Potential and economic implications*. https://www.resourcepanel.org/reports/resource-efficiency.
Vittersø, G., Klepp, I. G., Tobiasson, T. S., & Kviseth, K. (2017). *Opprinnelsesmerking av norsk ull*. Retrieved from Oslo: www.hioa.no/content/download/139130/3967899/file/OR5%20-2017%20-%20opprinnelsesmerking%20av%20norsk%20ull.pdf.
Wistuba, M., Sady, A., & Poręba, G. (2018). The impact of Wallachian settlement on relief and alluvia composition in small valleys of the Carpathian Mts. (Czech Republic). *CATENA, 160*, 10–23. https://doi.org/10.1016/j.catena.2017.08.017.

4

Slow and Indigenous Approaches to Textiles Arts

Lorrie Miller, Kjellaug Isaksen, Rebecca Burgess, Ingun Grimstad Klepp, and Tone Skårdal Tobiasson

Sustainability is often primarily linked to the material resource and its extraction from the land and the impacts to the land and related flora and fauna. In addition, the well-being of livestock is also now considered (Vičiūnaitė, 2020, p. 14). In discussing the consequences of the

L. Miller (✉)
University of British Columbia, BC Vancouver, Canada
e-mail: lorrie.miller@ubc.ca

K. Isaksen
Museum Department at the Davvi álbmogiid guovddáš/Center for northern peoples, Samuelsberg, Norway

R. Burgess
Fibershed, San Geronimo, CA, USA

I. G. Klepp
Consumption Research Norway (SIFO), Oslo Metropolitan University, Oslo, Norway
e-mail: ingunk@oslomet.no

I. G. Klepp and T. S. Tobiasson (eds.), *Local, Slow and Sustainable Fashion*,
https://doi.org/10.1007/978-3-030-88300-3_4

ecological and climate impact of the globalised textile industry, issues concerning the connection between the producer and local communities, whether they are consumers, producers or others impacted by proximity, is less discussed. As humans we are physically rooted in our landscape along with our place-in-time; this affects our choices whether conscious or not. With raised awareness, can we make conscious and better choices about the materials we use, for crafting and in our lives? This chapter highlights the textile traditions of several cultures, in particular, Indigenous ones, including coastal Salish peoples from the Pacific Northwest, Native Americans within the USA, as well of those of the Sea Sámi of northern Norway. It considers how textile art and craft production are part of cultural sustainability.

Drawing on Aboriginal scholar, Tyson Yunkaporta (2020), we keep in mind that 'Indigenous knowledge is any application of those memories [from those living sustainably on and a part of the land] as living knowledge to improve present and future circumstances' (p. 36). When contemplating our material world, and sustainability, we need to take into account Indigenous knowledge and lived experience. Global industrialisation has, on the other hand, had a broad impact on communities and cultures along with the environment.

The histories of various peoples migrating, settling, in times of peace and conflict or for other reasons tied to The Law of the Land (Yunkaporta, 2020), are a part of the global picture, also of textiles and fibres. We all come from somewhere and these places and our relationships with the land, and with one another have impacted our cultures, traditions and current state of affairs. Those who have been at the receiving end of colonialism have felt the brunt of globalised industrialisation. For instance, the Sámi and the other Norwegians settled in what is now Norway over multiple centuries beginning after the last major ice age, and have co-existed and inter-related since then. However, the Sámi were subjected to colonialisation from the eighteenth-century missionaries, later also by explorers, and Norwegianisation from the middle of the

T. S. Tobiasson
Nordic Initiative Clean & Ethical Fashion, Oslo, Norway

nineteenth century. Though the policy of Norwegianisation[1] was phased out during the twentieth century, the demolition of land previously used for Sámi livelihoods continues. Together, these processes led to the loss of own faith, musical instruments, diversity of language, self-esteem and access to land (Hætta Isaksen, 2021). Today, efforts are being made to remedy the damage this policy has caused.

Indigenous peoples of the Americas significantly pre-dated the settlers from Europe (the peoples of North and South America can be dated from the Pleistocene era and anthropological records have dated 20,000 years of place-based histories) and were kept separated[2] from settler societies through colonising practices and policies. This history of separation and discrimination is the same for many Indigenous peoples and, for the Sámi, and Indigenous peoples in Canada and North America, there is much work to be done to effectively reconcile previous wrong-doings (TRC, 2015). One small way to carry on the work of reconciliation is to be sure to meaningfully include the work and the true voices of Indigenous artists and scholars within research and publications.

The authors of this chapter are from both North American settlers, and Norwegians with and without Sámi background. Here, we turn our attention to the similarities, differences and intersections of textile practices in both historic and contemporary times. In addition, we recognise the limitations of written text, and of the language with which we are writing. English, for all its fluidity and ability to morph, is not our only language, and there are times when one's mother tongue may offer a more exacting nuance. The words related to textiles and textile tools are rich, but not always easily understood and used, and even less when translated between our different tongues. We have had to call upon experts inside and outside of the industry and crafts in order to find

[1] Norwegianisation was a deliberate policy of assimilation from about 1850 to 1980. Henry Minde (2005) tells us: 'The policy conducted in respect of the Sami minority in Norway was for a long time synonymous with a policy of assimilation or fornorsking, which literally means "norwegianisation' (p. 6).

[2] (term of 'kept separated' wouldn't apply to Spanish colonisation where they forced breeding (rape) to create a hybrid population aligned with Catholicism. Later influence from central and northern Europe decimated native populations via militarism and the most pronounced land theft via the reservation and boarding school system).

a semblance of meaning. Nålbinding and wadmal[3] are two such words, both of Norse origin and related to crafting wool. In addition, language, when written is different from when spoken, where the essence of care may be conveyed with a pause, a lowered tone and a hand gesture. So, we ask that readers allow their imagination to open to the moments described, to link their own feelings and stories to what we write and hope that they may be able to co-create meaning within this text, as we also co-create as we craft this chapter.

Grounded in local crafting and textile practices, the authors remind the readers that we learn from one another and alongside one another by showing and sharing (Yunkaporta, 2020). In Yunkaporta's book, we are introduced to the compelling concept of 'yarning', a conversational mode of forming, storing and passing on knowledge verbally alongside activities. In particular, Yunkaporta identifies ancestral knowing, which consists of both material and immaterial aspects. Here we are connecting this to textile traditions such as knitting or weaving with wool, something that is meaningful, and, we would argue, that impactful learning and teaching uses both telling and showing, with stories and technical skills. Such practice encourages genuine engagement and care. In addition, we are humbled by the knowledge, skills and wisdom of those who have come before us, and recognise that it is not welcome to be an 'expert' in another's culture (Yunkaporta); and with that, we are beginning where we each are and by understanding our own culture(s) traditions, privilege and vantage points.

Our World Today

Hollenbach (2019) tells us how '[c]raft poses an opportunity to explore the world we live in today, to understand the space we take up in it, and to recognise our responsibility in crafting tomorrow' (p. 29). In

[3] Nålbinding and wadmal: Nålbinding is a technique where loops are sewn together with different stitches to make garments; whereas wadmal (vadmal) is a dense and finely woven wool (often tabby or twill) that is then pounded and felted into a durable cloth that is both wind and water resistant.

that light, we turn to traditions from our own heritages, our neighbours, regional elders and local Indigenous makers. It is important to take the time necessary to learn from those before us and around us, and keep in mind the future's children. We position ourselves and our practices in a global context, both in place and time. We are living at a time of unprecedented environmental damage, including climate change, biodiversity loss and spreading of toxic chemicals, and caused by human action; a time when we, from many countries, work with local Indigenous communities towards healing and genuine reconciliation; we are at a time of a once-in-a-century global pandemic.

We understand that not all knowledge, including visual symbols, are available to everyone, at times these are restricted to members of specific cultural communities, and even to specific individuals (Yunkaporta, 2020). Here, we include more generalisable meta stories and showing cross-sections and intersections where they exist. Yunkaporta is critical of those who claim to learn *from* Indigenous knowledge and ways by latching onto pre-colonial examples of Indigenous ways or artefacts. Instead, he offers insights to 'Indigenous pattern thinking process to critique contemporary systems and to impart an impression of the pattern of creation itself' (p. 17). We consider this as we highlight some Indigenous textile practices in connection to cultural sustainability, cultural craft and art-making, across generations, and into the future.

When crafting and textile practices are grounded in one's local and sustainable fibreshed we are better able to connect with our place in the world (Burgess & White, 2019). This is further supported by recognising that 'craft cannot be removed from the social and historical reality of its geographic location, ubiquity and function, collective labour and collaborative design, trade and industry, commerce and consumption' (Hollenbach, 2019, p. 29). When we, in Chapter 2, discuss both the Higg Index MSI and EU's PEF initiative, it is interesting to note that the tools available to describe the environmental impact of different textiles completely disregard the values that lie in the raw material's place in culture, tradition and craftsmanship.

There is not one single way to do, or to make; it is an emergent practice that is grounded in experience, respect, culture, and care. By examining traditional wool practices, we can inform our practices today, not to simply repeat or romanticise the past, but to inform our present. By looking back, we can access the infinite knowledge buried in the past and we can better understand how we came to where we are today, and influence where we go from here.

Textile Traditions

The notion of 'tradition' according to Miriam Webster dictionary (2021) includes: 'the handing down of information, beliefs, and customs by word of mouth or by example from one generation to another without written instruction… cultural continuity in social attitudes, customs, and institutions'. Each of us can think of some skill, knowledge, belief, story that we have via tradition. Yet, there have been gaps in such traditional transmission, in this era of globalisation, mechanisation, fast fashion, and even more so for those impacted by colonial oppression where the intent by the oppressor was to break tradition, language and ultimately, culture. Yet, many groups, organisations and individuals have reinvigorated cultural textile traditions. Following, we highlight the work of two Coastal Salish weavers from the west coast of Canada, and also the work of Sámi weavers from Northern Norway and a cultural festival reviving cultural textile traditions.

How have the rich variety of traditions of making with wool manifested and continue to live on today within Indigenous communities? Debra Sparrow, θəliχ^{w}əl^{w}ət (Thelliawhatlwit) is a master weaver from Musqueam, in Vancouver, BC. She and her sister Wendy Grant-John (Connor, 2013) were instrumental in reviving Salish weaving. Without a local weaver to study under, they turned to books on Salish weaving, and to the raw wool, spindles and looms to learn this work. When contemplating this task, she asked: 'Could I spin myself from this world to another? Could we as a group use these tools to help understand how we got to where we are today?' (p. 152). Over time, new Salish weavers and spinners began to relate to the weavers and spinners from the past who had woven tapestries and weavings that had so inspired them. This was one of the ways of 'bridging the past to bring forward an understanding of what was happening in the present and how things might work in the future' (p. 152).

For one to understand the importance of spinning and weaving with wool, one must put one's own hands to work. Only by interfacing directly with the materials, can one really understand the challenges, and the time necessary for making. Debra Sparrow wanted to know how to weave and ended up with the answer of why she needs to weave and to teach others to weave. Another contemporary Coastal Salish weavers, Angela George (qʷənat), has taken the tradition of weaving from her culture and home community and brought it to contemporary understanding of law, and business. George describes the importance of this work in an interview for the Salish Sea Sentinel (McKenna, 2020), 'This is our set of laws. This is a document. Just because it's unwritten it doesn't mean it's any less valuable'. In the end, this woven document was also a major part of her master's thesis for her MBA. To put her work further into context, Angela George explains (Fig. 4.1):

> I am very passionate about weaving and feel a great responsibility to reconnect our people to this and other cultural practices that connect us to our laws of the lands and waters. Our Weavings are artifacts, encyclopedias and our holders of knowledge, and we the weavers, storytellers and translators of Knowledge. Revitalization of these important practices are reconnecting us to our sustainability mechanisms that our ancestors wove into all facets of our social systems and structures. (Angela George in email with Lorrie Miller May 2021)

Weaving was important in the past and remains so today, though mainly in industry; *craft* practices such as knitting and crocheting that are easier to bring along and do anywhere, have seen more of a resurgence (Klepp & Tobiasson, 2017). We cannot, or ought not, look at such objects of art and craft from behind glass display cases, preserved as merely historic artefacts decontextualised from our current way of living and being. Still staying in Canada; however, closer to Greenland than mainland Canada, we travel to the dramatic scenery featured in the opening scene of the James Bond movie, *The Spy Who Loved Me*. This

Fig. 4.1 Angela George (qʷənat) (Courtesy of Angela George 2020. *Photo credit* Angela George) Lorrie Miller

is the home of the Pang crocheted hat, with its iconic tapestry pattern. The hamlet that gave its name to the hat, is Pangnirtung, where Inuit, and their ancestors, have lived in the Cumberland Sound region for thousands of years. The weaving masters at the Uqqurmiut Centre for Arts & Crafts take orders from all over the world and have this as a side-line. As mentioned above, crocheting can be done anywhere; while the looms stay put at the Centre for Arts & Crafts. They use worsted wool, making the patterns vibrant and clear-cut. However, some locals also use synthetic yarns to bring the price down. No one remembers the origin of the hats, but their similarity to the tapestries that are woven locally are obvious.

History, beyond large societal, or global events and the documents and analysis of such events, includes daily life activities and events from an earlier time. If we look at it another way, we can see that today is tomorrow's history. With that thought in mind, what will our artefacts tell future generations about our habits, values and cultures?

And even if they may not come with a clear storyline, the artefacts can give us clues. Spindle whorls have been found all over the world, as have the stones for the warp-weighted looms; weaving the tale of the knowledge surrounding fibres and weaving as one intrinsically bound to our human history. Interestingly, it was a Viking spindle whorl that offered proof that the Norse travellers who settled in L'Anse aux Meadows in Newfoundland also brought their Old Norse Sheep over the oceans, and most probably also their women—as the plan was to build a settlement. Interestingly, wool-sheep were not Indigenous to the North American continent, even though the Mouflon—the mother of all sheep who looks more like a hefty deer—had travelled with others across the Bering Strait. However, they were never domesticated and therefore soft sheep wool was not part of the Indigenous peoples' textile repertoire before the 1650s brought European sheep to the continent. However, some of them may have gotten a taste of sheep's wool from the Vikings (Coulthard, 2020).

Coulthard paints a picture of the Vikings and the Inuit having a 'spinning bee', where they may have swapped techniques. Perhaps they even taught them *nålebinding*, for all we know. Or felting the wadmal. The author envisions 'the Norse women learning how to use hair from other animals such as musk ox, foxes and arctic hares, alongside their own imported sheep' (Coulthard, 2020, p. 141). The communal exchange of knowledge did not, however, save the settlement. The Vikings and their sheep died and left behind a spindle whorl.

Community Taking Centre Stage

Rebecca Burgess, tells us that one of the profound lessons learned from her work researching her 2019 book, *Fibershed,* is the understanding how communities are empowered through the process of grounding:

> [T]heir livelihoods in material culture that is grown, processed and utilized from their regional soils and in honor of the existing human cultural heritage, the strategies for how we design and implement solutions for many of our most pressing challenges – including climate change and wealth inequality – become more precise and effective. These textile cultures by their very design are durable and resilient. (Burgess & White, 2019, p. 13).

Localised inquiries with Indigenous communities can help our collective understanding of balanced human-earth practices needed to rebuild our soils, begin the work of halting climate change and drawing down carbon, alongside respond to regional economies in ways that retain the balance we need for a sustainable future (Burgess & White, 2019). It is through such authentic dialogue that we see building greater relationships across communities and cultures, continuing the pathway towards reconciliation that is called for throughout the world. This includes responding to the United Nations recognition of Indigenous Rights, in particular: 'Recognizing that respect for [I]ndigenous knowledge, cultures and traditional practices contributes to sustainable and equitable development and proper management of the environment' (UNDRIP, 2007, p. 4).

Considerations of Material in Relation to Culture

The more one works with wool, the clearer it becomes that one variety of wool is different from the next. Within each breed, the variety is also marked, depending on local geographical prerequisites, where on the animal the wool stems from, how it is sheared and further downstream treatments (Solitude Wool, 2021; Klepp & Tobiasson, 2017). There has been an uptick in the interest in small and speciality wool producers and collectives, some of which are described in Chapter 5. Supporting small-scale wool producers adds to the diversity within the system, resulting in a wider variety in the available woollen yarns, as described in more detail in Chapter 1; this also opened up for saving breeds that were in danger of extinction, those more suitable for harsher climates they had adopted to.

Navajo shepherd, Kelly Skacy describes the importance of being a Navajo-Churro[4] shepherd, 'To me, it's carrying on a legacy. Not everyone sees the value of the wool, to me it's everything' (Herring & Breeden, 2019). Her colleague, weaver and shepherd, Drake Mace states that 'Weaving is something I'm really passionate about. It's an aspect of the sheep life that I love so much, and it ties me to my history' (Herring & Breeden, 2019). The connection to culture, land and sheep though, is intensely important to these shepherds and weavers, they also express a desire to share this knowledge with others, regionally and beyond.

An example of how this knowledge has been shared comes to us via Burgess & White (2019), who introduces us to Katherine Jolda—a textile artisan—who spent six transformational years on the Navajo reservation in Arizona, primarily with shepherding and farming families. It was this experience that informed her textile practices and ethics. Jolda was also 'a member of Black Mesa Weavers for Life and Land, which works to bring together cosmopolitan and Indigenous fibre artisans' (p. 72). However, funding ran out. Jolda also founded *Felt the Sun* through which she offers classes and workshops on ecological wool felting that features her invention, the *Cyclocarder*. This human-powered bicycle drum-carder enables her to card, on average, six ounces of combed wool in just four to five minutes. With little access to equipment and manufacturing, when she was living with the Navajo, she was able

[4] Navajo-Churro is the first domesticated breed of sheep in the Americas, having been introduced in the early 1500s. This breed evolved and adapted to the dry desert area of American Southwest, but was subject to deliberate extinction by the USA army, under Kit Carson, who ordered to relocate the Navajo and destroy their flocks. Today, however, the Churro are being nurtured back as a breed.

to use parts from an old bicycle in order to develop a rather elegant solution. This merging of Indigenous and settler knowledge illustrates how low-tech and small-scale can be crucial in elevating crafts and artisanal development.

Jolda took up the 2019 Fibershed challenge of creating a '147-mile' felted winter coat (Burgess & White, 2019). Felting is a process where water, wool, soap and human hands create an immediate textile, without going the route of spinning a thread or yarn. The wool, however, still needs to be carded before it can be felted; and Jolda's Cyclocarder, as seen in Fig. 4.2, eased the process. Slow cloth, or slow stitch movements are not that different from the slow food movement that grew out of Italy as a response to fast food industries (Honoré, 2013). Slow cloth practices, as the Cyclocarder and the 147-mile winter coat, illustrate what is possible with more manual based technology, collaborative practices and sharing knowledge. Through 'Felt the Sun' she does not offer public workshops, but instead through the school system in California and weaves her understanding of textiles into her work as a middle school teacher.

Cultural Sustainability: Looking to the Sámi

When we look at each of our own local fibresheds, and we contemplate our positionality in the world; environmental sustainability is often part of that consideration including both land and water impacts. Here, however, we also consider social and cultural sustainability. Let us look to an area where heritage breeds have been and are continued to be supported, by the Sámi, one of the Indigenous people of Norway, Sweden, Finland and Russia. Trade, for the Sámi in these countries, was initially based primarily on hunting, fishing and wild reindeer. While some Sámi developed nomadic semi-domestic reindeer husbandry with large flocks, others settled and became permanent residents. The Sea Sámi, differing from their northern counterparts, live along the coast and have embraced livelihoods based on a combination of fishing, agriculture and crafts, among other things based on wool (Fig. 4.3).

Fig. 4.2 The Cyclocarder was 'invented' by Katherine Jolda. It is in essence a human-powered bicycle drum-carder which enables her to card, on average, six ounces of combed wool in just four to five minutes (*Photo credit* Rebecca Burgess)

The 'Norwegianisation' of the Sámi culture in Norway was stronger in this sub-set because their way of life did not clearly differ from their non-Sámi neighbours. Reindeer-herding Sámi culture has been perceived in society at large as being 'proper' Sámi. The Sea Sámi have, therefore, been the subject of double oppression (Hermanstrand et al., 2019). Today there is a revitalisation of Sámi culture, including the Sea Sámi culture, and textile traditions are an important part of this. This has also happened in other places, as noted earlier with the Salish.

Fig. 4.3 The Norwegian cross-bred sheep. Wool from this breed is often used in Sámi handicrafts (*Photo credit* Tone Skårdal Tobiasson)

The rátnu (also known as *grener*), as seen in Fig. 4.4, have for centuries been of significant importance to the Sámi. This weaving reflects the mountain Sámi's perpetual need for water-resistant blankets (covers) and tent doors. Half-worn rátnu were sewn together for loavdda, tent cloth in the bealljegoahtien/winter home. They were particularly suitable for this due to the heat-insulating properties of wool, even in wet conditions. To function as a door, the rátnu was laid in a pyramid shape and transverse wooden 'pins' were sewn on to keep the shape. The rátnu was used as an extra coverlet to sleep under, alongside the aforementioned many other purposes that offered cover from the varied weather. The doors also were in use for 'gammer' (clay huts), and even houses. The tent-like material pieces have been used as travel rátnu. It was a permanent

Fig. 4.4 Rátnu (*Photo credit* Torun Olsen Wernberg. Davvi álbmogiid guovddáš—Senter for nordlige folk)

part of the sleigh of the coachman and in the reindeer sleigh and 'pulk[5]'. Throughout the nineteenth century, they were part of the equipment in the Lofoten 'chest' in the boat, and from Kola we know that they could be used as sails if necessary.

Weavers use handspun wool both in the warp and the weft when weaving a rátnu on a simple warp-weighted loom, 'rátnostuolet'. Specific to this Sámi loom, natural stones keep the warp in a vertical stretch. In addition, the warping method has a specific and strong starting border and gives the rátnu weave a three-sided selvedge. Though aspects of this weave are unique to the Sámi, weighted vertical looms and weaving

[5] A pulk is a Sámi sled to be pulled behind (http://www.laits.utexas.edu/sami/diehtu/siida/reindeer/Reindeer/reindeer_main.html.

methods date back to Ancient Greece, and are highlighted in the story of Penelope's loom, and have been in continuous use in northern-European areas both by Sámi and others. The rátnu has existed at least since the years 600 and 700 (AD). Since the 1950s, this cultural tradition has mainly been preserved in the Sámi village Olmmáivággi/Manndalen in Gáivuotna/Kåfjord and among Skolte Sámi in Sävättejärvi, Finland.

The specialisation in various trades and practices within the Sámi population laid the foundation for barter and exchange, also gave the Sea Sámi a secure source of income via trade. The reindeer-herding Sámi, who followed the large domestic reindeer herds, had few other livestock, but good access to meat and hides, though not to wool or textiles. Textile work, including the traditional weft-faced wool weaving, the *rátnu,* see Fig. 4.4, was included in this trade both directly between 'friend families' with different products they could barter with, and in permanent marketplaces with large annual markets, where textiles including rátnu were important goods (Koslin, 2010).

Rátnu weaving is a *duodji*[6] form that creates close connections between people and place, as described earlier in the chapter, because the whole production and further processing of wool, as well as weaving, is done locally in an unbroken tradition. Deep roots in and connections to their surroundings and the fact that people have been self-sufficient in the supply for wool for rátnu, has been important for maintaining cultural tradition. Those who cannot weave themselves would bring their wool to a weaver, who then would receive some payment for the work. This is tied to old commission systems, but also to a contemporary upswing in this type of small-scale service provided by the growing number of mini-mills, as described in Chapter 1. The wool carding facility in Kåfjorddalen, the practice of spinning and rátnu weaving and not least the use of the *gákti* or 'kofte', shawls and other aesthetically engaging Sámi clothes create opportunities for pride and community, an arena for learning, sharing and developing cultural community.

---

[6] Doudji: is Sami for 'handicraft' where items are made with both aesthetics and functionality in mind.

Cultural Pride and Identity in Relation to Textile Traditions

The unbroken rátnu weaving tradition in Manndalen has supported a market for un-scoured, carded wool for hand-spinning, a product that is not produced by other companies in Northern Europe. Lanolin-yarns are normally made from lightly scoured wool, not un-scoured wool. Kåfjordalen wool carding mill, established in 1954, produces a pre-yarn that is then spun by hand spinners, and it does not mass-produce yarn itself. The spinning mill has now received a major boost and is developing new products based on the unique raw material and local traditions. This upswing is due to both increased interest in hand-spinning and local wool, and new forces that have begun to work in the company. Rátnu and other textile craft traditions are important in Manndalen. The sense of regional pride, in connection to these textile traditions, is clear as the municipality has fostered cultural and textile-related activities, and a municipal coat of arms as seen in Fig. 4.5.

The Riddu Riđđu Festivàla, an international Indigenous festival, takes place annually in Manndalen. Since 1991, Riddu Riđđu has worked to

Fig. 4.5 Gáivuotna-Kåfjord municipal coat of arms

Fig. 4.6 The Sámi shawl (*Photo credit* Ingun Grimstad Klepp)

create greater awareness and pride about and for Sámi (Sârghe, 2019). This open-air, family-oriented, festival includes international Indigenous artists along with local Sámi artists. 'The Riddu Riđđu festival supports personal connections to a place, contributes to forming the identity of the Sami participants in general and youth participants in particular, and enables the use of Sámi language' (Sârghe, 2019, p. 6) (Fig. 4.6).

The young Sámi singer and environmental activist Ella Marie Hætta Isaksen (born 1998), who in 2018 won the Norwegian talent competition called 'Stjernekamp' (Stars, stars), is often seen wearing the Sámi shawl as part of her stage outfit. Both the Sámi *joik*, the traditional technique for singing, is combined with modern impulses and popular music and with increasing impact (Hætta Isaksen, 2021). Here, Sámi language, the gákti and shawl are lifted up with pride. This cultural pride is a key part of such celebrations. Hansen (2015) reminds us that 'Saminess is not monolithic' (p. 105). Hansen's (2015) study of the Riddu Riđđu festival, identified some key reasons for holding such an event:

> Several people also said that the reason for Riddu Riđđu was to give the youth of Gáivuotna something positive to focus on, something to keep

Fig. 4.7 Sámi *gákti* or 'kofte' (and shawls) worn during Riddu Riđđu festival (2019) (*Photo credit* Torun Olsen Wernberg. Davvi álbmogiid guovddáš—Senter for nordlige folk)

> them in the area and to draw attention to Coastal Sami issues. There was a clear goal to include older people in the teaching of youth and children about aspects of local Sami culture. This intergenerational focus meant that all age groups could be involved in projects and that people from many age groups attended the festival. (p. 110)

In relation to the Riddu Riđđu festival, more specifically textile-based, the Spinnvill 'rokk[7]' festival is a fun, annual event where hand-spinning is central, as the festival hosts the Norwegian Spinning Championships, with separate divisions for children. There are workshops for all ages, in various textile techniques, spinning, repairing spinning wheels and more. The 'spinnvill' festival attracts people interested in spinning from all over the country and helps to market Kåfjorden as a textile craft centre. All the activities in Kåfjorden elevate Sea Sámi textile traditions, and the colourful Sámi gákti/kofte (see Fig. 4.7) and shawl contribute to a vibrant textile atmosphere.

In the work of restoring cultural pride and identity, both textiles and music are central. The Sámi gákti/kofte is used more today than just a decade ago and in many more settings. This use can be in the form of a full costume outfit from head to toe, or items put together with ordinary 'global contemporary' clothes, often called 'Western dress'. One of the elements that is used a lot is the shawl, a checkered, woven shawl in wool with clear contrasting colours often dominated by green and red, or blue and green, as described in Fig. 4.6.

Connecting Beyond the Surface

From looking to the festivals, and more specifically with textile practices, we can see that the relationship between the maker, their craft, the materials, are all entwined with culture, relationship, and the passing on of these skills, knowledge and ways. If the warp threads of a cloth were the land and the materials, and the weft were the people and their ways,

---

7 Rokk has a double meaning here—rock'n'roll and spinning wheel—as both have the same pronunciation in Norwegian. Spinnvill likewise connotates 'Crazy for spinning' and just plain crazy.

when woven together, they become a cultural expression of deep integration. It is a relationship with one's past, present and future, through the engagement with materials, with textiles. All of this is part of a greater narrative.

The Vicuña Poncho is a traditional piece of clothing produced at Laguna Blanca, Catamarca, in the Andes, and is an object with a deep symbolic character that is representative of a specific community. The artisans show their sense of belonging, unity and values through this garment. As they continue with these practices based on the vicuña fibre, they can teach the most exquisite technique and reflect the ancient knowledge of their ancestors—the Indigenous communities of the region (Amarilla et al., 2020).

Just as the Old Norse Sheep, the vicuña was threatened with extinction, but there is a major difference between the so-called 'Wild Sheep' and the wild camelids; the vicuñas have not been domesticated. So, in order to shear the exceptionally soft fibre, the animals are rounded up every three years with a system called *chaku,* which is a celebration of the sacred animal that dates back to Inca times. They were considered sacred beings which belonged to the deities, and only the son of the Sun and his family and the most loyal chiefs were allowed to wear garments made from these animals (Amarilla et al., 2020).

Cooperative Mesa Local Laguna Blanca, which is described in detail by Amarilla et al., has for all intents and purposes re-instigated the activity called 'vicuña *minga*', which involves expertise, learning and social interactions between women in close, trusted relationships—and which reminds us of 'yarning'. Such collective efforts around specifically the most time-consuming part of the process, the yarn-spinning by hand, include symbolic compensation that celebrate the mutual help and cooperation relationship: regional dancing and dining. When it comes to both shearing and weaving, both men and women traditionally perform the functions. Therefore, the vicuña poncho is both history and context, associated with geographical place and ecosystem (Amarilla et al., 2020).

As it encompasses tradition, homeland, culture, skilled craftmanship and Indigenous roots, the vicuña fibre is only handled by few and very knowledgeable artisans in Peru and Argentina. It is knowledge that sits in the hand and transferring the knowledge is not done through a YouTube video. Weaving, on the other hand, is almost an instinctual craft. We have also observed children being taught the art of spinning wool, and how their eyes glisten at the mastery of creating a yarn. Mastering a craft is in many ways a spiritual experience, as one creates something from a raw material that through the intervention of our hands and other body parts becomes something else—and hopefully something of utility and beauty.

Artisanal objects have become valuable in an economic market, having started their historic life as currency in trade, this includes the rátnu, the wadmal (Old Norse *vaðmál*) textiles and the aforementioned woven textiles from the Americas. We also know that what we today call 'Norwegian sweaters', are also called both 'Icelandic' and 'Faroese' sweaters, as they were knitted by skilled pre-industrial cooperatives and traded by 'The Icelandic Company' in the North Atlantic region (Klepp & Tobiasson, 2018). Offering the unique warmth of the wool, with a quicker and newer technique, which was knitting, these many objects and textiles were still in the fibre discovered by people in as different locations as the Andes and the North of Norway, in Mongolia and also in Canada. The common thread is the fibres we are privileged enough to weave, crochet, knit or nålebind with.

Sylvia Olsen (2010) tells the story of Cowichan knit sweaters. It is not that she discovered, nor invented these knitting patterns. She married a Coast Salish man and moved with him to Tsartlip First Nation. Her book, *Working with Wool*, is a tribute to the history, and the current traditions of Coast Salish wool workers, from weaving to a national obsession with the Cowichan sweater and patterns. The Cowichan were weavers but adopted a knitting style from settlers, the exact origin is unknown, and then the knitters added patterns of their own creating a distinct style. It is not the science of the wool, nor the tracking of mountain goat breeds, or even the demise of the Salish People's little woolly dog breed; it is the very human stories Olsen shares that are captivating. It is through these narratives that we can connect and care about people and their practices, as well as the warming textiles that are the result.

Intangible Cultural Heritage

The warp and weft of culture and textile traditions are more than inextricably bound together, they are felted and fused into a singular cultural cloth. This idea of an intangible cultural heritage that deserves protection and fostering is well documented. UNESCO (2021) tells us that cultural heritage 'includes traditions or living expressions inherited from our ancestors and passed on to our descendants, such as oral traditions, performing arts, social practices, rituals, festive events, knowledge, and practices concerning nature and the universe or the knowledge and skills produce traditional craft'. Throughout this chapter we have focused on these wool traditions in relation to culture and heritage. Traditional and contemporary practices exist together, 'intangible cultural heritage does not only represent inherited traditions from the past but also contemporary rural and urban practices in which diverse cultural groups take part' (UNESCO, 2021). The Norwegian national costume, the bunad, which we describe in Chapter 1, has a plethora of NGOs working on an application to receive status under this UNESCO protection, where, as far as we know, only Portuguese embroidery has a standing as of now.

We each have an opportunity to participate in our cultural environment, and to do so, we need to be curious and keep learning; we need to be brave enough to ask questions and to wonder 'what-if', then patient enough to listen carefully, and finally to care deeply. By taking time to settle into a practice and a place, and to be with the materials, we can forge a relationship to the land, to the material we work with, to the people we are from, to our neighbours and settle into a pattern of helpful humanity. We are a part *of* this earth, not apart from it. Textile practices that foster sustainable societies and cultures are the ones that can endure.

References

Amarilla, R., Gardetti, M. A., & Gabriel, M. (2020). Sustainable luxury, craftsmanship and vicuna poncho. In M. Á. Gardetti (Ed.), *Sustainable luxury and craftsmanship* (pp. 25–43). Springer.

Burgess, R., & White, C. (2019). *Fibershed: Growing a movement of farmers, fashion activists, and makers for a new textile economy*. Chelsea Green Publishing.

Connor. (2013, June 19). Entrepreneurs with tradition: How history weaves a path of success for Musqueam. *Vancouver Sun*. https://vancouversun.com/Business/2035/entrepreneurs-with-tradition-how-history-weaves-a-path-of-success-for-musqueam?r

Coulthard, S. (2020). *A short history of the world according to sheep*. Apollo.

Hætta Isaksen, E. M. (2021). *Derfor må du vite at jeg er same*. Cappelen Damm.

Hansen, K. (2015). *Being Sami: An ethnography of identity through the lens of the Riddu Riđđu festival* (Unpublished PhD dissertation). The Australian National University.

Hermanstrand, H., Kolberg, A., Risto Nilssen, T., & Sem, L. (Eds.). (2019). *The indigenous Identity of the South Saami: Historical and political perspectives on a minority within a minority*. Springer Open.

Herring, H., & Breeden, L. (2019). *The Navajo-Churro Shepherds in Stetson*. http://blog.stetson.com/the-navajo-churro-shepherds/

Hollenbach, J. (2019). Moving beyond a modern craft: Thoughts on white entitlement and cultural appropriation in professional craft in Canada. *Studio Magazine* (spring/summer). https://www.studiomagazine.ca/articles/2019/moving-beyond-a-modern-craft

Honoré, C. (2013). *The slow fix: Solve problems, work smarter and live better in a world addicted to speed*. Random House.

Klepp, I. G., & Tobiasson, T. (2017). *Strikk med norsk ull: Vormedal forlag*.

Klepp, I. G., & Tobiasson, T. S. (2018). *Norsk strikkehistorie*. Haugesund: Vormedal.

Koslin, D. (2010). The way of Sami Duodji: F y of Sami Duodji: From Nomadic Necessity t om Nomadic Necessity to Trademarked Lifestyle. In the *12th Biennial; Textiles and Settlement: From Plains Space to Cyberspace*, conference proceedings, Textile Society of America, https://digitalcommons.unl.edu/tsaconf/

McKenna, C. (Ed.). (2020). *Artist weaves Tsleil-Waututh governance model*. Salish Sea Sentinel. https://salishseasentinel.ca/2020/01/artist-weaves-tsleil-waututh-governance-model/

Minde, H. (2005). *Assimilation of the Sami—Implementation and consequences*. Aboriginal Policy Research Consortium International (APRCi). 196. https://ir.lib.uwo.ca/aprci/196

Norway Govt. (2019). *What defines Indigenous people*. Ministry of Local Government and Modernization. https://www.regjeringen.no/en/topics/indigenous-peoples-and-minorities/Sami-people/midtspalte/What-Defines-an-Indigenous-People/id451320/

Olsen, S. (2010). *Working with wool: A Coast Salish legacy & the Cowichan Sweater*. SonoNis Press.

Sârghe, O. (2019). *Cultural sustainability in indigenous people's festivals: Cultural impact of Riddu Riddu Festival, Norway* (Unpublished Master's thesis). University of Jyväskylä. http://urn.fi/URN:NBN:fi:jyu-201912125239

Sparrow, D. (1998). A journey. In I. Bachmann & R. Scheuing (Eds.), *Material matters: The art and culture of contemporary textiles* (pp. 149–156). YYZ Books.

Solitude Wool. (2021). *Types of wool*. https://solitudewool.com/pages/types-of-wool

"Tradition." *Merriam-Webster.com Dictionary*, Merriam-Webster, https://www.merriam-webster.com/dictionary/tradition. Accessed 7 May. 2021.

TRC. (2015). *Truth and reconciliation commission of Canada: Calls to action*. https://ehprnh2mwo3.exactdn.com/wp-content/uploads/2021/01/Calls_to_Action_English2.pdf

UNESCO. (2021). *Intangible cultural heritage*. https://ich.unesco.org/en/what-is-intangible-heritage-00003

UN General Assembly. (2007, October 2). *UNDRIP: United Nations declaration on the rights of Indigenous peoples: Resolution adopted by the General Assembly*, A/RES/61/295, https://www.refworld.org/docid/471355a82.html. Accessed 13 March 2021.

Vičiūnaitė, V. (2020). *Moving towards sustainability: Business models and entrepreneurship in the Norwegian wool industry* (Philosophiae Doctor thesis 2020). Norwegian University of Life Sciences School of Economics and Business.

Yunkaporta, T. (2020). *SAND TALK how Indigenous thinking can save the world*. Harper One.

5

Setting a New Stage: Small Scale as a Way Forward

Ingun Grimstad Klepp, Rebecca Burgess, Maria Ehrnström-Fuentes, Mafalda Pacheco, Jane Philbrick, and Tone Skårdal Tobiasson

When Covid-19 hit the world, one of the first problems was related to a lack of personal protective equipment (PPE). How to ensure enough face masks and infection protection coats for everyone who was in the front

I. G. Klepp
Consumption Research Norway (SIFO), Oslo Metropolitan University, Oslo, Norway
e-mail: ingunk@oslomet.no

R. Burgess
San Geronimo, CA, USA

M. Ehrnström-Fuentes
Hanken School of Economics, Vasa, Finland

M. Pacheco
Lisboa, Portugal

J. Philbrick
Redding, CT, USA

T. S. Tobiasson (✉)
Nordic Initiative Clean & Ethical Fashion, Oslo, Norway

I. G. Klepp and T. S. Tobiasson (eds.), *Local, Slow and Sustainable Fashion*,
https://doi.org/10.1007/978-3-030-88300-3_5

line in health care and later also for the general population when travelling, in stores, in schools and all sorts of public spaces? From the outset, China had enough with producing these items for their own market, and the Norwegian textile companies and small sewing facilities made a quick turnaround. It soon became clear that there was an acute lack of crisis preparedness for both textiles and sewing capacity. There weren't readily available knowledge on the materials or testing facilities either; these had been closed down earlier, in favour of out-sourcing.

The lack of available PPE did not last long. China increased its production, but protective equipment and face masks are still sewn locally and on a small scale in Norway and many other countries. Covid-19 did, however, increase awareness of local production and global uncertainty (Cappelli & Cini, 2020; Gereffi, 2020). Agriculture, fishing and construction sites, industry and health institutions depend on labour that commutes across borders and problems arose once the borders were closed. For Norwegian consumers the crisis increased the interest in buying Norwegian, supporting local business. Among the companies that did best in Norway in 2020 and 2021, were hand-knitting yarn manufacturers and Norwegian producers of wool underwear. Our spinning mills spun like never before: the largest spinning mill in Norway—Sandnes Garn—increased sales close to 20%, with 13.7 million balls of yarn sold. Many other spinning mills in Norway report a similar upswing in business (Tobiasson, 2020a). Everyone wanted local wool. Knitting became a way to find peace and meaning in new everyday life, as it has done earlier during wars and other times of acute crisis (Klepp & Tobiasson, 2018; Stannard & Sanders, 2015). In particular, 'knitting provided Icelanders (literally and metaphorically) an opportunity to take the difficult times into their own hands and produce something of value' (Coulthard, 2020).

Local production of clothes thus contributed two important elements in managing the crisis: protective textiles and meaningfulness. This was possible through the fact that there was already an infrastructure, people and companies, despite a marked out-sourcing policy, that we will return to in Chapter 6. To meet the demand, there were old family businesses and newly established ones. Many of these were in various ways part of a development, where local wool and small-scale production were at the core. It is therefore worth asking: Who are these actors, and what do they want and what can they do? What made them stay, or get involved in textile production based on a local fibre? To answer this, we will mainly use examples from Norway, but also show how the same story is repeated in many other places and locations. The sources for these examples are diverse and consist of conversations with actors in the whole value chain, and in many countries, alongside earlier descriptions of these in texts we and others have written. We have also used sources such as web pages, conference presentations and feature articles; however, foremost based on having been privy to much of the on-goings through our contacts in the global 'wool family' for over a decade.

A Place to Call Home

In our travels to describe these developments, we start in Lofoten, Norway. Lofoten Wool is a small company that develops yarns, produces and sells knitwear, based on the breeds grazing on this archipelago of islands in northern Norway. We have already mentioned the company in Chapter 1 when we wrote about wool and origin labels. Lofoten boasts steep mountains, beautiful beaches and abundant fishing, a paradise for surfers and a perfect backdrop for movie productions. Ragnhild Lie came here because of an interest in theatre but stayed on because it had become her home. But what can a textile artist live off in such a remote area? The company Lofoten Wool, established in 2014, was developed in response to this question. Here there were sheep, with colourful black, brown, grey and surprisingly white wool. There were also tourists more or less year-round, and growing local production of food based on seaweed, herbs, salt and all that the land and sea offer. If we lift our gaze, we see that the same thing is happening elsewhere as well. Talented, well-educated people are leaving secure jobs and a hectic life in favour of proximity to nature, tranquillity and opportunities to produce on a small scale the products they believe in.

Lofoten is not the only place where there are old breeds and young people fascinated by nature and new opportunities. We first turn to an example from Finland and Janne Rauhansuu, a Finnish windsurfer who, while living in Davos in Switzerland, spotted a myssy (Finnish for knitted beanie) on a friend and tried to buy it off her; however, to understand his story, we need to describe the situation for Finnish wool. Finnsheep or Finnish landrace, which is the national breed, has exceptionally soft wool even though it is not at all kept for its fleece. About 80% of the country's 155,000 sheep are members of this indigenous, old breed that has been traced 4000 years back in time and therefore has many valuable breeding traits. Of the estimated 572 tonnes of wool produced, the national Finnish Natural Resource Centre believes that somewhere between 70–90% of all the wool is waste (Haaksluoto, 2020). Two other estimates are lower, but still say it can be as much as 70% (Lehto, n.d.; Valta, 2019).

70% of the knitting yarn sold on the domestic Finnish market comes from abroad (Lehtonen, 2018). Yet, this might be rapidly changing due to increased consumer demand and an increase in the price paid for local wool by local spinners. There is not enough good quality wool for the rapid surge in demand on the local market (Torikka, 2020). For knitting yarns, the main ingredient for at least one of the major mills, is increasingly Finnwool, though some qualities still mix in crossbred wool as well. As mentioned, Finnwool is soft, with an even staple, often compared to Merino-softness, with a brighter lustre generally only found in the other short-tailed breeds. The lambswool is fine enough to be worn next-to-skin for most people today.

Janne Rauhansuu's friend was however not willing to part with it the myssy, no matter the price. So Janne taught himself to knit and within a short time, he was knitting beanies for sale. Fast-forward to Janne moving back to his family farm with roots back to the nineteenth century in Pöytyä with his wife Anna and discovering the wonders of the Finnsheep wool. Since they wanted the beanies to be handknitted, they enlisted local grannies. The Finnsheep are mainly white, but also with naturally pigmented wool, varying from black to fawn. This gives some of the wool a heathered hue. The lustre and wonderful colours are very much in play in the beanie hats knit by local grannies that have made Finnwool famous all over the world: Myssyfarmi.[1] The rest is history. 'We would

[1] https://myssyfarmi.fi/en/pages/the-story-of-myssyfarmi.

actually like to make a larger quantity of hats and employ more grannies, but the spinning mills in Finland can barely keep up with the demand', explains Anna Rauhansuu, who is the head designer and ensures the yarn is hand-dyed on the farm. Anna and Janne are also trying to garner enough media attention and interest in the local wool resource to wake up Finnish authorities, who have not given a single euro to encourage Finn's role in the current Nordic wool revival. There is a call for reinstating the national wool collection and building a scouring mill; both are seemingly very much in the blue.

These two examples from rural Finland and Norway are both colourful and both illustrate successful physical moves to rural areas. They have also shown entrepreneurial and enterprising skills that can inspire other micro-businesses. In a textile sector that is dominated by many and global giants, this offers optimism. If we return to Norway, we have a much more urban example. Laila Yvonne Henriksen quit her safe job at the University of Oslo and took the big step into the unknown. She also followed a dream, albeit her new 'home' was originally created in the middle of Oslo's trendiest neighbourhood, often called Oslo's SoHo, later she moved shop a little further north to a new, trendy area. In her cosy shop, knitters gather for 'knit & wine' evenings, to learn how to dye yarn or to peruse her carefully selected Norwegian-spun wool yarns that she also dyes in the brightest colours in her workshop (Klepp & Tobiasson, 2018) (Fig. 5.1).

A Circle of Collaboration

In California in 2010, Rebecca Burgess came up with the idea of calling clothes produced from local raw materials and production systems within a given geographical area a 'fibreshed'. She first spent a year exploring dressing only in clothes from local fibre sources and producers, which led to the following questions: Is it possible to build local value chains, not individual companies, but coherent networks of producers within a specific geographical area? Is it possible to be regionally self-sufficient? In the book *Fibershed*, she describes how she defines a '...fibershed. Similar to a local watershed or a foodshed, a fibershed is focused on the source

Fig. 5.1 From inside the knitting shop *Værbitt,* located at Sagene in Oslo (*Photo credit* Tone Skårdal Tobiasson)

of the raw material, the transparency with which it is converted into clothing, and the connectivity among all parts, from soil to skin and back to soil. (….) many of these cropping and livestock systems are showing benefits that we are just beginning to document in detail, such as ameliorating the cause of climate change, increasing resilience to drought, and rebuilding local economies' (Burgess & White, 2019).

The initiative aimed to transform the fibre and dye systems from the soil up. For Burgess, it was a vision that embraces everyone involved, including farmers, ranchers, grassroots organisers, designers, manufacturers, cut-and-sew talent, crafters, fashion pundits, investors and the wearer, the consumer. Her vision was to challenge the power structures and begin putting decision-making into the hands of the communities' members. The resulting place-based textile sovereignty would aim to include rather than exclude all the people, plants, animals and cultural practices that compose and define a specific geography (Burgess & White, 2019).

Burgess acknowledges how local and slow food, Farmers' Markets where customers and producers could meet face-to-face, also inspired her: 'Fibershed systems borrow considerable inspiration and frame work design from the Slow Food movement' (Burgess & White, 2019). This movement can be traced back to 1986 when Italian farmer Carlo Petrini, organised a protest against the opening of a McDonald's chain restaurant near the Spanish Steps in Rome. He was quoted as saying: 'A firm defence of quiet material pleasure is the only way to oppose the universal folly of Fast Life'. Hence the name 'Slow Food movement'. The questions he posed have guided the mission statements of thousands of non-governmental organisations (NGOs) focussing on reforming food systems, and perhaps the new question is then, can the same happen for our clothing. Burgess believes firmly that a grassroots movement is afoot to change this, led by those exact people and small-scale firms she set out to galvanise. Interestingly, some large pundits are sniffing around her ideas as well, perhaps because they too are having their awareness raised 'on the undeniable fact that the soil that feeds us is also the soil that clothes us' (Burgess & White, 2019).

One of Burgess' more profiled forays that showcased how local wool could enter the supply chain of a large sports brand, The North Face's first taste of regenerative fashion started in 2017 with its Climate Beneficial™ line, the Cali Wool Collection.[2] These wool products, which were mainly beanies, were produced in partnership with one of the few US

[2] https://sustainablebrands.com/read/supply-chain/trending-the-north-face-timberland-vans-scaling-regenerative-supply-chains.

sheep ranchers that practise carbon farming, Bare Ranch, who worked closely with Burgess to achieve the outcome. The ranch sequesters 4,068 metric tonnes of CO_2e annually. The drawdown rate effectively offsets 6 to 9.3 times the greenhouse gas emissions associated with Bare Ranch wool production each year and over 20 years, that's equivalent to the emissions of 23,740 cars (Burgess et al., 2020). Despite being a pilot program—the Cali Wool Collection was extremely successful and was a finalist for a World Changing Ideas award two years in a row by Fast Company. Burgess has several other ongoing projects with other California ranches that are finding good uses for the local wool, that Burgess had discovered was underutilised.

In Connecticut, also in the US, Wear Wool New London has taken a cue from Burgess and Fibershed and is currently building a vertically integrated, 'soil-to-shoulder' wool clothing business, as part of the Fibershed family, with North-Eastern American sheep farmers, A small group of New England-trained bio-material scientists and New York City-trained fashion designers have created a network in order to build upon New York and New England's pool of design, scientific, manufacturing and agricultural knowledge. The plan includes sourcing wool from grass-fed Northeast sheep breeds, then scouring, spinning and weaving these locally in ways that optimise their use for fashion-forward and place-specific accessories, garments and shoes. These will be sold directly to consumers in the region in a distribution model that minimises truck delivery. The products will have a *terroir*-affiliation, like a good wine, and the wearer will know where it comes from and how it is made.

Wear Wool New London commissioned three Parsons graduates to produce capsule collections that debuted in a 2019 Ecological Fashion Summit in Stamford, CT. The Summit received extensive coverage in the fashion press (Frame, 2020), establishing them as a player in what could be called ecological fashion. They have received additional grant funding to conduct a feasibility study for building a wool scouring operation in a former newspaper printing plant in New London, CT. Wool scouring is here, as in many other places including Norway, the critical missing infrastructure required to unlock the potential for a completely local value chain.

The eagerness to invest locally can easily be confused with protectionism, as with Trump's 'America First', Brexit and other political undercurrents with or without strong support from far right-wing forces. Therefore, it is possible that gathering around something global, as one common name, actually gives strength. Whatever the reason, we see that both the name and the idea from California are spreading. In Norway, it has happened in the form of Fibershed Nordenfjeldske, which was recently started by Årolilja Jørgensrud based in Tingvoll (a township we will return to in Chapter 7), who also invited Burgess to Norway the first time she visited here. Jørgensrud is cooperating with Selbu Spinning Mill on this venture. We are also privy to plans emerging in Finland, Denmark, Switzerland and, in the UK three Fibresheds[3] (with the British spelling) have already been established (Marshall, 2021).

As we mentioned Tingvoll, one of the driving forces in the work for local wool and with a burning desire for implementing the whole value chain locally, is Arnar Lyche, a sheep farmer and employed in the region's farmers' cooperative. Lyche knows his mathematics and calculated how much it cost to shear the wool of his small flock, and what he as a farmer was left with after he received the government subsidies and payment from the wool station. The calculation clearly showed that the wool did not provide for a financially 'profitable operation'. He went on to develop an idea for creating a local sweater from Norwegian Old Spæl sheep, sorted by colour and undyed. The initiative, which he dubbed Tingvoll Wool and established as a company in 2019, has all along been based on local forces, amateurs, the joy of being together and the belief that together we can achieve goals if we put our mind to things. For three years in a row, Tingvoll Wool has invited local amateur knitters to make their version of first a Tingvoll-sweater, then a Coastal Culture sweater and in 2021 a sweater celebrating the farmer, all made from yarn spun at Selbu Spinning Mill with Lyche's flock's wool. A catwalk-show, with young and old models, and a humorous presentation of the creations, is part of the package.[4] We hasten to mention that several of the people active in the Amazing Grazing project volunteered as models, designers

[3] https://www.thelandmagazine.org.uk/articles/fibreshed-comes-britain.

[4] https://www.tingvoll-ull.no/.

and knitters, as the main seat for the project bearing the name, which we have mentioned in Chapter 2, is actually Tingvoll.

The project Amazing Grazing: sustainable food and fibre from Norwegian sheep rangeland-grazing systems[5] will explore how products from rangeland-grazing sheep can gain a higher value by communicating how they contribute to biodiversity, healthy soils and a natural carbon cycle—and thus to more sustainable meat and wool. By looking at how products from rangeland grazing are marketed and how this affects consumer behaviour, the goal is strengthening value creation for sheep farmers, but also for those who process and sell products from grazing animals. The aim is also to influence the discussion about red meat and textiles—especially wool—and the environmental footprint of these, both how the media discusses this and how policies are shaped. This will be done by studying various measuring tools for environmental impacts associated with grazing systems and other feeding models, in addition to further processing in the value chain, including consumption, for wool or skins. What we discussed in Chapter 2, will be the basis for this. Fibershed is an important partner in this project and this shows how global networks can contribute to local adaptions that enhance soil and carbon-sequestration, if adjusted to place-specific factors within a given biosphere.

However, it is not only in the US, the UK, Finland and Norway, we see new developments and ideas for local wool and small-scale production. The WOOLUME project in Poland, described in Chapter 3, will certainly be trialling small-scale operations—at least to start with. In many local communities or geographical areas, we see a growing interest in cooperation and a wish to create a good life, fetch inspiration from history and nature. Many have seen the same as we have: It is very wrong to waste wool, and it is very hard for the global, large-scale industry to meet our current challenges.

We are therefore happy that research bodies, such as the Norwegian Research Council and the grant programs within Europa, such as EEA Norway Grants, and the Norwegian Agricultural and Food Industry Research Fund have understood that we need to look at better solutions

[5] https://www.nibio.no/prosjekter/amazing-grazing-baerekraftig-kjott-og-ull-fra-sau-som-beiter-i-norsk-utmark.

for local value chains, community-building, and taking care of valuable resources. The 'Save the Portuguese Wool' Association was created in 2015 with the aims of promoting the sustainability of the wool and safeguarding the culture and heritage traditions related to wool in Portugal. This association took the initiative to the hiWOOL project—Network for heritage and innovation for the future of WOOL—funded by the Bilateral Relations Fund EEA Norway Grants and started in 2021. The project focuses on the exploitation of wool products for small producers of local, indigenous sheep breeds. As is the same for many wool projects, it is important to get an overview of the current situation. What type of wool is being produced in Portugal, and how much? Such questions must be answered in order to find good uses. More than other projects, hiWOOL is grounded in cultural history. The aim is to investigate wool traditions and thus also includes using museums and archives, companies and researchers in the two countries Norway and Portugal. Again, some of the authors in this book, are involved in the project. The ambitions are high, and this and other small initiatives wish to join forces for a strong network—with the ultimate aim to submit an EU application for funding.

Portugal has an important wool history to tell. Together with Spain, they are an important piece in the jigsaw puzzle of the Merino sheep's role in Europe. According to one theory, Merino sheep were first introduced in the Iberian Peninsula in the late twelfth century from North Africa, and in the thirteenth and fourteenth centuries, Merino breeds were developed to produce fine wool, with a fine fibre monopoly in Portugal and Spain between the twelfth and sixteenth centuries. In fact, before the eighteenth century, the export of Merinos was a punishable crime, but sheep were smuggled out during this time. Once one opened for export of Merinos, they became the basis of fine wool growing in Australia, New Zealand, South America and South Africa. In the project, we are seeking more knowledge about the black Merino sheep's demise, against the backdrop of the expenses and chemicals involved in dyeing processes. In addition, we want to know more about the good use of grazing-lands and transhumance practices and how country borders made this difficult.

In the sad story, we have described in Chapter 3, for the fate of wool in Europe, Portugal is no exception. Like the rest of Europe, most of the coarser or coloured wool is wasted. This is a result of the import of cheaper fibres and standards set by the industry on uniformity. Thereby the local production with traditional processes is being forgotten. Through the disappearance of the wool industry in Portugal, sheep breeders were forced to sell the wool to foreign industries; however, the small-scale breeders have not been able to produce sufficient quantities at reasonable prices, and it ends up as waste (Pacheco & Bazaraite, 2018).

There are around 15 local sheep breeds in Portugal, each with a unique set of properties, which tells a piece of genetic and wool-quality history. These traditions maintained a great breadth of qualities. As in Poland, wool is today mainly a by-product from milk or meat production. Wool from the different Portuguese breeds varies in texture, colour and softness among other properties. This is in a clear contrast to the one-sided classification system that exists today, where wool is either 'good' or 'bad'. An important goal is therefore to change these criteria. Wool which is unacceptable as a raw material for clothing might be suitable for other artisanal purposes and products.

Artisan craft is an important element in hiWOOL. During the first half of the twentieth century, these artisanal crafts continued to thrive, not least in the Azores (e Sousa & Pacheco, 2020), but once the industrial giants introducing cheap and accessible textiles and clothing of low quality, this led to abandoning natural and local fibres. One of the aims of the initiative is to offer knitters and designers yarn differentiated by the sheep breeds, enriching the market with more options, and thus avoiding wool waste. In the same way as we discuss in Chapter 4, this will be based on personal meetings between tradition bearers and younger people, so that knowledge can be transferred uninterrupted and thereby contribute to a revival of woollen textile crafts as part of local identity.

The idea is to produce with our own hands, serving both as therapy and a way to fight overconsumption. These thoughts have become more and more prevalent during the last decades. People look for handmaking activities, yearning for capacities to both plant their food and make their clothing. During the last decade, a global renaissance of interest in knitting and spinning has inspired several start-ups in Portugal. Besides various public meetings involving knitting and spinning enthusiasts, the small-scale wool industry has restarted. The small-scale production seeks to find uses for wool of various sheep breeds, offering new quality products for knitters and spinners. Some larger factories have also started producing clothing and homeware infused with a local identity, and employing workers who had been let go in the late 1990s and now have an opportunity to apply their knowledge once again.

Salva a Lã Portuguesa, is now working to find a solution that can work between big scale industry and small-scale artisanal groups, bringing to life old machinery that is still functional and able to solve the challenges facing the local sheep farmers and artisans, in part inspired by the development the KRUS project facilitated in Norway. hiWool will contribute with seeking a way out of the massive production also here, of waste.

The Nordic Region

Before we embark on more examples of these small and brave micro-sized enterprises, we will take you to Iceland—a country that has understood the value of wool and marketing its unique qualities to tourists. As we've mentioned in Chapter 1, Icelandic designers were part of the VikingGold project, and in cooperation with the textile museum on Osterøy in Norway, Ásthildur Magnúsdóttir at the Museum of Design and Applied Art (Hönnunarsafn Íslands) has modernised the 'varafeldur' weaving process and made some stunning pieces using this old Viking-tradition. The resulting covers, also called 'rya' or 'gråfell' (gray fleece), were originally woven on warp-weighted looms, which are still in use in Kåfjorddalen in northern Norway by Sea-Sámi craftspeople, as described in Chapter 4. A Norwegian design duo also used the technique to create accessories—wrist-warmers and a neck-warmer—as the Japanese market had expressed interest in the rough look and Viking history. They never went into production, as the price-point proved to be prohibitive (Klepp & Tobiasson, 2013) (Fig. 5.2).

In Snorre's Sagas of the Norwegian kings, one can read the story of how the varafeldur became an Icelandic export item to Norway. The

Fig. 5.2 The Norwegian design label With & Wessel took inspiration from the varafeldur and made prototypes with the Japanese market in mind. These two products are the results. They were never actually produced (*Photo credit* Tone Skårdal Tobiasson)

story, which took place sometime before the year 1000, tells how an Icelandic ship laden with 'gråfells'[6] arrived in Hardanger in Norway, and that no one wanted to buy them. The King, Harald, however, was given one (the world's first product placement?) and started wearing it; and suddenly they sold like hot cakes. Harald thus became King Harald Gråfell. They became a big export item until other woven wool materials, usually felted, took over (Klepp & Tobiasson, 2013).

The raincoat effect of the Old Norse sheep breeds' coarse cover-wool, is also an asset in the Icelandic lopapeysa knitted sweater, mainly used when Icelanders are out riding, which comes in handy in the constantly shifting weather. Lopapeus[7] stands as an important symbol of Iceland's

[6] Grey fleeces, they were, however, woven and not actual fleeces.

[7] Icelandic for wool sweater.

cultural heritage, with long traditions through generations of knitting patterns for creating the sweater (Coulthard, 2020). The recent small-scale upstart mill, Uppspuni,[8] sells their own lopapeysa design with horseshoes as part of the yoke pattern. Most of the yarns from Uppspuni are named for the Icelandic mythical fairy-creatures for which are very much present in cultural expressions.

Building from the bottom up, the continuation of handicraft traditions and new forms of tourism go hand in hand in Iceland. Another new spinning operation, Ullarvinnslan Gilhaga, got their spinning machines in February 2020, right before the world closed down. According to Hulda Brynjólfsdóttir they also crowd-sourced in order to start up. As things have opened up again; Ullarvinnslan Gilhaga can operate at full capacity. Perhaps they can also join 'The Woollen Circle', which is the Icelandic version of The Wool Heritage Route in Norway,[9] which has a plant-dyeing studio (Hespa) and a speciality yarn shop (Thingborg) on their itinerary. Knitting tours are quite the tourist-thing to do in Iceland, many of them are led by the famous knitting book author Hélène Magnússon, and combine knitting and hiking.

Denmark has neither a large wool production today nor well-organised systems for taking care of their local wool; however, we see a growing interest in local wool, which may even result in a Fibershed upstart here, as mentioned. Historically, on the other hand, Denmark was an early powerhouse for spreading knitted, woollen wares in Scandinavia, with home-based industry and travelling salesmen who peddled hats, socks and other items from 1600 and especially in the 1700s when the local townships Lysgaard and Hammerum in Jutland gave employment to 40,000 knitters through the so-called 'putting-out' system (Klepp & Tobiasson, 2018).

300 years later, Danish designer Stine Sandermann was shocked when she followed her mother on a wool collecting trip to local farmers. Her mom used the wool for hand-spinning and the designer asked what happened to the wool they didn't collect. 'It's burned', she was told. Stine has turned it all around, the hard way. Working closely with local

---

[8] https://www.uppspuni.is/.

[9] http://thewoollencircle.com/.

sheep farmers in the district, she collects the wool she wants to process herself and then sends it on to Hjelholdt mini-mill on the island of Fyn. 'They accept as small volumes as 15 kilos, while Henrichsens Spinning Mill who also spins on commission have a much higher minimum', Sandermann explains (Tobiasson, 2020b).

She started her project in 2014, when she was finishing her master's degree at Chelsea College of Art, and has since developed her brand Sandermann with two fully fashioned knitting machines and with a 'SyLab'—a sewing lab cooperative trialling robot-sewing. 'It has been a challenge to get the farmers to handle the wool so it is clean and not full of vegetable matter. (..) I have to sort the wool myself, and as we have at least 27 different breeds in Denmark I've been in touch with many different breeders here to find good wool. My main partner is Lystbækgaard, which is a heathland-based, organic farm'. Her business model has been on-demand production and this has been more successful abroad than in Denmark; however, the yarns she has commissioned are selling even better with her knitting designs and she is currently looking at a new approach: 'I make more money selling the yarns and designs than the finished products, so the plan is to do more of that and less of production. I set out to prove that Danish wool doesn't have to be a waste product and I think I've converted a fair number of customers' (Tobiasson, 2020b).

If Danes don't properly appreciate their local wool, the Faroe islanders certainly do. An old proverb says that 'ull er færøya gull' which means wool is the Faroe gold. For over 100 years, knitted woollen garments were the main commodity exported and traded for necessities such as salt, sugar and coffee. Everyone, old and young, men and women, knitted. But then the name of the islands is derived from the old Norse 'Færeyjar', which literarily means Sheep Island.[10] The oldest code of law here from 1298 deals mainly with sheep husbandry. The Faroe sheep are descendants from the Old Norse breed and was crossbred with imported sheep from Iceland and the Scottish Isles in the seventeenth century. They are a wide variety of colours: white, grey, light and dark red, chestnut brown and black or some mixture thereof (Tobiasson, 2020b).

[10] https://www.faroeislands.fo/nature-environment/fauna-flora-vegetation/the-sheep-islands/.

Snældan is a traditional woollen mill and knit factory, and is open for factory visits. It was founded in 1949 and three generations still work together under the same roof, by the fjord of Stendur. At the heart of their production is local wool and tradition, coupled with new developments. On these islands, junior high school students are taken into the wool sorting facility and taught the craft of sorting the wool according to colour, which ensures that knowledge passes on to the next generation.[11]

Greenland has a large population of sheep. However, they also have a large muskox population and yarn production from this unique and soft wool. Going 20 years back in time, this local resource, also known as qiviut, was burned as waste. The muskox is not native to Greenland, so they used the meat, but understood little of the value of the wool, until Anita Høegh, a local woman took things into her own hands. Høegh learned how to spin and also how to separate the coarser guard hairs from the soft underwool from the pelts she bought from the hunters. Muskoxen do not willingly lend themselves to being shorn, for obvious reasons. 'It's a pretty smelly process', she explains. The result, however, is spun gold and the yarn commands a high price because of the many hands-on processes. Once the tourists have been told the story, they willingly pay the high price. This goes to show once again how local value creation can create jobs, beautiful yarns and contribute to waste-reduction.[12] As we wrote in Chapter 4, the Inuit have embraced yarn-based handicrafts, such as crocheting, as well.

Sweden is the 'just do it' country of the Scandinavians that has built industry and global companies, also for textiles (we assume H&M and IKEA's home textiles have not evaded attention), and even though their wool value chain has been on a death-bed for many years, things are potentially changing: Companies like Fjällräven, Filippa K, Gudrun Sjödén, Tiger of Sweden, Acne and even H&M have embraced wool as of late. The marked difference between the wool-loving Norwegians and Swedes, when it comes to the use of wool, including finer Merino next-to-skin products, has been analysed earlier (Klepp et al., 2016). It is therefore an important development that all of these companies,

[11] https://snaldan.fo/.

[12] https://www.qiviut.gl/om-qiviut/.

except for H&M, are part of a newly started Swedish Wool Initiative. While the Norwegian projects have been funded by the Norwegian Research Council, which again is funded by the government; the Swedish projects that have proliferated since 2010, have eked out funding from local municipalities and enterprises. There is little to no governmental support; however the AxFoundation in Sweden has recently stepped up to the task.[13]

As Sweden lacks a functioning infrastructure, shearing-competence and a classification system, 'this is first priority', according to Elin Larsson, formerly responsible for sustainability in Filippa K who spearheaded 2019s successful experiment where the iconic fashion brand ended up selling out 140 numbered sweaters in 100% Swedish-scoured local wool which otherwise would have been destroyed[14]; where they themselves had to follow through from shearing, scouring and spinning—and finally knitting, something fashion brands very seldom do. They sold out almost immediately, and they plan to continue with small capsule collections in the same artisanal-minded way. For now, Sweden is very concerned with building competence, as Annkristin Hult, who is a national developer for the National Swedish Handicraft Council explains: 'We have finally got in place the first education for a wool advisor, and we already have a student who started in the fall of 2021. It will be a two-year vocational education and the students can decide what part of the wool industry they would like to specialize in'.[15]

So, what kind of wool does Sweden have, now that all of 30% of the wool clip is going into the Swedish pipeline and is being refined, according to the Swedish Sheep Breeding Association? As they are hoping to create a cooperative organisation that can operationalise the value chain, so that each farmer and company does not have to go through all the value chain stages themselves, this is vital knowledge. Other hurdles are the lack of wool presses, the lack of production machinery, as most of the industrial machines were sold to the Baltic countries several years ago. This is exactly what emerging Swedish wool enthusiasts want to address.

---

[13] https://www.axfoundation.se/en/projects/the-swedish-wool-initiative.

[14] https://fashionforum.dk/2019/10/29/filippa-k-recirkulerer-svensk-restuld-med-eksklusivt-sweatersamarbejde/.

[15] Based on personal communication with Annkristin Hult, May 2021.

Grey Gotland[16] has been a 'black sheep' in the family, as it is naturally grey and therefore not an industry favourite. This wool has given its name to a new project which aims to find uses for this lustrous wool that can give heathered or naturally pigmented wool. It is, however, challenging to spin because of its shiny, slippery surface. It has been bred mainly for wool fleece pelts, where spinnability has not been an issue. Gotland is the home of 70,000 sheep, of which 80% are of the breed Gotland sheep.

The prices commanded for Swedish wool vary from 1 to 50 SEK per kilo, some wool is as high as 100 SEK. The farmer, if he or she sells the wool to the newly established wool scouring facility Ullkontoret,[17] first gets paid six months after they have delivered the wool; once the wool has been scoured and they have established the quality of the wool; which may explain some of the lack of engagement. Jenny Andersson, co-owner of Ullkontoret: 'We are anxious for the situation now, because we need to sell the scoured wool to customers in order to pay the farmers and with the Covid-19 situation marketplaces for selling the wool have ceased business'.

Not all wool needs to end up in clothing, though. Current and past projects have tried to find the best use for the Swedish wool. Their approach has been a little different than the other countries, even though knitting yarns, sweaters, throws and fabrics for national costumes have been part of both past offerings and current developments. Yoga mats, horse covers, sitting mats (a huge market for all the Nordic countries where hiking is big), jacket insulation, sound absorbing elements for public spaces, building insulation and the latest venture is wool pellets for soil-enhancement that Ullkontoret is experimenting with for the wool that is full of vegetable matter and that has been piling up. This is also part of what the WOOLUME project is exploring.

There is a patchwork of companies functional in the wool value chain within the Swedish borders that haven't given up and sold out, and that now see increased interest. The National Swedish Handicraft Council did apply for a grant to start up a worsted mill, but the authorities deemed

---

[16] https://faravelsforbundet.se/kunskap/gotlandsfar/.

[17] http://www.ullkontoret.se/ULLKONTORET/Start.html.

this to not be 'innovative' enough as the technology already is known. Bureaucrats tend to think that anything that can't be patented is not innovation. Despite this, an independent wool station in the far north of Sweden has opened, there is also a carding mill (Åddebo), five mini-mills and five more established spinning mills that are, however, also fairly small in size. And then again, a Fibershed project is emerging, with very local, long-abandoned mill facilities in a small county.

Communities for Change

So far, we have mostly described cooperation and communities in one country or in one area, or in the form of companies or research and development projects. The breadth of the nascent interest in wool is great and also embraces conferences and organised festivals and trips that bring together a praetorian of activists, companies and enthusiasts. The North Atlantic Native Sheep and Wool Conference is such a conference. It wanders between the countries in the North Atlantic region: Iceland, Faroe Islands, Orkney, Shetland, The Hebrides, Greenland and Norway, and contributes to spreading knowledge through lectures, exhibits, markets, social media presence and much more. The aim of the conference (and network) is to make progress for the development of local wool, and specifically in the area where the conference is being held. It is thus not only a community, but rather a tool in the work of promoting and supporting local companies and initiatives. Central in this work, is Karin Flatøy Svarstad. She has strived to promote the use of old breeds by arranging wool and knitting trips, and through her own workshop with arts and crafts products in felted wool.

There are also newer Nordic collaborations, one which includes the Baltics: The Baltic Wool Conference in Gotland, Sweden, which takes place in the fall. During the pandemic, they have arranged these as digital and hybrid conferences. Wool Days and Wool Weeks have been inspired by the Campaign for Wool's similar events around the world; Oslo has its annual Wool Day in the fall, and the West Coast in Norway has a Wool Week. Most impressive when it comes to the number of participants, is probably the Kil Fårfest[18] (sheep festival) in the spring in Sweden. We have yet to visit the South Iceland Wool Week (fall) and the Finnish Wool Week (fall). When that is said, a European Wool collaboration recently announced the European Wool Day as the 9th of April.

There are so many knitting festivals that only in Norway there is one for nearly every town and city, and many of them also focus on wool. These are found in other countries as well, too numerous to mention here, but the Fanø Knitting Festival, in Fanø, Denmark is one of the more important ones. In other words, there are plenty of opportunities for real and virtual encounters, whether the interest is wool, felting or knitting, whether you are an amateur, producer, researcher or activist. Part of the strength of the wool work is precisely its anchoring in the love for the animals, for the material and the will to change through local production and community. As we shall see in the next chapter, such popular movements can be important agents for change, something that is truly needed.

References

Burgess, R., & White, C. (2019). *Fibershed: Growing a movement of farmers, fashion activists, and makers for a new textile economy*. Chelsea Green Publishing.

Burgess, K. & Tobiasson, T. (2020, September). *The role of wool in a post-covid world*. Presented at Virtu-Wool Conference.

Cappelli, A., & Cini, E. (2020). Will the COVID-19 pandemic make us reconsider the relevance of short food supply chains and local productions? *Trends in Food Science & Technology, 99*, 566–567. https://doi.org/10.1016/j.tifs.2020.03.041

Coulthard, S. (2020). *A short history of the world according to sheep*. Apollo.

e Sousa, P. S., & Pacheco, M. (2020). The woollen manufacture industry in the Azores islands (1850–1930). In *Textiles, identity and innovation: In touch* (pp. 76–83): CRC Press.

[18] https://farfestikil.com/.

Frame, M. M. (2020). Clothes minded. *STAMFORD*. https://wearwoolnewlondon.com/stamfordmagazinearticle

Gereffi, G. (2020). What does the COVID-19 pandemic teach us about global value chains? The case of medical supplies. *Journal of International Business Policy, 3*(3), 287–301. https://doi.org/10.1057/s42214-020-00062-w

Haaksluoto, M. (2020). *Järjetöntä haaskausta! Suomalainen villa päätyy jätteeksi, ei vaatteisiin – nyt muutos on tulossa*. https://www.iltalehti.fi/muoti/a/feca0170-87ef-483a-8031-0b81f6345fff

Klepp, I. G., Laitala, K., & Tobiasson, T. S. (2016). *Woolbed—Sweet dreams in merino*. Retrieved from Oslo. http://sifo.no/files/file80443_oppdragsrapport_no_2_2016_-_woolbed_final.pdf

Klepp, I. G., & Tobiasson, T. S. (2013). *Ren ull*. Aschehoug.

Klepp, I. G., & Tobiasson, T. S. (2018). *Norsk strikkehistorie*. Vormedal.

Lehto, M. (n.d.). Lampaanvilla. Määrä, laatu ja hyödyntäminen Suomessa. Uutta liiketoimintaa sivutuotteista -hanke. 2017–2021. https://uusivu.weebly.com/uploads/1/0/5/1/105123013/villa_hyödyntäminen.pdf. Accessed 25 March 2021.

Lethonen, S. (2018) *Novita luopui täysuomalaisesta villalangasta. Maaseudun Tulevaisuus*. Published on January18.

Marshall, J. (2021, May 27). Simply thread: The North West England Fibreshed on exploitative fast fashion and changing the world. *Lancashire Post*. https://www.lep.co.uk/business/simply-thread-the-north-west-england-fibreshed-on-exploitative-fast-fashion-and-changing-the-world-3240122

Pacheco, M., & Bazaraite, E. (2018). *Sustainability through traditional processes: Strategy of "Salva a Lã Portuguesa" for revival of natural wool.* Paper presented at the Textiles, Identity and Innovation: Design the Future: Proceedings of the 1st International Textile Design Conference (D_TEX 2017), November 2–4, 2017, Lisbon, Portugal.

Stannard, C. R., & Sanders, E. A. (2015). Motivations for participation in knitting among young women. *Clothing and Textiles Research Journal, 33*(2), 99–114. https://doi.org/10.1177/0887302x14564619

Tobiasson, T. (2020a). *Coping with Covid-19 in the cold: A wintery and wooly wonderland*. https://southwritlarge.com/articles/coping-with-covid-19-in-the-cold-a-wintery-and-wooly-wonderland/

Tobiasson, T. (2020b). Wool, yarn & beyond. *Wool2Yarn Global*. Retrieved from https://issuu.com/ely12155/docs/wool_2_yarn_global_2020

Torikka, T. (2020). *Lampurit jaksavat lajitella ja pakata villoja, kun hinta nousee ja keräily toimii – kotimaisen villan kova kysyntä pienentää vähitellen hävikkiä*. https://www.maaseuduntulevaisuus.fi/maatalous/artikkeli-1.1256406

Valta, L. (2019, January 11). *Puolet suomalaisesta lampaanvillasta päätyy roskiin samalla, kun Suomeen tuodaan villaa ulkomailta*. Yle Uutiset -sivusto. https://yle.fi/uutiset/3-10588584. Accessed 25 March 2021.

6

Rethinking the (Wool) Economy

Tone Smith, Maria Ehrnström-Fuentes, Sophia E. Hagolani-Albov, Ingun Grimstad Klepp, and Tone Skårdal Tobiasson

The modern, global growth economy is increasingly called into question due to its many problematic aspects. The climate crisis and biodiversity

T. Smith (✉)
Wien, Austria
e-mail: tone@degrowth.no

M. Ehrnström-Fuentes
Hanken School of Economics, Vasa, Finland

S. E. Hagolani-Albov
University of Helsinki, Helsinki, Finland

I. G. Klepp
Consumption Research Norway (SIFO), Oslo Metropolitan University, Oslo, Norway
e-mail: ingunk@oslomet.no

T. S. Tobiasson
Nordic Initiative Clean & Ethical Fashion, Oslo, Norway

I. G. Klepp and T. S. Tobiasson (eds.), *Local, Slow and Sustainable Fashion*,
https://doi.org/10.1007/978-3-030-88300-3_6

loss are only the tips of the iceberg of the myriad problems caused by our current system. Some problems are not as obvious, including proneness to crises, unemployment, alienation in production processes, and the exploitation of labour in the global South. In addition, there are ethical concerns related to the poverty and inequality that accompany textile and other systems of clothing production and consumption. This book looks more closely at the apparel and textile sector, which are both key sectors in the industrialisation that has occurred, first in the global North and later the global South. The apparel and textile sectors are currently in the midst of the discussion about whether measures of 'green growth' and circular economy will remedy the situation or whether a more radical paradigm shift is needed to ameliorate the problematic aspects of these sectors. This chapter address a variety of the base issues that surround the textile and apparel industry, beginning with energy and fossil fuels and their role as the base of industrialisation.

Environmental Problems: A Biophysical Economy Perspective

The current level of industrialisation would not have been possible without access to fossil fuels. Hence, they are a foundational element of our current economic system. Ecological economists claim that access to this specific energy source lies behind the enormous increase in material living standards across much of the world in the last two centuries. Such a perspective, however, runs counter to the general understanding that the current living standards are caused by high 'productivity'. Instead, labour productivity has increased first and foremost because human and animal labour has been substituted with fossil energy and machines, not because of an increase in efficiency or smarter working. Hence, modern living standards and the modern growth economy are possible because of easy access to large amounts of cheap fossil fuels. While the development of the fossil-fuel-based economy has provided the opportunity for producing enormous amounts of goods and material wealth, these same processes have led to a rampant degradation of the natural environment, including excessive amounts of greenhouse gases in the atmosphere (Spash, 2017). This is the main paradox of the modern growth economy.

When moving away from fossil energy, the same level of energy use cannot be maintained. This is because renewable energy production necessitates large inputs of raw materials and energy. Compared to fossil fuels, renewables have a lower energy return per energy unit used in the energy production. In addition, many of the raw materials needed to produce the components accompanying a transition to renewable energy are not abundant, and they are often extracted under problematic social and environmental conditions, mostly in the global South, but increasingly also in the global North (Kröger, 2016a). Another important implication of a shift to renewable energy is that many 'climate solutions' simply shift the problems to other environmental areas, which creates socioecological consequences for communities in those areas. For example, large windmill parks degrade the local natural environment, especially through the construction and road infrastructure needed for maintenance (Dunlap & Correa Arce, 2021). The presence of the windmills might also threaten local species and traditional ways of life (Normann, 2020). Constructing windmills is not carbon-free, as large amounts of concrete are needed for the construction. The production of biofuels is another problematic example of renewable energy as the production of the raw materials needed for biofuel often requires the establishment of plantation-style agricultural production. In many places, like Brazil, these plantations are carved out of existing forest areas (Kröger, 2021). This deforestation, in addition to reducing the biodiversity in the affected areas, can reduce food security as the producers focus on the production of fuel rather than food (Kröger, 2016b). As these examples demonstrate, industrial renewable energy is often wrongly labelled as 'clean' or 'green' energy. As with all (industrial) production processes, there are serious social and environmental side-effects in the communities where renewable energy projects are located. Thus, the focus should not be on shifting the source of energy, but on reducing the total use of energy and raw materials (Smith, 2020).

The first law of thermodynamics, which is a basic law of physics, is also called the law of conservation of energy and materials and it has serious consequences for Earth's living system. Thermodynamics is the branch of physics that addresses the qualitative transformation of energy and materials. Understanding this law is vital to understanding the energy-related challenges of the energy transition. Energy is the capacity to exercise mechanical work. Although energy, like materials, cannot disappear, it can be converted to forms that are unavailable for human use. Fossil energy has a unique density and a high capacity to carry out mechanical work. However, this energy source can only be used once for such purposes, after which it dissipates. Unlike materials, energy cannot be recycled. In this respect, all transformation processes are characterised by irreversibility (Georgescu-Roegen, 1971).

One implication of this law is that an absolute decoupling between economic growth and environmental load is impossible since efficiency cannot increase eternally. There is always a minimum amount of resources and energy inputs that are needed in a production process, and some waste will always be produced. Thus, the environmental load of production processes cannot be completely removed. Another implication of this law is that innovation cannot unilaterally 'save us', as every new production technology comes with its own side-effects, e.g. new waste products. Further, beyond each separate transformation process that is related to producing a good, there are similar processes related to the energy and material resources used as inputs to the production process. The inputs must also be generated or extracted, which requires the use of energy and material resources, which will create waste products.

Economies, at their most fundamental level, are embedded within the biophysical systems of the Earth. One could say that the economy is bounded by the limits of the biophysical because it is biophysical. All economic activities or transformation processes (like the industrial activities described above) require an input of resources and energy to make products. In addition to the manufactured products, the production process generates waste. It should be noted that not all waste products are equally problematic, and some of them can become side-streams and by-products, such as wool, which in many countries is a by-product from meat and/or dairy production, as discussed in Chapter 3. Whether or not the waste products from an industrial process are problematic depends on the type, amount and concentration of the waste. In general, biological waste can be more easily assimilated through natural processes than synthetic waste. However, even biological wastes can be a problem when they are introduced to the environment in high concentrations. An example is the large amount of whey disposed of by most European dairy farmers, which while an effective fertiliser, requires special management in some regions because of its high saline content (Prazeres et al., 2012).

Wool Inputs and Outputs

Wool as a waste product has already been described extensively in this book. However, from an environmental perspective, wool waste should be regarded as a wasted resource instead of strictly a pollutant. Unlike other industrial by-products, it needs to be deposited in huge amounts or in a way that pollutes significantly (e.g. burning) to create an environmental problem. Hence, wool waste is a slightly different kind of waste than the wastes described and problematised within a biophysical economy perspective. It is a biological by-product of meat and/or dairy production, which only becomes wasted when it has low economic value in the global market. However, the viability of utilising the wool that is a wasted product needs to be assessed based on the energy that is needed to manufacture that wool. Thus, it is not a straightforward resource *or* pollutant. One must assess the total impact of the transformation processes and the required use of resources along the value chain to convert wool to textiles or other types of materials.

Many of the transformation processes associated with the wool value chain (e.g. animal husbandry, shearing, scouring, carding, spinning, knitting or weaving, cutting, sewing and a slew of other processes including dyeing) require high amounts of resource and energy inputs and produce different types of waste. Many resource-intensive processes must take place before the wool is even ready to be refined. The breeding and rearing of live animals require the use of agricultural machinery and other inputs, regardless of whether the sheep feed from rangelands, fields and pasture or from the imported feedstock. Energy is also used for the transportation of sheep or feed. The scouring of the wool involves many inputs, such as warm water and chemical cleaning agents, resulting in the by-product lanolin, which can either go to waste or can be further processed. If the wool is dyed and/or bleached, this involves the addition of further chemical treatments.

Shearing, as an activity, can exemplify in more detail some of the resource uses involved. Shearing can be done with scissors and thus with human energy, or with electricity-driven mechanised shearing instruments. In both cases, the equipment also needs to be produced, which in turn requires energy and raw materials. In addition, the shearers themselves are often seasonal workers from New Zealand or Australia. They are a specialised labour force, travelling around the world to shear sheep, following the different seasons. This means a lot of air travel, and thus dependency on fossil fuel energy sources is high. Other transportation activities are required to move the people and materials to and from the various production facilities, including yarn-spinning, knitting, weaving, cutting and sewing, transport to and from the store or storage unit, and finally, of course, the transportation of the consumer to and from the shop (or for the delivery to the consumer).

One of the few life cycle assessment (LCA) studies that has looked at all stages in a clothing item's life cycle, analyses a lightweight Merino woollen sweater. It showed that the use of fossil fuel energy was dominant in wool processing, with substantial impacts also coming from retail and garment care (Wiedemann et al., 2020). In terms of greenhouse gas emissions, the highest impacts came from the wool production on sheep farms, followed by contributions from processing and garment care. Impacts on water stress varied less across the supply chain (Wiedemann et al., 2020). Yet, what is most important with this study is that it shows how the most influential factor in determining environmental impacts was the number of times each garment was used and for how long. Similarly, in another study comparing the best and worst case scenarios for use and care of a wool sweater, Wiedemann et al. (2021) found that garments reused by one or multiple users increased the lifespan of the garment and reduced its impacts by 25–28% across all indicators. The largest effects came from increasing the number of wears from 109 to 400 per garment, which decreased the environmental impacts by up to 68%. In addition, implementing the best care practices for prolonging the usable life of the sweater resulted in a 75% reduction in impacts across all indicators. Unsurprisingly, worst case scenarios increased impacts dramatically; for example, using the garment only once before disposal increased the greenhouse gas impacts over 100 times (Wiedemann et al., 2021).

These results clearly indicate that any improvements in energy use and material inputs in the production process will not result in actual reductions of environmental impacts unless the growth of consumption is reversed. This study showed that the wearer of the garments (i.e. the consumers) had the largest capacity to reduce the overall impacts to the environment by maximising the active lifespan of their woollen products. This also suggests that to downscale the production processes, it is important to produce quality products that last longer.

In line with this, we observe a wide variety among producers in the wool industry, which is highlighted in several chapters. There are those who use biodegradable natural dyes that decompose in water, while others use artificial, synthetic dyes that cause widespread pollution and even hormone disruption, which can lead to disease (Srivastava & Singh, 2019). In this way, the type of inputs in the production plays a role in the waste that is produced and whether it is problematic or not.

What we want to stress with these examples is that environmental problems emerge as effects of both the specific *structure* and the *scale* of the value chains that make up an economy. For example, different energy systems allow for different kinds of consumption patterns, which in turn lead to different environmental effects. A qualitative difference between agricultural or hunter-gatherer societies and today's industrial economies is that in the former, the provisioning systems were largely locally based, and their energy systems were based on the direct biological conversion of solar energy. This solar energy served to sustain human and non-human life without the need for external inputs. Arguably, this could be framed by industrialists as a less 'productive' way to power society. Modern, industrial economies are made possible only through access to external energy inputs, which in this era is fossil energy. Fossil minerals are an energy source that was created through the accumulated inflow of the sun to the earth over millions of years, yet the industrial economy has managed to consume almost all of them within the past 200 years. Resource use in earlier types of societies provides a perspective for today's economies. Estimates show that industrial economies use between 25 and 50 times more material resources per person per year than hunter and gather societies used (Krausmann et al., 2016, p. 67). When looking at energy consumption, the picture becomes even starker, as this is several orders of magnitude higher (Simmons, 1989). At the same time, the world's human population has greatly expanded. This makes it clear that the human economy is taking up and appropriating an increasingly larger share of the 'ecological space' on Earth. This has impacts on ecology, biodiversity, and more generally for living nature. The web of life that supports both human and non-human life is often severely threatened long before any absolute limits of resources or energy supply are reached. Furthermore, the constant expansion and conversion of land to support this continued industrialisation (i.e. through monocultural agriculture, infrastructure, and the spread of buildings) continuously contributes to shrinking the habitats available for other species. Ecologists generally agree that land use change is now the most important direct cause of biodiversity loss. Even more importantly, there is increasing agreement that the Earth is entering the 6th era of mass extinction of species, which is the first one caused by human activities (Ceballos et al., 2017).

One of the major problems that even moderate economic transitions face, is that the economy is structured around wage labour intimately tied to the industrial mode of production, which depends on a large throughput of energy and materials. This means that simply maintaining the current production level, without any additional growth of economic activity, demands a high level of resources. However, this is near impossible to change, because economic growth is at the core of many national, corporate and intergovernmental strategies for future economic development and societal well-being as we see in United Nation's SDGs.

Problematic Social Aspects of the Current Globalised Economy

Western material living standards are made possible by an economy based on high energy and materials use, which is fuelled by the exploitation of nature. Yet, this is only one aspect, as modern growth economies are not only exploiting nature; they are also socially exploitative (Spash, 2021). This can be observed on many levels, particularly in the global textile industry. Since colonial times, international trade has evolved based on an unequal economic exchange between the global North and South. The globalisation of production in the textile industry has been known throughout history for its exploitative and unsafe working conditions in garment factories. This is a structural issue that has caused consumer boycotts and protests, particularly since the Rana Plaza collapse in Bangladesh in 2013 (Korica & Bazin, 2019). While some corporations have sought to tackle these issues with improved ethical standards (Arrigo, 2013) and social auditing of factory compliance, to date such actions have been rather toothless in improving the exploitative conditions in global textile supply chains (Reinecke & Donaghey, 2021). Instead, elite interests continue to override the voices of marginalised victims in negotiations to create fairer systems of global trade (Chowdhury, 2017). An example is discussed in detail in Chapter 2, as there is the danger that comparing products based on selective and not representative environmental impacts further contributes to destroying local industries in both the global North and South.

Western living standards have been referred to as a modern 'imperial mode of living' (Brand & Wissen, 2021) since they are based on a disproportionately high share of global consumption taking place in the global North. This includes consumption of products and resources, but also of so-called 'environmental sinks'. Rich countries are importing cheap goods from poorer countries, and they also outsource the pollution caused by production and waste treatment. This situation is made possible due to the underlying structures of colonialism and colonial land relations that continue to this day, which enables the polluters of the global North to outsource their waste including hazardous waste to rural and Indigenous communities in the global South (Liboiron, 2021). These injustices are key to many environmental and social conflicts worldwide and are central to the fight(s) of the global environmental justice movement (Temper et al., 2018). Textiles are not an exception, and while this export is seen as 'gifts' from the global North and as an important contribution to the idea of the circular economy, the global second-hand textile market is already beyond capacity. More than 100,000 tonnes of used textiles are collected yearly from the Nordic countries alone and around three-quarters of these end up on the global markets (Watson et al., 2016). Currently, there is no technology or recycling industry ready to utilise the textiles not suitable for reuse (Watson et al., 2020).

The prevailing economic growth model in countries throughout the global North is premised on extraction from the global South (and increasing also from the global North, see Kröger [2016a]). Thus, addressing these issues properly goes far beyond national redistribution. Any serious attempt to move the economy towards more sustainable and just production models must include considerations about the fundamental workings of the current globalised economic system. That is an economic system that is built on growth and exploitation, which does not account for its biophysical limits and its direct effects on marginalised communities.

It is these interlinked externalised environmental and social costs of the globalised textile industry that have enabled an exploding production of cheap, low-quality products that do not last. Fast fashion is a prime example of this development. Hence, even the claim that modern, industrial and global economies have provided the richer segments of society a higher material living standard, can be contested in many respects. It is difficult to claim that we are more well-dressed or more content with our outward appearance than we were 20 years ago (Klepp & Laitala, 2015), but consumption of resources has doubled (Ellen MacArthur Foundation, 2017). Hence, change is urgently needed in how we produce, consume and relate to our clothes and other textiles, but this change must be accompanied by the right actions, insights and strategies to avoid replicating past mistakes.

The Inadequacy of Political Responses

Addressing the problems related to the current globalised economic system, which is built on growth and exploitation, is far from the agenda of today's politicians. Instead, the dominant political position is to prop up the growth economy at all costs. As the unavoidable environmental problems are becoming increasingly clear, the prevailing idea of how to tackle these issues is to provide 'green growth'. The dream of green growth is that by a combination of innovation and more efficient technologies, we will be able to decouple the level of production from the amount of pressure and load placed on the environment. This is not really a new idea as it was already presented during the establishment of sustainable development in the late 1980s. In 1987, the Brundtland Report (Brundtland et al., 1987), proposed that old ideas about economic growth, which is growth that came at the cost of the environment, should be left behind. Instead, the new idea was to 'change' the content and type of growth. Ideally, this would mean aiming for immaterial growth, through a structural change in the economy, from industrial production to more services. However, what actually happened, was that the richest countries did not procure fewer industrial products, but instead outsourced these sectors to poorer countries, and simultaneously added more procurement of services (e.g. restaurant visits, tourism and yoga classes) on top of the previous procurement.

These changes can also be seen in the textile industry, which quickly outsourced from the global North to the global South, as a result of the introduction of both free trade for fibres (Scheffer, 2021), and increased requirements for environmental control of textile production in many places in the global North. However, these same strict requirements did not apply to imported goods. In Chapter 3 we showed how this impacted Polish wool. A similar description for Norway is found in the article *Nisseluelandet* (Klepp & Laitala, 2018), which describes why parts of the wool industry could not be outsourced in the same way and managed to survive the onslaught of cheap imports. Both family-owned businesses steeped in tradition and the distinctive market in Norway for knitting yarns and woven woollen fabrics for the Norwegian national costume, the 'bunad', contributed to this situation, as described in Chapter 1.

There are no signs of people in richer countries reducing their basic material consumption, rather the opposite. They are simply buying more services in addition, with higher income and cheaper prices for items like those that broadly constitute fast fashion. Hence, empirically, there is no sign of either 'changing the content of growth' or of global decoupling

(Haberl et al., 2020). Based on the previous explanation about the basics of the biophysical economy, this is not surprising. Production needs raw materials and energy inputs and produces waste, no matter how innovative or efficient the industrial processes become. In Chapter 2 we pointed to the report by the Biomimicry Institute which underlines that the side-streams and waste from any industry are either a pollutant, a nutrient, or both; alongside the fact that so many of the many finishing processes in the textile industry, even for natural fibres, result in toxic chemical outputs.

A Push for New Innovations and Subsidies

In recent years, governments and interstate systems of cooperation have created several policies to find ways of addressing the dire consequences for the environment through strategies of green growth. First, to tackle the issue of climate change, there has been a push for new innovations and subsidies that enable the transition from fossil to renewable energy sources. The underlying assumption of this strategy is that if industry and society could manage this transition, then the economy could continue as before. However, as argued above, renewable energy production is not without its own set of problems.

Another addition to the green growth agenda is the idea of creating a circular economy that seeks to address the challenge of the current and expected future shortage of a range of material resources. The main argument for the implementation of a circular economy is that current rates of recycling are very low. What needs to happen is a shift to reusing products to a larger extent (through e.g. repair), coupled with a push to recycle much more material, including taxing virgin resources. Various proposals already exist in many countries for recycling a larger amount of the material resources circulating in the economy, while ideas for reusing and reducing material input to the production phase is explored by companies and researchers.

While, for most people, it is intuitive that there cannot be endless growth in a finite material world, the concept of a circular economy is thornier. The notion itself hints at a system based on biological cyclical processes that endlessly renew themselves. It also suggests that products and by-products from manufacturing processes, which would otherwise be 'wasted', can serve as a source of economic growth by reusing, remaking and recycling. In practice, industrial or other human-led production is much more energy-intensive than nature's own production (Giampietro, 2019). Given that materials in small amounts are hard to recover from products, recycling requires a lot of energy, and materials eventually lose their properties, thus, reduced energy and materials use is the only way forward. Intensive industrial energy production and the continued growth of economies are not challenged within this paradigm. Instead, the circular economy serves to legitimate the growth economy by suggesting that all 'waste' can be eternally circulated as materials for production (Valenzuela & Böhm, 2017). This way of thinking about sustainability does not question the amount of materials and energy that circulate in the system, nor does it account for the environmental impact caused by the extraction or recycling of these resources.

Related to the circular economy is the notion of the 'bio-economy', which has been presented as the solution to replace non-renewable fossil materials with renewables sources (e.g. a move from synthetics to cellulose fibres in clothes). A key aspect of the bio-economy is whether the production is based on non-renewable, and hence exhaustible, rather than what are presented as renewable sources of energy and materials. In this respect, any fossil-based supply chain (e.g. plastics) by definition has a more detrimental starting point than a biologically based supply chain (e.g. wool). However, while the move towards a bio-based economy can appear to present a solution to the concurrent crises of the twenty-first century, on deeper inspection it is apparent that for example, viscose sourced from monoculture industrial tree plantations will require a high amount of water, chemicals and energy input in order to be converted into textiles (Ehrnström-Fuentes, 2019). That said, while both the circular economy and the bio-economy have potential, neither should be blindly implemented without embedding the solutions on the ground. Although the basic raw material of the value chain is biologically based, the rest of the supply chain might be just as resource intensive as synthetic production, if based on e.g. long transportation, heavy machinery, or high energy use. In addition, the prospect that we would substitute our current consumption of plastic products with an equal consumption of products made from natural materials like wood fundamentally misses the point, which is a reduction in overall consumption. To simply change our current plastic consumption to wood as a 'green' solution, obscures the reality that deforestation would increase, or large tracts of land would need to be dedicated to plantations to support the increased wood production.

The latest ideas within this mode of thinking have been the various proposals for a Green New Deal (GND), which aims to simultaneously address concerns of climate change, economic stagnation and unemployment (Smith, 2021), by promoting a combination of state intervention and investment to accelerate the sustainable transition while also creating jobs (note in the policy documents this transition is sometimes referred to as a green transition). The discussion surrounding the EU's Product Environmental Footprint (PEF), discussed in Chapter 2, is a component in this type of policy work.

A problem with all these new paradigms or 'solutions' to the environmental impacts of the current economic system, is the lack of realism in addressing the environmental crisis and a lack of respect for the basic laws of physics (i.e. the thermodynamics elaborated earlier) and biology. Understanding energy is important to understand both the key enabling factor and the deep challenges of modern, industrial economies. A transformation of our energy system needs to take into account the extent to which our modern, industrial economies are enabled by easy access to cheap fossil energy. While at its core the production of wool is based on solar-fuelled biological processes, the actual manufacturing processes that convert wool to textiles will still need to detach from much of the industrialised input and globalised ancillary services to reduce the dependency on fossil fuels and to become more aligned with the biophysical reality of Earth's living system. Taking the biophysical aspects of the economy seriously will also make it clear that an economic system is completely unsustainable if it promotes limitless economic growth via unlimited raw material extraction, material consumption, and waste releases (Ergene et al., 2020). Hence, there is a need for a deep transformation of the whole economic system. However, how to enable the deep transformation described above is still a highly debated topic.

The Need for a Deep Economic Transformation

The implication of the biophysical understanding of the economy as outlined above, is the need for a radically transformed economy, one that sets limits to growth. One of the difficulties in initiating this type of change is that it must be done from within the system that is in need of change. That is, capitalist societies depend on economic growth to avoid recession and the associated problems (e.g. increased unemployment, social unrest). While this problem seems intrinsic to capitalist dynamics, socialist economies might be more flexible as there is often not as direct a need for return or profit on all investments, although historically socialist countries have also pursued growth and wealth accumulation. Socialism, which has been considered the main alternative to capitalism for the last century or so, has also not fared well in terms of environment or democracy. A question that remains is to what extent true sustainability, which respects the biophysical limits of Earth, is possible within either of these systems, or even within economic systems that rely on a mix of elements from these two systems (e.g. the Nordic Welfare State). To make things even more difficult, the globalisation process itself has transferred a lot of decision-making power to global corporations and stripped national governments of their capacity to regulate business conducted beyond their own jurisdiction (Scherer & Palazzo, 2011). These factors and many more, suggest that traditional politics between the left and right within the nation-state system may not provide answers on how to enable the kind of deep transformations needed to change the rules of the game.

In recent years, a range of social movements and scholars have urged for the transition to new, alternative economic systems that give primacy to social, ecological and subsistence concerns over the primacy of profit maximisation and growth (e.g. degrowth, commoning, buen vivir, and post-development). Anthropologists, like David Graeber (in Sahlins, 2017 [1972]), have argued for learning from historical systems (e.g. tribal economies, primitive communism or medieval peasant economies), and combining the positive elements in an attempt to develop something new, appropriate for the challenges and values of modern times. Already in 1944, Karl Polanyi (2001) explained in his landmark book, *The Great Transformation*, how market culture in the seventeenth through nineteenth centuries gradually replaced kinship, custom, religion, morality and community to become the primary ordering principle of society. He pointed out how all economies prior to market capitalism were socially embedded in their context and 'organized either on the principles of reciprocity or redistribution, or householding, or some combination of the three' (Polanyi, 2001 [1944], p. 57). It is this transformation that must be reversed to align the economy with Earth's living system. There is also a well-explored body of knowledge on alternatives that draws on ecofeminist (see e.g. Salleh, 2009) and Indigenous (Kuokkanen, 2011) perspectives of economies as an integrated part of the socioecological life in the community. In Chapter 4, we also explored Tyson Yunkaporta's work.

Yet, while these more philosophical debates are valuable in that they may be able to give birth to new imaginaries and explain alternative economic thinking, they still provide limited understandings of how change that takes us in this direction can occur. More grounded examples of community economics from across the world show how civil society actors through 'grassroots innovations' (Seyfang & Smith, 2007) have skilfully organised themselves to intervene in globalised production and consumption patterns, in order to localise and 'take back' (at least part of) the economy from global capitalist markets (e.g. Gibson-Graham et al., 2013). Such examples provide valuable insights to how at least some degree of change (if not system change) can happen from the grassroots level, when people with common interests or concerns come together to enact change 'from below' (Misoczky et al., 2017). Chapter 5 provides some relevant examples, and in the rest of the chapter, we will discuss how to understand the emerging wool economy, its sustainability and limits, from such a grounded perspective, where grassroots actors come together to initiate change. We start by re-focussing our attention on the potentialities in place.

The Integral Part of Place in Creating an Alternative System

In the creation of local alternative systems of production and consumption, everything starts with and in place (Ehrnström-Fuentes & Leipämaa-Leskinen, 2019). The available technologies and infrastructures as well as place-based normative frameworks and inherited or acquired competencies will influence the ways through which people interact and create alternative solutions to the global system of trade (Ehrnström-Fuentes & Leipämaa-Leskinen, 2019). Thus, all local initiatives that emerge from specific places are imbued with specific socioecological and socio-technological meanings and relations, which makes them 'place-based' (Vanclay, 2008). However, theories on entrepreneurial ventures do not often account for how place plays an intrinsic role in the sustainability performance of an organisation (Shrivastava & Kennelly, 2013). In fact, social theories overall do not usually integrate the crucial role of place, as an agentic force that shapes the creation of economic systems, cultures, environments and the daily lives of the people (Escobar, 2008). Thus, we need to pay attention to place in order to understand how local wool economies emerge.

Burgess and White (2019, p. 49) write on the power of place in the making of California's Fibershed:

> From my hands-on learning journey. . .I learned about textile making that was, for the most part, not reflected in today's industrial economy. Instead I found geographic pockets of time-tested indigenous practices and approaches towards textile making that existed symbiotically with ecosystem health and function. In Northern California, for example there is a thirteen-thousands-year-old (some say longer) history of weaving with plant species such as willow, hazel, deer grass, sedge, and many others. Baskets in this region are created for all types of function – watertight vessels for food, cradle boards to carry babies, and burden baskets for harvest. . .With their intricately woven design and sturdy structure the Californian baskets embody an ecological code of conduct.

Kuokkanen (2011) has noted how these inherited and symbiotic relations between people and place are the cornerstone of Indigenous economies and an entirely different economic system that is not centred on exchange for profit and competition, but on the sustenance of individuals, families and the community. As Kuokkanen (2011, p. 219) explains:

> The key principles of indigenous economies – sustainability and reciprocity – reflect land-based worldviews founded on active recognition of kinship relations that extend beyond the human domain. Sustainability is premised on an ethos of reciprocity in which people reciprocate not only with one another but also with the land and the spirit world. Indigenous economies are thus contingent upon a stable and continuous relationship between the human and natural worlds. Individuals and communities acquire special knowledge, skills, and a complex understanding of. . .the local environment through their various subsistence activities.

Yet, much of this local knowledge is either on the brink of going extinct or can only be found, with some luck, in museums and history books covering local artisanal practices. As Burgess and White (2019) point out, these traditional ways of weaving and producing textiles through such a symbiotic relation with place exist only as small pockets in today's modern consumer societies, often mixed with capitalist markets. Kuokkanen (2011) also notes how these economic activities at present exist side by side with the market economy as 'mixed economies' characterised by a mix of subsistence, commodity production, wage labour and entrepreneurial activities. Thus, the industrialisation and globalisation of the textile industry have left most local communities across the world without the crucial infrastructures and competencies needed for a well-functioning and flourishing local economy. In fact, if the whole circle of infrastructures associated with the soil-to-soil processes of the material flows that circulate in the wool economies (Burgess & White, 2019) is to work smoothly, many parts of the puzzle will literally need to be put back in place. Hence, what is needed is a directed effort to localise all the different processes that go into the making of wool fibres, yarns, textiles and garments through the whole chain from production, to process, to consumption. This kind of re-localisation effort of production-consumption is a well-known phenomenon in the agri-food sector, which can serve as a proxy to understand the processes involved. For textiles and apparel, the Fibresheds emerging around the world (see Chapter 5) have come the furthest in this process. A thing that enabled KRUS' success, was that the mapping and description of the value-chain already had been done.

Localising Economies–Experiences from Alternative Food Networks

Within the debate on the sustainability promise of local food systems, the general perception is that by re-embedding food production in the local sphere and by reconnecting producers with consumers, it is possible to improve a host of problems associated with long supply chains and the corporate-driven conventional food system. For example, it is suggested that such local systems can increase farmer incomes, build communities, provide healthier foods to consumers, increase the sustainability of farms, and reduce carbon dioxide emissions and energy used (Forssell & Lankoski, 2015). Yet, as many critics have warned such simplifications risk conflating spatial relations with desired outcomes, rather than examining the actual consequences of localisation (Born & Purcell, 2006). Some have even pointed at the dangers of solutions that practice a type of 'defensive localism' in which the local economy is driven purely by the self-interests of local elites rather than by some socially just and sustainable ideals (Hinrichs, 2000; Winters, 2003).

Recent debates have increasingly acknowledged how pre-existing infrastructures and structural inequalities prohibits the development of systems that would include the concerns of disadvantaged and marginalised groups (DuPuis & Goodman, 2005). They also point at the challenges of assessing the ecological impact and energy use in localised systems of production, transportation and consumption, as these are 'as reliant on fossil fuels as are long distance foods' (Mariola, 2008, p. 193). Others have pointed at the dangers of equating local with simplified definitions (e.g. distance travelled, see Trivette [2015]), or representations of a particular place, (see Bowen and De Master [2011]) as it does not give room for 'a deeper holistic description of local processes, voices, and landscapes (natural, cultural and political)' (Delind, 2011, p. 280). There is also a danger of juxtaposing local and global as dichotomies when most systems are hybrid and include components and influences from both sides (Mount, 2012). For example, many producers sell to both local and conventional markets, just as most consumers purchase from both (Mount, 2012). The material conditions (e.g. machinery) for local solutions are also shaped by global markets. In essence, what these debates show is that the outcomes of localisation involve many different actors with various interests, and they are shaped by the existing (infra)structures and inequalities of the globalised and industrialised systems of trade.

What is also noteworthy is how the research on local food systems often evaluates the success and failures of these systems based the triple bottom line (TBL) of social, environmental and economic sustainability (Galt, 2013; Maxey, 2006). The TBL framework was originally developed for global corporations' sustainability reporting with the base function of communicating how their environmental and social impacts could be integrated to the bottom line, based on a win–win logic (Elkington, 1994). While it is true that most local market-based systems will have to sustain a certain degree of profits to stay in business, it is worth keeping in mind that the TBL framing does not describe deeper processes of change that seek to alter the mal-practices of the current system. In comparison to the conventional industrialised system, which seemingly has everything rigged in its favour (e.g. competitive advantages, ready-made efficient logistical solutions, cheap labour, regulations that favour large scale solutions), these alternatives may appear unsustainable when assessed based on metrics designed for the global system. Such framings do not account for the nuances of what is taking place, on the ground, or when people engage in setting up alternative systems respectful of Earth's living system. This also applies to what we described in Chapter 2 regarding the current evaluation tools being used by industry on products, such as the Higg Index and potentially the EU's PEF .

This, certainly, is also true for local wool economies. Many new local wool ventures emerge from a different logic than that of the industrial corporations for whom the sustainability framework of TBL was designed. Their very *raison d'etre* has to do with finding ways to reverse the destructive features of the global textile industry, which is a continuous process of change. Through collaborative and place-based practices grassroots initiatives seek to find alternatives that can heal and regenerate healthy ecosystems and communities (Burgess & White, 2019). Also, many small or micro-sized enterprises are managed by entrepreneurs whose primary motive is not about maximising profits, but their passion for local breeds of sheep, wool fibre traditions, craftsmanship (Vičiūnaitė, 2020), and their desire to sustain the heritage of the family's farm despite economic difficulties to make ends meet (see Chapters 1 and 5). Thus, to truly understand the localising efforts of these actors we need to find ways of describing the economy which they are engaged in building in ways that reflect their locally situated reality.

Hence, what is going on in the emerging wool economies, and the directions they are taking cannot be addressed through conventional economic and sustainability frameworks as they encapsulate not just novel, but also pre-industrial ways of producing and consuming goods. Through their doings, these wool ventures connect that what we wear next to our skin with the living landscape where sheep graze and regenerate grasslands. This means that many of the nuances of what it means to be sustainable need to be adjusted to the biophysical realities of the living landscape in place. Rather than trying to relate to abstract and inadequate concepts borrowed from the corporate-driven growth-based global economy, we suggest redirecting our attention towards how the living landscape plays an important role in how these alternatives are made.

Living Economies in Living Landscapes

Local wool economies are neither static nor homogeneous, rather they embody a living economy situated in a living landscape composed of myriad interactions of human and non-human beings. The story of wool begins long before the fibre is traded and put in the hands of craftspeople to make garments or other objects for sale. In fact, it stems from the domestication of sheep as they learned to live alongside their shepherds, spreading together across the microclimates of the ancient world, adjusting together to different temperatures, precipitation patterns and terrain (Burgess & White, 2019). Heritage breeds of sheep, for example, are the result of the sheep's interactions with humans and the land. These different breeds of sheep produce different varieties of wool that offer different use-values according to the properties that they possess (Burgess & White, 2019). In Chapter 1 we have described some of the challenges with pigmented or indigenous breeds that do not fit the large-scale, industrialised needs of uniformity, but in small-scale production result in gourmet yarns that have found an enthusiastic following among knitters. The forte of the yarns is that they are 'different' (Klepp & Tobiasson, 2017).

The quality of the wool itself is influenced by how the sheep are cared for and where and how they have grazed and how they have lived over millennia in what kinds of climate and with which systems of mutual influence between the human culture and animal genetics in their locale. Thus, how humans care for sheep will impact both the living landscape they graze and the fibres in textile products. Examples of this can be found in the intricate relationship between the Norwegian Old Spæl sheep breed and the protection and management of the Heathland areas along the coast of Norway.[1] This vulnerable, resilient and interdependent system between humans, animals and place is practised by most Indigenous peoples, though for a long time in many places, this has been illegal or impossible. The return of this practice in Australia and California (by Fibershed), and other places, offers hope.

Seeing the emerging wool economy as the result of the living landscape in which it resides allows for adopting an economic view that takes into account these complex and dynamic relations between humans and other living beings. Thus, under the conceptualisation of a living economy, the resources of the Earth do not exist solely to serve the purpose (and whims) of humanity at any cost. Instead, a living economy is organised

[1] https://muho.no/lyngheisenteret/en/about-us.

in ways that integrate the biophysical aspects and the laws of thermodynamics through the living relations that sustain the whole production process. This is a complete shift from the logic of the growth economy, which as discussed above does not account for these dynamics, rather it treats nature as a reserve of raw materials, or natural resources, that can be extracted for value and returned as waste.

This living aspect of the economy is clearly visible at many sheep farms across the world where wool producing growers follow principles of holistic planned or Adaptive-Multi-Paddock (AMP) grazing (Teague & Barnes, 2017). Also, traditional ways of keeping sheep are respectful of the living landscape in the way that the animals are moved around to graze in different places according to seasons, often called transhumance. Many old and well-developed grazing systems in mountain areas, for example in Norway and Poland, are organised in a way that animals are taken to the mountains where they can graze on new grass during the summer before the same route is followed back as the high mountains become inhospitable in the fall. These systems depend on commonlands, without fences and where the seasons dictate where the animals graze. Similar practices still exist in the archipelago areas of Finland and Norway, where sheep are taken out to islands to graze during the summer.

Research suggests that such grazing principles, where the farmers or rangers follow nature's own principles can quickly restore the health of ecosystem functions, by enhancing soil health, improving water cycles above and below the ground, while also creating more biodiverse landscapes that sequester a large amount of carbon in the soil (Fenster et al., 2021; Gosnell et al., 2020; Teague & Kreuter, 2020). These regenerative practices point towards a growing trend of acknowledging how particular human-non-human relations and the biophysical dynamics of the Earth itself have implications for the material output of the economy (Krzywoszynska & Marchesi, 2020). How people organise together with the living landscape plays a role in reducing the need for external inputs of raw materials and energy. How and what is 'cared for' (Puig de la Bellacasa, 2017) in specific ecologies and human-non-human entanglements (e.g. human-sheep relations) will have material (and potentially regenerative) effects on the living landscape.

Yet, equating the local wool economy with regenerative practices risks leading into the trap of assuming that just because something is local, it possesses certain desired qualities (Born & Purcell, 2006). As Burgess and White write, the standard management scheme on most of the world's ranches and farms is still continuous grazing, where 'livestock are allowed to disperse uncontrolled across the same pastures day in and day out year after year, eating their favourite plants down to the ground ignoring less well-liked ones, which cause severe damage to the land' (p. 88). Such short-sighted land management practices leave behind 'the degradation of soils, long term declines in plant productivity, decreased biological diversity, a negative impact on farmer income and an overall reduction in the resilience of the system' (Burgess & White, 2019, p. 89). Thus, there is also a danger that instead of bringing about deeper transformative changes to the economic realm, localisation initiatives that are not premised in regenerative practices could transform 'nature' into labour that serves to sustain the growth economy without questioning the exploitative relations it upholds (Krzywoszynska, 2020). Such accounts of local wool risk painting an idealised perspective of a living economy, and do not actually describe the deeper transformative processes involved in the creation of a healthy regenerative system that nurtures diversity and complexity (Wahl, 2016).

An essential question is how to match what is locally consumed with the potentialities and limits of the living landscape in a way that does not push for more growth. One major difference between the local food economy and textile fibres is that the community's need for food may be easier to pair with the seasonality of available products. However, this view is ignoring the fact that natural fibre production is very much tied to seasons: The wool is mainly sheared in the autumn when flax was also harvested. In pre-industrial Norway, the weaving loom was set up after Christmas, and the finished textiles bleached and laundered in the spring. The major difference is that the time span for making the textiles from natural raw materials are much longer and could last more than a year. Food is also perishable and often does not have a long and complicated use phase (Fletcher & Vittersø, 2018).

Local food traditions and household cooking are still, at least to some degree, embedded in the ecology of place. This also creates an understanding or guidance about what kind of food products can be consumed within the biophysical limits of the community. In addition, the energy from solar fuelled 'overproduction' at the farm can easily be returned to the soil as compost. Such, farm level overproduction does not increase the use of fossil energy and does not worsen the biophysical load of the economic activity. This means that alternative food researchers have not always been outspoken about the need to also 'degrow' the economy and its associated activities, as what is produced is converted into food for people or the microbes in the soil, and as such is not 'wasted' energy. Thus, instead of debating how to reduce the overall level of consumption, the food debate has been more concerned about the issues of accessibility and justice when trying to get people to eat 'real' or 'good' food instead of industrially processed 'junk' (for a critical view see Guthman [2008]). And while food waste has been increasingly targeted, the wasting of textiles has received little policy attention.

The above-described differences in the situation for fibre production are fuelled by designer houses and the fashion industry's luring temptations of short-sighted whims. The whole textile industry is built on a system wherein people seem to have lost touch with how their clothing relates to the living landscape, the enormous distances their garments have travelled, and all the hands that have dedicated their time to fashion them. Thus, if we are to transition away from the whims of fast fashion and re-embed all aspects of the production in the place-based biophysical economy, the central question is how to shift production so that it prolongs the lifetime of each garment and meets the real needs of the community. Without a clear vision of what and how much should be produced, the risk is that localisation worsens the effects on the biophysical economy. This will be further explored in Chapter 7. In fact, under localisation, energy use might actually increase per single unit produced, due to the need to break with the optimisation of production and economies of scale. Furthermore, local wool entrepreneurs have been tied to specialised and luxury products for global markets (Amarilla et al., 2020). While such production of wool luxury products may sustain traditional practices, it does create problems associated with social justice and accessibility and does not necessarily replace fast fashion items in a typical wardrobe. So how then are we to understand the sustainable change in these place-based living economies?

Creating Sustainable Change Through Collaborative Efforts

In the sustainable transitions literature, new green solutions are assumed to emerge as a result of (state-subsidised) new technological innovations (Schot & Geels, 2008), the market-forces, or by consumers demanding greener products (Stolle & Michelletti, 2013). However, such assumptions should be handled with caution. There is the problematic issue of technological fixes that require more material extraction from Earth and greater use of energy. Furthermore, to date, technological innovations that would contribute to the re-localisation of the textile industry and wool production have not been supported by state subsidies, rather the contrary as wool from local sheep farms within the EU are categorised as by-products and end up as waste, and thus may become ineligible for agricultural subsidies.

Furthermore, due to the undervalued status of local wool, it is common that many wool ventures are not (at least initially) motivated by hopes of an increase in demand and profits. Although it is clear that consumers are becoming increasingly aware of and concerned about the socioecological footprint of their clothing habits (Pookulangara & Shephard, 2013), such awareness is not necessarily translated into action (Carrington et al., 2010). Thus, to state that change in consumption habits act as the driving force of the (re)localisation processes is probably quite far from the truth in most places. Just as with the pockets of local wool knowledge that remain stored in the deposits of local memories in specific communities, so too can local wardrobes be found in small circles of very engaged citizens (see Burgess & White, 2019) or in the few Indigenous communities whose self-sustained land-to-clothing practices remain intact despite the forces of globalisation.

Perhaps the clearest picture of what is going on is in the geographic pockets where local wool economies are already emerging. Traditionally, the organisations that are suggested to shape the economy are those with clear boundaries between the inside and the outside, and these boundaries are established through certificates that give them the legal status of being, for example, an entrepreneur, small business or a corporation (Czarniawska, 2018). The driving force of change and innovation in these types of economic organisations is profit and competition as firms seek to appropriate the benefits of innovation to move ahead of competitors to capture market rents (Schumpeter, 1961).

Yet, the emerging wool economy is nothing of the sort. The wool entrepreneurs typically start their business with other base motivations. Such motivations may include making use of wool that otherwise would be wasted, reducing reliance on large-scale global supply chains with dubious certification schemes, recovering lost traditions of craftsmanship, and rescuing heritage breeds from becoming extinct (this is described in more depth in Chapters 1 and 5). No matter the primary motivations of the individual entrepreneurs, the economic logics that underlie the market-based system still create difficult trade-offs that entrepreneurs make to stay in business within the dominant system. To overcome these trade-offs, many of the activities within this sector are based on self-organised collaboration among a disparate set of both formal and informal organisations (e.g. entrepreneurs, activists, knitters, and persons who have this as a side job or a hobby).

The products are also likely to be more expensive to cover higher costs (as these producers are not participating in the globalised system of trade built on cheap labour), which can make it difficult to provide goods at a 'fair' price that is accessible to the consumers. Thus, for these processes to be both just and sustainable, they will also need to include some form of planned strategic direction that breaks with the injustices of the current system of trade, while creating a wardrobe that is aligned with the living landscape in place, its natural seasonal processes, weather-patterns and the socioecological and climate impacts. A 'reflexive' (re)localising process (Dupuis & Goodman, 2005) should start from the fundamental question of how the local wool economy can contribute to a good life for all members of the community. Thereby, the question that emerges is how the relationship between the price and lifespan of the product, as well as the additional socioecological benefits that are produced, can be communicated to the consumer. Another central question to be asked in these discussions is how to design products with local materials that are durable and adjusted to the climate, while also attractive to wear. These are questions that we will return to in Chapter 7.

The key to overcoming the barriers to a just transition might go through the development of 'co-creative spaces' and other systems that are built around already produced apparel. An example of an apparel system that is produced and maintained in cooperation between producers and consumers is discussed in Chapter 5. We see an increased interest in repair among artists, activists and consumers (Klepp & Tobiasson, 2021). Even the industry itself has discovered that their customers are something more than just sources of potential profit. These changes in practice include new meeting-places (e.g. community Fab Labs for clothing) and internet spaces in which shared learning takes place, but also new business models with an emphasis on repair and maintenance (Klepp & Tobiasson, 2021). There is a lot of enthusiasm and new ideas about these topics. Yet, these practices are not considered 'economic' because they do not contribute to the GDP and have not garnered support from policymakers (e.g. handicrafts produced for households, or the praxis of repair in households with or without help from the producers) (Klepp & Haugrønning, 2021). Despite their current non-economic status, these practices have very tangible impacts on locally produced wardrobes.

In Chapter 5, we have described many such local initiatives, such as the ongoing activities in Tingvoll, a communal endeavour based on a *dugnad*[2] among local enthusiasts with a common wish to showcase locally anchored clothes and better use of wool from local Norwegian Old Spæl sheep. The aim is that the production will garner a surplus for the local sheep farmers and local producers, but there is also value in the communal cooperation for developing beautiful products. The very close cooperation between the farmers, mill and knitters is the very basis for the local anchoring such an initiative can garner.

Finally, a note on the role of online communities that act in support of these place-based collaborative efforts. Escobar (2004, p. 4) points

[2] Norwegian expression describing community work.

out how anti-globalisation movements are 'strengthened by the self-organising dynamics of the new information and communication technologies (ICTs)'. This is also relevant for the emerging local wool economies, as their activities are not just rooted in place, there is also a lot of shared learning that occurs through global communities on social media (e.g. Fibershed, online-community groups, the Ravelry discussion forum), paradoxically underpinned by the corporate, digital economy. Some even suggest that the Internet fuels many of the activities associated with local wool economies (Hudson, 2010). The shared knowledge in these online communities helps local actors become inspired and find solutions to the problems that arise as they seek to put everyday wardrobes back in place.

Conclusions

In conclusion, three main points emerge from this reflection on the urgent need for deep transformations of the globalised textile industry, which is dominated by fast fashion and growth logic, and the emergence of a local wool economy.

First, the local wool economy does not by itself challenge the global fast fashion and textile industrial complex built on economic growth. To truly dismantle the structural problems of the growth economy, there needs to be much more structural support from society at large. This includes the development and adoption of governmental policies, which are aimed at a true attempt at de-growing the economy by supporting small-scale local solutions wherein materials circulate from soil to soil mostly via solar energy. A widespread social movement is also needed to push for change in consumers' fast fashion addiction (e.g. similar to the flight-shaming campaign in Sweden that has had a notable influence on travel behaviour in the population).

Second, the inherited injustices between the global North and South will not 'go away' just because the global North relocates its production/consumption and its environmental impact back home, sometimes called 'on-shoring' or 're-shoring'. The question remains of how to support the workers attached to the global industry for wool so that they can also sustain their lives in place-based economies. Social injustice and the divide between rich and poor will only grow greater if their income is stripped away. It is clear that also in these communities, there is a need to take back the economy to build local economies around locally sourced solar-fuelled materials. Tackling these injustices requires a much broader approach to social change than just changing consumption/production behaviours and policies. There is a need for an environmentalism that builds alliances between the global North and South and truly challenges the colonial legacies and land-grabbing that the global economy relies on. Presently, this is not given much attention in the debates on the need to re-localise wool production, but there is a need to build such networks or connect to already existing ones (e.g. the global Food Justice Movement organised through La Vía Campesina).

The third conclusion comes back to the promise of the agency that resides in place and self-organised collaboration. New economies that break with the current logics of the growth economy do not emerge 'from below' by chance. They require hard work, strategic planning and visions, collaborative efforts at multiple levels and scales. Therefore, for these types of collaborative efforts to move towards a common goal in the long term, they also need the support of meta-organisations such as Fibershed. Also, other enterprises that manage to engage and create networks can play such a role, for example, Selbu Spinning Mill's engagement with the local community described in Chapter 1 (Lennon, 2017) and Tingvoll Wool, which is mentioned above. These networks connect disparate actors and create an overarching narrative of an alternative logic that enables the actors to work beyond the market logic. It is through such alternative forms of organising that barriers to change can be overcome by replacing self-interest and competitive mindsets with shared learning and collaboration.

Although it is clear that these new ventures need to be assessed based on their biophysical and social impact, we also must be mindful that trying to break with old systems does not happen overnight, but is work that is 'under construction', delinking from the old economy happens gradually. Thus, we as researchers and educators that write books about these emerging initiatives have a responsibility in how we assess what is going on in the emergent alternatives and what sustainability means in economic ventures that follow a different logic than that of maximisation of profits prevalent in global markets. Focussing on all the non-monetary benefits and values that these ventures produce can lend visibility and (political and economic) support to the people who against all odds are doing the hard work of reconfiguring the textile systems from within the place and living landscapes they are part of. We need to care more for the land and each other, which is also manifested as caring for the socio-environmental impacts of our clothes.

References

Amarilla, R., Gardetti, M. A., & Gabriel, M. (2020). Sustainable luxury, craftsmanship and vicuna poncho. In M. A. Gardetti & I. Coste-Manière (Eds.), *Sustainable luxury and craftsmanship* (pp. 25–43). Springer.

Arrigo, E. (2013). Corporate responsibility management in fast fashion companies: The Gap Inc. case. *Journal of Fashion Marketing and Management, 17*(2), 175–189.

Born, B., & Purcell, M. (2006). Avoiding the local trap: Scale and food systems in planning research. *Journal of Planning Education and Research, 26*(2), 195–207.

Bowen, S., & De Master, K. (2011). New rural livelihoods or museums of production? Quality food initiatives in practice. *Journal of Rural Studies, 27*(1), 73–82.

Brand, U., & Wissen, M. (2021). *The imperial mode of living. Everyday life and the ecological crisis of capitalism.* Verso.

Brundtland, G. H., Khalid, M., Agnelli, S., Al-Athel, S., & Chidzero, B. J. N. Y. (1987). *Our common future*. Oxford University Press.

Burgess, R., & White, C. (2019). *Fibershed: Growing a movement of farmers, fashion activists, and makers for a new textile economy.* Chelsea Green Publishing.

Carrington, M., Neville, B., & Whitwell, G. (2010). Why ethical consumers don't walk their talk: Towards a framework for understanding the gap between the ethical purchase intentions and actual buying behaviour of ethically minded consumers. *Journal of Business Ethics, 97*(1), 139–158. https://doi.org/10.1007/s10551-010-0501-6

Ceballos, G., Ehrlich, P.E., & Dirzo, R. (2017, July 10). Biological annihilation via the ongoing sixth mass extinction signaled by vertebrate population losses and declines. *PNAS*. www.pnas.org/cgi/doi/10.1073/pnas.1704949114

Chowdhury, R. (2017). The Rana Plaza disaster and the complicit behavior of elite NGOs. *Organization, 24*(6), 938–949.

Czarniawska, B. (2018). On meshworks and other complications of portraying contemporary organizing. In L. Gårseth-Nesbakk & F. Mellemvik (Eds.), *Dealing with expectations and traditions in research* (pp. 109–127). Cappelen Damm Akademisk. https://doi.org/10.23865/noasp.42.ch7

DeLind, L. (2011). Are local food and the local food movement taking us where we want to go? Or are we hitching our wagons to the wrong stars? *Agriculture and Human Values, 28*, 273–283.

Dunlap, A., & Correa Arce, M. (2021). 'Murderous energy' in Oaxaca, Mexico: Wind factories, territorial struggle and social warfare. *The Journal of Peasant Studies*. https://doi.org/10.1080/03066150.2020.1862090

DuPuis, E. M., & Goodman, D. (2005). Should we go "home" to eat? Toward a reflexive politics of localism. *Journal of Rural Studies, 21*(3), 359–371. https://doi.org/10.1007/s10460-010-9263-0

Easterlin, R. A. (1995). Will raising the income for all increase the happiness for all? *Journal of Economic Behavior & Organization, 27*(1), 35–47.

Ehrnström-Fuentes, M. (2019). Confronting extractivism–the role of local struggles in the (un)making of place. *Critical Perspectives on International Business*.

Ehrnström-Fuentes, M., & Leipämaa-Leskinen, H. (2019). Boundary negotiations in a self-organized grassroots-led food network: The case of REKO in Finland. *Sustainability, 11*(15), 4137. https://doi.org/10.3390/su11154137

Elkington, J. (1994). Towards the sustainable corporation: Win-win-win strategies for sustainable development. *California Management Review, 36*(2), 90–100.

Ellen MacArthur Foundation. (2017). *A new textiles economy: Redisgning fashion's future*.

Ergene, S., Subhabrata B. B., & Hoffman, A.J. (2020). (Un)sustainability and organization studies: Towards a radical engagement. *Organization Studies*, https://doi.org/10.1177/0170840620937892

Escobar, A. (2004). Beyond the Third World: Imperial globality, global coloniality and anti-globalisation social movements. *Third World Quarterly, 25*(1), 207–230. https://www.jstor.org/stable/3993785

Escobar, A. (2008). *Territories of difference: Place, movements, life, redes*. Duke University Press. https://doi.org/10.1215/9780822389439

Fenster, T. L., LaCanne, C. E., Pecenka, J. R., Schmid, R. B., Bredeson, M. M., Busenitz, K. M., Michels, A. M., Welch, K. D. & Lundgren, J. G. (2021). Defining and validating regenerative farm systems using a composite of ranked agricultural practices. *F1000Research, 10*, 115. https://doi.org/10.12688/f1000research.28450.1

Fletcher, K., & Vittersø, G. (2018). Local food initiatives and fashion change: Comparing food and clothes to better understand fashion localism. *Fashion Practice, 10*(2), 60–170. https://doi.org/10.1080/17569370.2018.1458496

Forssell, S., & Lankoski, L. (2015). The sustainability promise of alternative food networks: An examination through "alternative" characteristics. *Agriculture and Human Values, 32*(1), 63–75. https://doi.org/10.1007/s10460-014-9516-4

Galt, R. (2013). The moral economy is a double-edged sword: Explaining farmers' earnings and self-exploitation in community-supported agriculture. *Economic Geography, 89*(4), 341–365. https://doi.org/10.1111/ecge.12015

Georgescu-Roegen, N. (1971). *The entropy law and the economic process*. Harvard University Press.

Giampietro, M. (2019). On the circular bioeconomy and decoupling: Implications for sustainable growth. *Ecological Economics, 162*, 143–156. https://doi.org/10.1016/j.ecolecon.2019.05.001

Gibson-Graham, J. K., Cameron, J., & Healy, S. (2013). *Take back the economy: An ethical guide to transforming our communities*. University of Minnesota Press.

Gosnell, H., Charnley, S., & Stanley, P. (2020). Climate change mitigation as a co-benefit of regenerative ranching: Insights from Australia and the United States. *Interface Focus, 10*(5), 20200027. https://doi.org/10.1098/rsfs.2020.0027

Guthman, J. (2008). "If they only knew": Color blindness and universalism in California alternative food institutions. *The Professional Geographer, 60*(3), 387–397. https://doi.org/10.1080/00330120802013679

Haberl, H., Wiedenhofer, D., Virág, D., Kalt, G., Plank, B., Brockway, P., Fishman, T., et al. (2020). A systematic review of the evidence on decoupling of GDP, resource use and GHG emissions, Part II: Synthesizing the insights. *Environmental Research Letters, 15*(6), 1–42.

Hinrichs, C. C. (2000). Embeddedness and local food systems: Notes on two types of direct agricultural market. *Journal of Rural Studies, 16*(3), 295–303. https://doi.org/10.1016/S0743-0167(99)00063-7

Hudson, T. P. (2010). *Spin artists, and how the internet fuels the art yarn movement*. Paper presented at Textiles and Settlement: From Plains Space to Cyber Space, Textile Society of America 12th Biennial Symposium, October 6–9, 2010, Lincoln, NE.

Klepp, I. G., & Haugrønning, V. (2021). *Naturgarvet skinn i et miljøperspektiv*.

Klepp, I. G., & Laitala, K. (2015). His mother's dress—Growth in the number of clothes. In P. Strandbakken & J. Gronow (Eds.), *The consumer in society* (pp. 311–334). Abstrakt forlag.

Klepp, I. G., & Laitala, K. (2018). Nisseluelandet—The impact of local clothes for the survival of a textile industry in Norway. *Fashion Practice, 10*(2), 171–195. https://doi.org/10.1080/17569370.2018.1458497

Klepp, I. G., & Tobiasson, T. (2021). *Lettfiks. Klær med ni liv: Bokvennen Forlag.*

Klepp, I. G., & Tobiasson, T. S. (2017). *Strikk med norsk ull [Knit with Norwegian wool]*. Vormedal.

Korica, M., & Bazin, Y. (2019). Fashion and organization studies: Exploring conceptual paradoxes and empirical opportunities. *Organization Studies, 40*(10), 1481–1497. https://doi.org/10.1177/0170840619831059

Krausmann, F., Weisz, H., & Eisenmenger, N. (2016). Transitions in sociometabolic regimes throughout human history. In H. Haberl, M. Fischer-Kowalski, F. Krausmann, & V. Winiwarter (Eds.), *Social ecology human-environment interactions* (Vol. 5, pp. 63–92). Springer, Cham.

Kröger, M. (2016a). Spatial causalities in resource rushes: Notes from the Finnish mining boom. *Journal of Agrarian Change, 16*(4), 543–570. https://doi.org/10.1111/joac.12113

Kröger, M. (2016b). The political economy of 'flex trees': A preliminary analysis. *The Journal of Peasant Studies, 43*(4), 886–909. https://doi.org/10.1080/03066150.2016.1140646

Kröger, M. (2021). *Extractivisms, existences and extinctions: Monoculture plantations and Amazon deforestation*. Routledge.

Krzywoszynska, A. (2020). Nonhuman labor and the making of resources: Making soils a resource through microbial labor. *Environmental Humanities, 12*(1), 227–249. https://doi.org/10.1215/22011919-8142319

Krzywoszynska, A., & Marchesi, G. (2020). Toward a relational materiality of soils: Introduction. *Environmental Humanities, 12*(1), 190–204. https://doi.org/10.1215/22011919-8142297

Kuokkanen, R. (2011). Indigenous economies, theories of subsistence and women: Exploring the social economy model for indigenous governance.

American Indian Quarterly, 35(2), 215–240. https://doi.org/10.5250/amerindiquar.35.2.0215

Lennon, A. (2017). *Natural regional resilience: Determining the sustainable value of a local wool industry through actor-network theory* (Master's Thesis). Norwegian University of Science and Technology (NTNU). http://hdl.handle.net/11250/2469509

Liboiron, M. (2021). *Pollution is colonialism.* Duke University Press.

Mariola, M. (2008). The local industrial complex? Questioning the link between local foods and energy use. *Agriculture and Human Values, 25*(2), 193–196. https://doi.org/10.1007/s10460-008-9115-3

Maxey, L. (2006). Can we sustain sustainable agriculture? Learning from small-scale producer-suppliers in Canada and UK. *The Geographical Journal, 172*(3), 230–244. https://www.jstor.org/stable/3873966

Misoczky, M. C., Dormelas, G. C., & Böhm, S. (2017). Organizational practices of social movements and popular struggles: Understanding the power of organizing from below. *Qualitative Research in Organization and Management an International Journal, 12*(4), 250–261. https://doi.org/10.1108/QROM-09-2017-1567

Mount, P. (2012). Growing local food: Scale and local food systems governance. *Agriculture and Human Values, 29*, 107–121. https://doi.org/10.1007/s10460-011-9331-0

Normann, S. (2020). Green colonialism in the Nordic context: Exploring Southern Saami representations of wind energy development. *Journal of Community Psychology, 49*, 77–94.

Polanyi, K. (2001 [1944]). *The great transformation.* Beacon Press.

Pookulangara, S., & Shephard, A. (2013). Slow fashion movement: Understanding consumer perceptions—An exploratory study. *Journal of Retailing and Consumer Services, 20*(2), 200–206. https://doi.org/10.1016/j.jretconser.2012.12.002

Prazeres, A. R., Carvalho, F., & Rivas, J. (2012). Cheese whey management: A review. *Journal of Environmental Management, 110*, 48–68. https://doi.org/10.1016/j.jenvman.2012.05.018

Puig de la Bellacasa, M. (2017). *Matters of care: Speculative ethics in more than human worlds.* University of Minnesota Press.

Reinecke, J., & Donaghey, J. (2021). Political CSR at the coalface—The roles and contradictions of multinational corporations in developing workplace dialogue. *Journal of Management Studies, 58*(2), 457–486. https://doi.org/10.1111/joms.12585

Sahlins, M. (2017 [1972]). *Stone age economics.* Routledge.

Salleh, A. (Ed.). (2009). *Eco-sufficiency & global justice. Women write political ecology*. Pluto.

Scheffer, M. (2021) Interview with Michiel Scheffer/Interviewer: Fibre2Fashion.

Scherer, A., & Palazzo, G. (2011). The new political role of business in a globalized world: A review of a new perspective on CSR and its implications for the firm, governance, and democracy. *Journal of Management Studies, 48*, 899–931. https://doi.org/10.1111/j.1467-6486.2010.00950.x

Schot, J., & Geels, F. (2008). Strategic niche management and sustainable innovation journeys: Theory, findings, research agenda and policy. *Technology Analysis and Strategic Management, 20*(5), 537–554. https://doi.org/10.1080/09537320802292651

Schumpeter, J. A. (1961). *The theory of economic development* (3rd ed.). Oxford University Press.

Seyfang, G., & Smith, A. (2007). Grassroots innovations for sustainable development: Towards a new research and policy agenda. *Environmental Politics, 16*(4), 584–603. https://doi.org/10.1080/09644010701419121

Shrivastava, P., & Kennelly, J. J. (2013). Sustainability and place-based enterprise. *Organization & Environment, 26*(1), 83–101. https://doi.org/10.1177/1086026612475068

Simmons, I. G. (1989). *Changing the face of the Earth. Culture, environment, history*. Blackwell.

Smith, T. (2020, January 12). *Klimakrise og systemendring* [Climate crisis and system change], Forfatternes klimaaksjon. https://forfatterneskIimaaksjon.no/2020/01/12/klimakrise-og-systemendring-tone-smith/

Smith, T. (2021). Wie radikal ist der Green New Deal [How radical is the Green New Deal?] *Prokla, 202*(1), 9–30. https://doi.org/10.32387/prokla.v51i202.1928

Spash, C. (2017). Social ecological economics. In Spash, C. L. (Ed.), *Routledge handbook of ecological economics. Nature and society* (pp. 3–16). Routledge.

Spash, C. (2021). Apologists for growth: Passive revolutionaries in a passive revolution. *Globalizations*. https://doi.org/10.1080/14747731.2020.1824864

Srivastava, R., & Singh, N. (2019). Importance of natural dye over synthetic dye: A critical. *International Journal of Home Science, 5*(2), 148–150.

Stolle, D., & Michelletti, M. (2013). *Political consumerism: Global responsibility in action*. Cambridge University Press.

Teague, R., & Barnes, M. (2017). Grazing management that regenerates ecosystem function and grazingland livelihoods. *African Journal of Range &*

Forage Science, 34(2), 77–86. https://doi.org/10.2989/10220119.2017.1334706

Teague, R., & Kreuter, U. (2020). Managing grazing to restore soil health, ecosystem function, and ecosystem services. *Frontiers in Sustainable Food Systems, 4*, 157. https://doi.org/10.3389/fsufs.2020.534187

Temper, L., Demaria, F., Scheidel, A., Del Bene, D., & Martinez-Alier, J. (2018). The global environmental justice Atlas (EJAtlas): Ecological distribution conflicts as forces for sustainability. *Sustainability Science, 13*, 573–584. https://doi.org/10.1007/s11625-018-0563-4

Trivette, S. A. (2015). How local is local? Determining the boundaries of local food in practice. *Agriculture and Human Values, 32*(3), 475–490.

Valenzuela, F., & Böhm, S. (2017). Against wasted politics: A critique of the circular economy. *Ephemera: Theory and Politics in Organization, 17*(1): 23–60.

Vanclay, F. (2008). Place matters. In F. Vanclay, M. Higgins, & A. Blackshaw (Eds.), *Making sense of place: Exploring the concepts and expressions of place through different senses and lenses* (pp. 3–11). National Museum of Australia Press.

Vičiūnaitė, V. (2020). *Moving towards sustainability: Business models and entrepreneurship in the Norwegian wool industry* (PhD diss.). Norwegian University of Life Sciences.

Wahl, D. C. (2016). *Designing regenerative cultures.* Triarchy Press.

Watson, D., Palm, D., Syversen, F., Skogesal, O., & Pedersen, J. (2016). *Fate and impact of used textiles exports.* Phase One Report. Retrieved from Copenhagen. http://norden.diva-portal.org/smash/get/diva2:919621/FULLTEXT01.pdf

Watson, D., Trzepacz, S., Rubach, S., & Johnsen, F. M. (2020). *Kartlegging av brukte tekstiler og tekstilavfall i Norge* (OR.11.20). https://www.ostfoldforskning.no/media/2260/or1120-kartlegging-av-brukte-tekstiler-og-tekstilavfall-i-norge.pdf

Wiedemann, S. G., Biggs, L., Nebel, B., Bauch, K., Laitala, K., Klepp, I. G., Swan, P. G., & Watson, K. (2020). Environmental impacts associated with the production, use, and end-of-life of a woollen garment. *The International Journal of Life Cycle Assessment, 25*, 1486–1499. https://doi.org/10.1007/s11367-020-01766-0

Wiedemann, S. G., Biggs, L., Nguyen, Q. V., Clarke, S. J., Laitala, K., & Klepp, I. G. (2021). Reducing environmental impacts from garments through best practice garment use and care, using the example of a Merino wool sweater. *International Journal of Life Cycle Assessment*. https://doi.org/10.1007/s11367-021-01909-x

Winters, M. (2003). Embeddedness, the new food economy and defensive localism. *Journal of Rural Studies, 19*(1), 23–32. https://doi.org/10.1016/S0743-0167(02)00053-0

7

A Fashion Future: Fibre Diet

Ingun Grimstad Klepp, Vilde Haugrønning, Kirsi Laitala, Anna Schytte Sigaard, and Tone Skårdal Tobiasson

Throughout the book, we have argued for using all the wool that has already been produced. This is not the same as us wanting to use wool for everything, or increase wool production at the expense of other natural fibres. On the other hand, we want a debate on the amounts of textile fibre that are produced and how these are used. In this last chapter, the quantity will again be the topic, and wool will thus play a more modest role.

I. G. Klepp · V. Haugrønning (✉) · K. Laitala · A. S. Sigaard
Consumption Research Norway (SIFO), Oslo Metropolitan University, Oslo, Norway
e-mail: vildeh@oslomet.no

I. G. Klepp
e-mail: ingunk@oslomet.no

T. S. Tobiasson
Nordic Initiative Clean & Ethical Fashion, Oslo, Norway

I. G. Klepp and T. S. Tobiasson (eds.), *Local, Slow and Sustainable Fashion*,
https://doi.org/10.1007/978-3-030-88300-3_7

In the past 20 years, the consumption of clothing in Norway has increased by 37% (SSB, 2019), and 20% of clothing in Norwegian wardrobes is never or rarely worn (Klepp & Laitala, 2016). The same development is found in other affluent countries, and consumption of clothing is expected to increase even more in the coming years, especially in populous countries such as China. The increase is probably even greater, but less documented, if we look at the quantity of clothing produced, and the many clothes that end up as deadstock (Turnbull, 2019). Fibre, yarn, fabric and clothing become waste through the long, complicated and global value chains. Even clothes that have been sold can become waste before they are used, either as returned goods (Cullinane & Cullinane, 2021; Culliane et al., 2019), or lost in other ways.

As pointed out in Chapter 6, increased amounts of used clothing are collected, by NGOs, by fashion companies and others for reuse and recycling, and 97% of the collected textiles on the Norwegian market are exported. However, as the quantity has increased, the quality has decreased (Watson, Trzepacz, et al., 2020). This threatens the very business model in this industry where the sale of goods provides a profit for sorting, transport and proper handling of what is not saleable. Though recycling of post-consumer textile waste is marginal (less than 1% globally), and the global market for second-hand clothes is declining, the EU has decided that clothes should no longer be disposed of as residual waste. By 2025, textiles must be collected separately in all member states and more clothes must be reused and recycled.[1] Mandatory separate collection of textiles is mentioned for the first time by the EU in the 2018 proposal for a new waste directive (EC, 2018).

Is Second-Hand Actually Replacing New Purchases?

Reuse and recycling are key principles in what is referred to as the circular economy. As a political strategy, the goal is a circular model

[1] For more information, see the webpage of the European Parliament.

of production, consumption and disposal, where waste can be utilised as new resources. However, in practice, the circular economy is still an ambiguous concept that is often reduced to a matter of recycling (Kirchherr et al., 2017). And as we saw in Chapter 6, even if the systems can be improved, they will not be able to reach the goal of a closed-loop where no energy goes in and no waste goes out. It is also a question of whether reuse and recycling can make the clothing industry greener, or if this is just a way to camouflage waste exports.[2] The Covid-19 pandemic has caused several of the larger markets for used clothing to close down either due to collapsed consumer demands or fear of contamination in textiles (Glover, 2020a). It will be interesting to see what will happen to the surplus of clothes that the countries of origin now must deal with themselves.

The volume of used textiles sold for reuse compared to how much ended up as waste in pre-Covid-19 times has been studied (see for example Watson et al., 2016). However, to our knowledge, the lifespan for used clothes compared to new and thereby the totality of waste production is still relatively unexplored. We also do not know how reliable the knowledge we have actually is, as it is often presented by actors with a vested interest in the subject. Reuse of clothes as a principle can be discussed from a consumer perspective. If the acquisition of used clothes through purchase or inheritance is meant to reduce the environmental impact of clothing consumption, the purchase or inheriting of used clothes must replace the purchase of new ones. In Life Cycle Analysis (LCA) studies, this issue is handled as a replacement rate. Studies have found replacement rates for second-hand textiles in Europe to be divergent, with estimations between 28 and 75% (Castellani et al., 2015; Farrant, 2008). In Norway, results from a consumer survey showed that those respondents who buy a lot of used clothing, also tend to buy many new clothes (Laitala & Klepp, 2020a). We see the same if we compare countries. Denmark, for example, where the commercial second-hand market is bigger than in Norway, has the same market for new clothes (Watson, Hvass, et al., 2020).

[2] https://www.abc.net.au/news/2021-08-12/fast-fashion-turning-parts-ghana-into-toxic-landfill/100358702.

This picture looks different when viewed from the global South, however. In some countries, the market is dominated by second-hand trade while some markets have attempted different types of bans. In 2018, Rwanda, for example, banned imports of second-hand clothes as a means to revive the local textile industry (John, 2018). On a global scale, the trade in second-hand clothing represents a relatively small proportion of the clothing market. However, in sub-Saharan African countries, for example, it represents a dominant feature with more than 50% of the market. Second-hand clothes may replace the purchase of new, but the difference in ratio between these types of trade is largely affected by prices. Nørup (2019) found replacement rates in three African countries equal to or lower than those in Europe. The rate was especially low among respondents with lower economic purchasing power simply because they could not afford to buy new textiles. Thus, the purchase did not represent an actual replacement.

Another way to look at this issue is through the lens of interdependency. By this understanding, a dependency exists both within the human system and between humans and other systems as human lives are inseparably reliant on as well as intrinsically part of planet Earth and its resources (Fletcher & Tham, 2019). The distribution of these resources and the consequences of this are, however, brutally unevenly allocated. Selling second-hand clothing does not solve the problem of either the inequitable access to resources or the current global overproduction. However, if the production of clothing must decrease, the big question is how this reduction can happen, as long as growth remains the basic political premise, as discussed in the previous chapter.

The New Business Lynchpins

If production was in synchrony with the actual needs of the global population, then the sale of second-hand clothes, other good solutions for sharing, and good utilisation of the individual garments through repairs, etc. could ensure optimal use. These 'new business models' are generally promoted as the circular economy's lynchpin whenever one raises critique related to the focus on recycling either pre- or post-consumer surplus clothes and textiles. But to prolong the lifespan and use time of clothes within a system that already has too many, does not really make sense. For these reasons, we believe that the fundamental questions are what do we know about how much the industry produces, how much clothing do we, the population of this planet, have, and how much will we need in the future? And yes, we do recognise clothes' complex physical, social and historical significance, sometimes referred to as 'conventions of dress' (Entwistle, 2000).

Today, it is easy to forget that not very long ago, clothing were people's most valuable possessions, meticulously defined in the inheritance settlements (Ulväng, 2012, 2021), and an important element in the establishment of a global textile chain, such as the Silk Road from China. Developments in the global fibre trade have made two major leaps. Firstly, there was a leap in volume as a result of the slave trade and industrialisation which gave us cheap cotton and cheaper clothes. Secondly, there has been a leap as a result of the low price of synthetic fibres and rapidly growing production capacity linked to the free trade of fibres, mentioned in Chapter 6. The combination of the latter resulted in the rapid growth of synthetic fibres beginning in the 1980s. How much of the global fibre production ends up as clothes, we do not know, but clothes are the largest market, even though textiles are used in most industries such as interiors, transport, fishing and aquaculture. We know, however, that synthetics make up a large proportion of textiles used for clothing. A recent study from the UK shows that from 10,000 items being marketed online, on average 49% were made entirely of new polyester, acrylic, nylon and/or elastane—and as much as 88% contained at least some virgin plastic (The Royal Society of the Arts, 2021).

There is much we do not know about the size and composition of global textile production. One thing for which a reliable overview does exist is the quantity of produced textile fibres. We wrote in Chapter 2 that in 2019, polyester, polyamide and other synthetic fibres represented about 63% of the annual global fibre production, comprising about 66.6 million metric tonnes of plastic fibre (Textile Exchange, 2020). We also know something about the consequences of growth for the use of clothing. About 20% of garments in Norwegian wardrobes are either never worn or only worn a couple of times (Klepp & Laitala, 2016), and more than 30% of clothes in European wardrobes have not been worn in the last year (Šajn, 2019). Overproduction of textiles brought along a reduction in value. This reduction is visible in the form of declining prices, which make it hard to finance the sorting of used clothes (Glover, 2020b), as well as rental and repairing (Haugrønning et al., 2019). Growth itself thereby makes the 'circular' solutions unprofitable. A discussion with a starting point at the other end of the thread is needed.

In KRUS, one of the goals, as stated in Chapter 1, was to turn the discussions about sustainable fashion away from the one-sided so-called 'circular economy' debate and direct it towards a systemic change. During the project, it became increasingly evident that the growth ideology is the problem. However, we see that the narrow understanding of the circular economy is constantly gaining ground and is being promoted by politicians and businesses alike, precisely because it does not challenge economic growth and overproduction. Our position is therefore to begin from the opposite end; to show alternatives such as local production, but also to start a discussion about how big the production should actually be.

The Fibre Diet

Fibershed, which we have mentioned several times, works with this radical and local perspective and aims to become self-sufficient in fibre and dyes within a given geographical area (Burgess & White, 2019). This raises the question; how much is really needed? Burgess, Klepp, Fletcher and Tobiasson among others discussed this question at the concluding KRUS conference, in a discussion called *The Fibre Diet*, which underlines that the goal of fibre production is to dress the population so that they are both beautiful and warm, and feel well-dresses in their 'second skin'. The EAT foundation works with a similar mindset. Framed as a food diet, EAT is a non-profit organisation dedicated to transforming our global food systems. Based on nutritional physiology, it examines normatively how much food we need and how to compose our diets. This is further combined with the calculations related to a healthy and sustainable world. EAT has funded reports showing what an equitable distribution across a global 'carbon budget' for food could look like (Willett et al., 2019). The main message is that a diet with plenty of plant-based food and less animal-based foods will be the most beneficial for our health, but will also help to solve climate and environmental issues.

In the Norwegian public discussion, it was pointed out that the EAT report does not sufficiently take local cultural differences and circumstances into account.[3] This is interesting because if we transfer this mode of thinking to clothing, the current production system pays little attention to the local aspect. At the same time, our interest in a fibre diet springs from knowledge about just this: local clothes. These factors open up the emphasis on developing the local in a fibre diet in the same way that local and small-scale production must in one way or another enter into the work where comparisons of products and even food's environmental impacts are discussed.

One thing that is unique for the Fibre Diet, in the same way as EAT, is the vision for a fair and sustainable clothing system that suits all people and the planet.[4] Such a transition will particularly require the global North to address the wastefulness of today's clothing consumption, in alignment with UN SDG number 12 for sustainable consumption and production patterns. This is not the main responsibility of consumers, however, as it is the industry, such as the fast fashion system and its need for growth that has contributed to create an impression of 'more is more'. The 'I don't have anything to wear' mantra that has been a construct in the global North, while looking at an overstuffed wardrobe. Therefore, it becomes important to investigate how people wear clothes in order to better understand the increasing volumes of clothing, especially in wealthier societies, and the potential to reduce them. We will return to this point later.

---

[3] https://forskning.no/klima-kronikk-mat/mye-av-kritikken-og-fordommelsen-av-eat-lancet-rapporten-er-basert-pa-misforstaelser/1299197.

[4] See the official web page for EAT, eatforum.org.

Starting Out with a Budget

One way to obtain an overview of the consumption of clothes is to construct a budget. This is done in the Norwegian Reference Budget for Consumer Expenditures. The budget first appeared in 1987 but builds on a Swedish Consumer Agency (Konsumentverket) budget from 1978. The Reference budget calculates the cost of maintaining a reasonable level of consumption based on households of varying sizes, ages and gender composition. 'A standard budget approach can be described as a method to define the price tag of participation in ordinary activities in a given society' (Borgeraas, 2010). There is a close connection between empirical sociology, consumer studies, welfare studies and the development of statistics (Collette, 2000). Since the establishment of the Reference budget, interest in a material theoretical perspective, as well as consumption, has been forced into a marginal position (Borgeraas, 2010), which means that the development of knowledge, e.g. what kind of clothes we have and need, has lagged behind. There has been more emphasis on identity than materiality (Woodward, 2002) and the statistics available for clothing are poorly developed (Kassatly, 2020).

The Reference budget is one of few sources for a normative budget for clothing, which is also found in other European countries (Austgulen & Borgeraas, 2018). The budget is based on what goods and services are considered necessary for an acceptable standard of living, on a country-specific level. For clothing, the budget includes clothes (in addition to shoes and accessories) for ordinary sporting and leisure activities and formal occasions, and it takes into consideration that children and young people who are in a growth phase need clothes that fit. In the process of updating the Reference budget, it is decided what the different occasions are, where specific and new clothes are required, how much change is needed, and how long the clothes should last. A very typical example: Does the football team need new uniforms every season? The Reference budget also follows governmental advice for physical activity. The method used in the budget can be developed further to study additional costs, such as for consumer groups with specific challenges and needs, the sick and disabled (Laitala & Klepp, 2019), which thus shows costs related to being ill.

More recent developments where the quantity of clothes is central, do exist. As a result of the overabundance of clothing in wardrobes, tendencies for so-called 'voluntary minimalism' have appeared in affluent societies, exemplified by phenomena such as the 'KonMari method' by Marie Kondo (Kondo, 2014). Several books and blogs define modern minimalism as glamorous, and describe how 24 or 33 garments are enough and preferable (Klepp et al., 2019). Central to these movements is that the small wardrobes can still provide the possibility for full social participation. The minimalism is to some extent achieved through limited purchasing but mainly through decluttering of the current wardrobe. Therefore, minimalist wardrobes do not necessarily entail reduced environmental impact in total, it depends on if a person disposes of or purchases more or less (Klepp et al., 2019). The enthusiasm created by this phenomenon is, however, interesting as an example of challenging the number of clothes and throwaway culture, not mainly for the environmental impact. One of the results of such attempts is that it becomes easier to find something to wear and to gain an overview of the wardrobe and good outfits, and it may in general lead to slower consumption with less material acquisition (Chamberlin & Callmer, 2021). Another important topic to mention here is the concept of 'Consumption Corridors' that are defining minima and maxima of consumption that could be used to guide policy design and policy-making in sustainable consumption governance (Defila & Di Giulio, 2020; Vladimirova, 2021).

In the work of transitioning clothing production and consumption, a global snap-shot is essential, especially in terms of defining a fibre diet. Local conditions for clothing practices will become important. In some areas, there is overproduction, in others overconsumption and some areas are drowning in second-hand clothing. While the Reference budget has been developed within a welfare policy framework, the new perspectives on knowledge about the quantities and number of clothes we need to feel well-dressed will potentially transform the patterns that need to change, with the environment and Mother Earth's planetary boundaries as the overriding issue.

Wardrobe Studies Methods

In 2001, Klepp developed a new and ground-breaking method for studying the relationship between wardrobes and the use of clothing (Klepp, 2001). The method has been further developed in a Nordic collaboration (Skov, 2011), and as mentioned in Chapter 1 this resulted in a book in KRUS (Fletcher & Klepp, 2017). Wardrobe studies have gained importance for clothing research internationally since then, also for studying other consumer products (Fredriksen et al., 2013; van Nes & Cramer, 2006). The field of study has been useful for product development, teaching and design (Cramer, 2019), but above all, important in studies contributing to the environmental debate related to clothing. An important characteristic of wardrobe studies is that each garment is an analytical unit. Its history, use, value, shape, wear and materials are subject to systematic analysis.

In KRUS, the work related to these methods was further developed. Based on field studies in Tingvoll and Nordhordland in Norway, and Macclesfield in the UK, we looked at both wardrobes and the local infrastructure related to making, distributing, preserving and repairing clothes (Fletcher, 2018). The work also resulted in such diverse outcomes as a tour guide for Macclesfield, where Fletcher helped to raise awareness of the textile history and textile infrastructure through a walking map (*Fashion Ecologies Walk*). As there is little fibre or textile production left in this area, the walk centres around fabric suppliers, haberdasheries and businesses that support repair and making. Other results have been the Wool Heritage Route, also described in Chapters 1 and 5, which is much more a 'fibre to finished fully-fashioned product' approach. The latter will probably be more touristic and lead to shopping-sprees in factory-outlet stores, than the first one. That said, both 'tours' offer food for thought on where clothes originate and how local ecologies evolve. Perhaps those who participate will take an extra glance into their wardrobes to see what they actually own—and use, and how and with what their clothes are made—since this is the focus of the tours.

Subsequently, Klepp and Laitala have further developed wardrobe studies in collaboration with the Australian Wool Innovation (AWI) in a quantitative direction by using survey-based wardrobe audits, conducted by Nielsen AG, where wardrobes representing the largest global consumer markets were examined, namely UK, US, Germany, China and Japan. This has helped to improve knowledge about the use phase in LCAs and added to the general work with environmental comparisons as discussed in Chapters 2 and 6 (see for example Klepp et al., 2020; Laitala & Klepp, 2020b; Wiedemann et al., 2021). In possible future work with a fibre diet, geographical comparisons will be important. They will show both how clothing consumption differs, but also what types of textile history and environmental challenges exist, as well as what fibres belong to a *terroir*.

Burgess has started this work in California. What does the Californian wardrobe look like? To support the emergence of regional textile economies she needed a clear picture of the wardrobes across the community and where clothes come from and where they will end up when they are worn out. Fibershed and partners at @ecocitybuilders asked people to help through an online wardrobe survey. The plan is to aggregate this information to produce publicly available data that will bring about a healthier textile system that is rooted in ecological restoration and regional manufacturing. The system has been developed by a team of volunteer software engineers and non-profit partners.

We now know increasingly more about quantities and longevity related to clothing, as more and more variations of wardrobe studies have been conducted. An article about the Norwegian national costume and the sari (Klepp et al., 2014), found that while the traditional attire, bunad, in Norway is a one-time investment in a garment that at least ideally refers to where you are from, the Indian traditional attire, sari, is something that is expected to be replaced and varied for social occasions (Klepp et al., 2014). This indicates that it is not only in a system with frequent 'fashion changes', where change can be an established practice and create expectations, but also that there are clothes that are exempt from this requirement. The solutions for expectations of variation are also many, with informal networks, exchange and gifting involved, as well as renting and buying second-hand clothes. The difference between these practices still raises many unanswered questions: Why does age and perhaps even constant use over time give an outfit value, but for another items of clothing results in devaluation? Local clothing customs can include resources for change, where care, repair and the actual use of the clothes can be included. Since clothes have been seen and studied through a perspective where the change (i.e. fashion) has been a dominant discourse, there is a lot we do not know about clothes related to the persistence of use and how we actually can develop a true and meaningful relationship with our wardrobes over time.

Several of the contributing authors will continue to develop this suite of tools and the knowledge-base in the project CHANGE: Environmental system shift in clothing consumption. The project involves studies on how occasions and clothing standards in everyday life contribute to driving the volume of clothing, and thus how we can understand growth, not only as overproduction in general but also overconsumption of clothing. This research is in the tradition of a Social Practice Theory (SPT) approach (Shove et al., 2012), which provides analytical tools to study the relationship between the performance of practices and their social ordering (Mylan & Southerton, 2018), as constitutive elements that configure how clothing is acquired, used and disposed of. Clothing consumption will thus be studied through the relationship between 'occasions' (all practices, both ordinary and special occasions, that require clothing), the 'wardrobe' (clothes a person owns or has access to) and the volume of clothes acquired and disposed of, and thereby form a more solid base for future projects on a fibre diet. SIFO also continues the work on examining why and how clothes and textiles are disposed of, and the role synthetic textiles have in this, in the WASTED TEXTILES project.[5] Here, too, we will emphasise local solutions, so that discarded clothes and textiles are better utilised in local settings.

Missing Pieces and Further Work

When and if a policy change to reduce quantity actually takes hold, it is extremely important that information on the durability and functionality of clothes is easily accessible to consumers. This is because, when there

[5] More information on SIFO's projects can be found at clothingresearch.oslomet.no.

is less clothing on the market, the prices of both new and used clothing will increase and it also becomes more important to be able to recognise quality and durability. There is still a lot of work to be done here, but we believe that in the same way that obesity can be a result of poor nutrition, eating too much without actually getting what your body needs, we think that the over-consumption of clothes is related to the poor state of our clothes. Fletcher refers to this as a lack of 'good roots' (Fletcher, 2018). In line with ecological thinking, plants with short roots (in a typically non-regenerative agricultural system) will not be able to utilise the earth's resources or variations in water availability, etc. This is also the case with clothes, the short roots make them less resistant to changes in taste, less resilient related to our needs and they are therefore unsatisfactory and leave us less well-dressed. Thus, we return to the driving forces intrinsic to local actors, in order to find clothes and production methods with deeper roots. It is interesting to note that the word 'regenerative' in connection with fashion, seems to be increasingly on the menu.

In the work towards a global and local fibre diet, we will need to discuss the relationship between natural materials (fibre, dyes and other textile finishes), resources and human needs. It is not the case that wool—or another fibre—will be able to make up the entire 'diet'. We will probably have to keep producing and using synthetic textiles for some important purposes. We, therefore, need to start a discussion about what the different materials are best suited for. Is it an absolute certainty that cotton is best for bedding (Klepp et al., 2016)? And are synthetic materials the only alternative for providing waterproof, windproof and breathable clothing (Klepp & Haugrønning, 2021)? We need knowledge, discussion and product development. This is in many ways equivalent to the knowledge that EAT has gathered from specialists in nutrition. Knowledge about antioxidants, vitamins, proteins and the composition of calories and fibre has come a long way in the field of food, while clothing research has not received the same attention and has therefore not had the same resources to develop this breadth in understanding for the functions of clothing. This is ironic since we have one important element in common: Fibre.

The important thing, both in the work with a fibre diet and in the work with wool and other natural resources, is that in the future, we must find good ways to utilise and appreciate what we have and can use as locally as possible, and within the planetary boundaries. This means that we must use resources in the best possible way—and never use resources that are suitable or irreplaceable for other functions in a way that does not respect this. All this was once a matter of common sense. Perhaps we must learn to walk the talk once again. In Norwegian, we have a saying 'need teaches a naked woman to spin', which in English is 'necessity is the mother of invention'. We can hope the saying can be flipped so that we can use both the knowledge we have—and the knowledge we see is lacking—to solve the challenges that stand in the way of a good life for our descendants, who will hopefully be walking the Earth, also those on four legs, the off-spring of today's wool producers. We may not all have to learn how to spin, out of a dire need in the sense of being naked; necessity, in a world of diminishing resources, may however lead us to question exactly what we need to spin, how we weave our communities together… or even how we yarn a better future.

References

Austgulen, M. H., & Borgeraas, E. (2018). *Review of the Norwegian reference budget in light of similar initiatives across Europe*. Retrieved from Oslo. https://fagarkivet.oslomet.no/handle/20.500.12199/3860

Becker, J. (2016). *The more of less: Finding the life you want under everything you own*. WaterBrook

Borgeraas, E. (2010). Household standard budgets. In K. M. Ekström (Ed.), *Consumer behaviour: A Nordic perspective* (pp. 359–380). Studentlitteratur.

Burgess, R., & White, C. (2019). *Fibershed: Growing a movement of farmers, fashion activists, and makers for a new textile economy*. Chelsea Green Publishing.

Castellani, V., Sala, S., & Mirabella, N. (2015). Beyond the throwaway society: A life cycle-based assessment of the environmental benefit of reuse. *Integrated Environmental Assessment and Management, 11*(3), 373–382. https://doi.org/10.1002/ieam.1614

Chamberlin, L., & Callmer, Å. (2021). Spark joy and slow consumption: An empirical study of the impact of the KonMari method on acquisition and

wellbeing. *Journal of Sustainability Research, 3*(1), e210007. https://doi.org/10.20900/jsr20210007
Collette, J.-M. (2000). *Empirical inquiries and the assessment of social progress in Western Europe: A historical perspective.* Retrieved from Geneva.
Cramer, J. (2019). *The living wardrobe: Fashion design for an extended garment lifetime* (PhD). RMIT Univeristy.
Cullinane, S., Browne, M., Karlsson, E., & Wang, Y. (2019). Retail clothing returns: A review of key issues. In P. Wells (Ed.), *Contemporary operations and logistics: Achieving excellence in turbulent times* (pp. 301–322). Springer International Publishing.
Cullinane, S., & Cullinane, K. (2021). The logistics of online clothing returns in sweden and how to reduce its environmental impact. *Journal of Service Science and Management, 14*(1), 24. https://doi.org/10.4236/jssm.2021.141006
Defila, R., & Di Giulio, A. (2020). The concept of "consumption corridors" meets society: How an idea for fundamental changes in consumption is received. *Journal of Consumer Policy, 43*(2), 315–344. https://doi.org/10.1007/s10603-019-09437-w
EC. (2018). *Directive (EU) 2018 of the European Parliament and of the Council of the European Union amending Directive 2008/98/EC on Waste (Text with EEA Relevance).* https://www.europarl.europa.eu/meetdocs/2014_2019/plmrep/COMMITTEES/ENVI/DV/2018/02-26/AG-WFD_EN.pdf
Entwistle, J. (2000). Fashion and the fleshy body: Dress as embodied practice. *Fashion Theory: The Journal of Dress, Body and Culture, 4*, 323–347. https://doi.org/10.2752/136270400778995471
Farrant, L. (2008). *Environmental benefits from reusing clothes* (Masters thesis). Technical University of Denmark, Kgs. Lyngby. http://etd.dtu.dk/thesis/240978/
Fletcher, K. (2018). *Presentation at the warm threads conference in Oslo.* https://www.youtube.com/watch?v=aoKCwKe15tk&ab_channel=OsloMet
Fletcher, K., & Klepp, I. G. (Eds.). (2017). *Opening up the wardrobe: A methods book.* Novus.
Fletcher, K., & Tham, M. (2019). *Earth logic: Fashion action research plan.* JJ Charitable Trust.
Fredriksen, M., Graabæk, H., & Skjold, E. (2013). *Shoes—How we use them.* How we design them. https://www.designskolenkolding.dk/en/publications/shoes-how-we-use-them-how-we-design-them-0

Glover, S. (2020a, October 21). Pandemic 'hits garment supply chain hard'. *EcoTextileNews*. https://www.ecotextile.com/2020102126888/materials-production-news/covid-19-hits-garment-supply-chain-hard.html

Glover, S. (2020b). Pandemic closes down recycling markets. *EcoTextileNews* (97), 57.

Haugrønning, V., Klepp, I. G., Strandbakken, P., Laitala, K., & Throne-Holst, H. (2019). *Leve av å reparere? En studie av økonomien i reparasjonsbransjen for klær og hvitevarer*.

John, T. (2018, May 28). How the US and Rwanda have fallen out over second-hand clothes. *BBC News*. https://www.bbc.com/news/world-africa-44252655

Kassatly, V. B. (2020). Was it polyester all along? *Apparel Insider (14)*. https://www.veronicabateskassatly.com/read/was-it-polyester-all-along

Kirchherr, J., Reike, D., & Hekkert, M. (2017). Conceptualizing the circular economy: An analysis of 114 definitions. *Resources, Conservation and Recycling, 127*, 221–232. https://doi.org/10.1016/j.resconrec.2017.09.005

Klepp, I. G. (2001). *Hvorfor går klær ut av bruk? Avhending sett i forhold til kvinners klesvaner [Why are clothes no longer used? Clothes disposal in relationship to women's clothing habits]*. Retrieved from Oslo. http://www.sifo.no/files/file48469_rapport2001-03web.pdf

Klepp, I. G., & Haugrønning, V. (2021). *Naturgarvet skinn i et miljøperspektiv*.

Klepp, I. G., & Laitala, K. (2016). *Klesforbruk i Norge*. Retrieved from Oslo. http://www.sifo.no/files/file80519_fagrapport_nr._2-2016_rapport_klesforbruk.pdf

Klepp, I. G., Laitala, K., & Haugrønning, V. (2019). *Wardrobe sizes and clothing lifespans*. Paper presented at the Product Lifetimes and the Environment (PLATE), Berlin.

Klepp, I. G., Laitala, K., & Tobiasson, T. S. (2016). *Woolbed—Sweet dreams in merino*. Retrieved from Oslo. http://sifo.no/files/file80443_oppdragsrapport_no_2_2016_-_woolbed_final.pdf

Klepp, I. G., Laitala, K., & Wiedmann, S. (2020). Clothing lifespans: What should be measured and how. *Sustainability, 12*(15).

Klepp, I. G., Vramo, L., & Laitala, K. (2014). Too old: Clothes and value in Norwegian and Indian wardrobes. In M.-L. Nosch, Z. Feng, & L. Varadrajan (Eds.), *Global textile encounters* (Vol. 20, pp. 237–244). Oxbow Books.

Kondo, M. (2014). *The life-changing magic of tidying: A simple, effective way to banish clutter forever*. Random House.

Laitala, K., & Klepp, I. G. (2019). Dressing a demanding body to fit in—Clean and decent with ostomy or chronic skin disease. *Social inclusion, 7*(1). https://doi.org/10.17645/si.v7i1.1717

Laitala, K., & Klepp, I. G. (2020a). *Klær og miljø: Innkjøp, gjenbruk og vask* (3-2020).

Laitala, K., & Klepp, I. G. (2020b). What affects garment lifespans? International clothing practices based on a wardrobe survey in China, Germany, Japan, the UK, and the USA. *Sustainability, 12*(21), 9151. https://www.mdpi.com/2071-1050/12/21/9151

Mylan, J., & Southerton, D. (2018). The social ordering of an everyday practice: The case of laundry. *Sociology, 52*(6), 1134–1151. https://doi.org/10.1177/0038038517722932

Nørup, N. (2019). *An environmental assessment of the collection, reuse, recycling and disposal of clothing and household textile waste* (PhD). Technical University of Denmark, Kgs. Lyngby. https://backend.orbit.dtu.dk/ws/files/178411162/Thesis_online_version_Nynne_N_rup.pdf

Šajn, N. (2019). *Environmental imapct of the textile and clothing industry: What consumers need to know* (PE.633.143). https://www.europarl.europa.eu/RegData/etudes/BRIE/2019/633143/EPRS_BRI(2019)633143_EN.pdf

Shove, E., Pantzar, M., & Watson, M. (2012). *The dynamics of social practice: Everyday life and how it changes*. London: SAGE Publications Ltd.

Skov, L. (2011). Entering the space of the wardrobe. *Creative Encounters Working Papers Series, 58*. http://hdl.handle.net/10398/8277

SSB. (2019). *Table 08812: External trade in goods, by commodity group (two-digit SITC), country and mode of transport (tonnes) 1988–2018*. Retrieved from https://www.ssb.no/tabell/08812

Textile Exchange. (2020). *Preferred fiber & materials market report 2020*. https://textileexchange.org/wp-content/uploads/2020/06/Textile-Exchange_Preferred-Fiber-Material-Market-Report_2020.pdf

The Royal Society of the Arts. (2021). *Fast fashion's plastic problem: Sustainability and material usage in online fashion*. https://www.thersa.org/globalassets/reports/2021/fast-fashions-plastic-problem.pdf

Turnbull, S. (2019). *A qualitative study of the causes, implications, and potential solultions*. https://www.wornmorethanonce.com/

Ulväng, M. (2012). *Klädekonomi och klädkultur: böndernas kläder i Härjedalen under 1800-talet*. Gidlunds förlag.

Ulväng, M. (2021). Clothing economy and clothing culture: The farm wardrobe from a gendered perspective in nineteenth-century Sweden.

Gender & History, 33(2), 365–389. https://doi.org/10.1111/1468-0424.12543

van Nes, N., & Cramer, J. (2006). Product lifetime optimization: A challenging strategy towards more sustainable consumption patterns. *Journal of Cleaner Production, 14*(15–16), 1307–1318. https://doi.org/10.1016/j.jclepro.2005.04.006

Vladimirova, K. (2021). Consumption corridors in fashion: Deliberations on upper consumption limits in minimalist fashion challenges. *Sustainability: Science, Practice and Policy, 17*(1), 103–117. https://doi.org/10.1080/15487733.2021.1891673

Watson, D., Hvass, K. K., Moora, H., Martin, K., Nausėdė, V., Gurauskiene, I., & Akule, D. (2020). *Post-consumer textile circularity in the Baltic countries: Current status and recommendations for the future*. Nordisk Ministerråd.

Watson, D., Palm, D., Brix, L., Amstrup, M., Syversen, F., & Nielsen, R. (2016). *Exports of Nordic used textiles: Fate, benefits and impacts*. Nordisk Ministerråd.

Watson, D., Trzepacz, S., Rubach, S., & Johnsen, F. M. (2020). *Kartlegging av brukte tekstiler og tekstilavfall i Norge*. Retrieved from Oslo. https://norsus.no/wp-content/uploads/or1120-kartlegging-av-brukte-tekstiler-og-tekstilavfall-i-norge.pdf

Wiedemann, S. G., Biggs, L., Nguyen, Q. V., Clarke, S. J., Laitala, K., & Klepp, I. G. (2021). Reducing environmental impacts from garments through best practice garment use and care, using the example of a Merino wool sweater. *The International Journal of Life Cycle Assessment*. https://doi.org/10.1007/s11367-021-01909-x

Willett, W., Rockström, J., Loken, B., Springmann, M., Lang, T., Vermeulen, S., … Wood, A. (2019). Food in the anthropocene: The EAT–Lancet Commission on healthy diets from sustainable food systems. *The Lancet, 393*(10170), 447–492.

Wolfe, I. (2018). *Capsule wardrobes: How to build a sustainable closet for life*. https://goodonyou.eco/capsule-wardrobes-create-your-own/

Woodward, S. (2002). Book review: Making fashion material. *Journal of Material Culture, 7*(3), 345–353. https://doi.org/10.1177/135918350200700305

Correction to: Upping the WOOLUME: Waste Prevention Based on Optimal Use of Materials

Vilde Haugrønning, Jan Broda,
Ingvild Svorkmo Espelien, Ingun Grimstad Klepp,
Katarzyna Kobiela-Mendrek, Monika Rom,
Anna Schytte Sigaard, and Tone Skårdal Tobiasson

Correction to:
Chapter 3 in: I. G. Klepp and T. S. Tobiasson (eds.), ***Local, Slow and Sustainable Fashion*****,**
https://doi.org/10.1007/978-3-030-88300-3_3

The original version of this chapter was inadvertently published with incorrect figure credits for Chapter 3 (Figs. 3.2 and 3.3), which have been corrected now. The corrections to the chapter have been updated with the changes.

The updated version of this chapter can be found at
https://doi.org/10.1007/978-3-030-88300-3_3

I. G. Klepp and T. S. Tobiasson (eds.), *Local, Slow and Sustainable Fashion*,
https://doi.org/10.1007/978-3-030-88300-3_8

Glossary

Afforestation is when new trees are planted or seeds are sown in an area where there were no trees before, creating a new forest. Reforestation, in contrast, is planting where the number of trees in a forest has been decreasing.

Biosphere is made up of the parts of Earth where life exists. The biosphere extends from the deepest root systems of trees to the dark environment of ocean trenches, to rain forests and high mountaintops. Since life exists on the ground, in the air and in the water, the biosphere overlaps all of these spheres.

Bunad is a Norwegian term for a type of clothing and dress. The word comes from 'kledebunad' which translates into 'clothing outfit'. Unlike 'folk dress' ('folkedrakt' in Norwegian), it does not necessarily demand roots in traditional rural clothing, but can also be later revitalised or designed costumes. 'Kofte' or 'gákti', is an example of a Sámi bunad, and this is also a folk dress. The bunad movement has its roots in 19-century national romanticism, not only in Norway. In Norway the national romantic ideas had a lasting impact on clothing and bunad became an important form of dress. One has seen a similar development in the tartans and kilts in Scotland, relating to building national identity. We find around 450 distinct bunads in Norway today, and close to 80% of Norwegian women own one. Among men, more than 20% own a bunad, and the number is increasing.

I. G. Klepp and T. S. Tobiasson (eds.), *Local, Slow and Sustainable Fashion*, https://doi.org/10.1007/978-3-030-88300-3

Carbon–neutral or Climate-neutral are two promises increasingly made by countries, major companies and initiatives, specifically in the textile sector, which involves a date where this will define their business as a whole. The actual calculations involved are highly complex and can involve off-setting schemes, such as carbon offsets, which can be either voluntary or compliant. In the EU's Emission Trading Scheme companies, government, or other entities buy carbon offsets to comply with 'caps' on the total amount they are allowed to emit per year.

Climate-positive is a claim that goes beyond carbon–neutral and where the country, company or organisation claims to sequester carbon more than the total operation and activity actually emits.

Carding is a mechanical process that disentangles, cleans and intermixes fibres to produce a continuous web or sliver suitable for subsequent processing. The word is used both when carding by hand and in the industrial process.

Chaku is a system of rounding up vicuñas every three years, for shearing. The system includes celebrations and dates back to the Inca culture.

Commission spinning is a system where a spinning mill scours (though not always), cards and spins wool delivered from local producers and returns the result in the form of pre-yarn (tops), yarns and even finished products. This is an old system that is seeing a renaissance today; however not so much with finished products. This enables the production of local yarns, from local farms or regions, even though the region does not have a local infrastructure in the form of a spinning mill. (See **Out-putting**.)

Commoning is a verb to describe the social practices used by commoners in the course of managing shared resources and reclaiming the commons. It was coined by historian Peter Linebaugh.

Crossbred is a collective term for all sheep with even-length wool, and a long tail. Crossbred sheep are usually white, but can be pigmented. Crossbred has a slightly stronger, highly crimped wool, which has a higher micron count and therefore is not as soft to the skin. In New Zealand, this type of wool is called 'strong wool', and it is mainly used for carpeting, some knitting yarns and other uses that are not necessarily next-to-skin. 85% of sheep in Norway are crossbred.

Dual-coated wool describes a wool fleece with coarser **guard hairs** and a soft **inner coat**. This wool type is found on older sheep breeds and goats. It can be spun after the fibres have been separated into the two, partially or completely. In older times, when this was done manually, the wool had multiple resulting products. In industrial handling, this is harder, though 'dehairing' technology for cashmere fibres has been developed that could possibly work for the older sheep breeds.

Duodji means 'handicraft' in the Sámi language. It is today used about the traditional, Sámi crafts and artisanal crafts. Duodji-teaching was earlier an embedded part of the Sámi upbringing, similar to other Indigenous cultures' transfer of knowledge. Today the Sámi duodji label is a Nordic Sámi trademark that guarantees the provenance and use of traditional techniques and materials. 'Soft' duodji is connected with textile and leather products, 'hard' duodji are metal, stone, bone and woodworkings.

Fast fashion is a term used to describe a business model originally based on replicating catwalk trends and made profitable by mass-producing high-fashion designs at a low cost for the global market. This business model was made possible during the late twentieth century, with the rise of synthetic raw materials, the move of production to the global South with cheap labour and little control over pollution and other environmental and socio-economic consequences. The model, or production system, has been replicated for other clothing genres, e.g. activewear and childrenswear, and is characterised by the speed of the turn-over, and built-in planned obsolescence of the products.

Fibershed is a term coined by Rebecca Burgess in 2011 to describe a geographical landscape that defines and gives boundaries to a natural textile resource base. The production, use and disposal of textiles, or a textile economy, is inextricably linked to our food systems and watershed environments.

Finnsheep is the local breed in Finland with exceptionally soft wool.

Fleece is the word for the sheep's wool when sheared.

Fulling also called walking (in Norwegian 'valking', in the UK defined and sold as 'broadcloth') is a finishing process where the woven textile goes through a process where water, temperature and the most important component physical 'pounding', in order to thicken the fibres to give more strength and increase waterproofing. It is a similar process to felting, which produces a non-woven material.

Gamme is the Norwegian word for a goahti, a Sámi hut often covered with peat moss.

Gákti —(see kofte).

Greasy wool is wool that has not been scoured. The wool is heavier, feels greasier, as it contains lanolin.

Grene is the Norwegian word for the **rátnu**, a rectangular woven wool textile, produced on a warp-weighted loom with three selvedges. The grene is an important element in **Duodji**. The weave is thick and heavy and has had many end-uses. Today it is mainly used for wall decoration.

Grey Gotland sheep is the indigenous name for the Swedish island of Gotland. The breed is in the Northern European short-tailed sheep family and is thought to be a cross between the island's native landrace, Gute and other imported breeds, during the 1920s and 1930s. In Norway, the Pelssau breed is similar.

Grey Trønder sheep is a Norwegian crossbred sheep breed with a history that goes back to mediaeval times. The history is opaque, but as monks were early purveyors of sheep handling all over Europe, this breed has its story tied to a monk order in the Norwegian region of Trøndelag. The fleece is grey, so the wool is currently sorted by grades of grey in order to produce naturally pigmented yarns in different shades.

Guard hairs are the coarse outer coat wool in the fleece from dual-coated sheep.

Indigenous peoples as a concept is hard, and even impossible, to define; as they are our predecessors. However, bodies such as the United Nations, the Norwegian government and others have attempted, and here is our alignment of these definitions They are descendants of the original inhabitants of a territory, for example, defeated by conquest. They are focussed on eco-systems, maintain permanent or nomadic systems of farmers, shepherds, hunters and gatherers, fishermen or artisans, who adopt a strategy of multiple use of appropriation of nature. They practice small-scale rural production through intensive (non-industrialised) labour that produces few surpluses and in systems with low energy needs. They generally, but not always, lack centralised political institutions, and a feature is that they organise their lives at the community level, and make decisions based on consensus. They may also share values, beliefs, clothing and other identifying characteristics, as well as a relationship with a particular territory. In addition, their world-vision had been expressed as a non-materialistic custodial attitude towards the land and natural resources based on symbiotic exchange. The concept can also be defined as a member of a community retaining memories of a life lived sustainably on a land base, as part of that land base. Thus, Indigenous knowledge is any application of those memories as living knowledge to improve present and future circumstances.

Innercoat is the soft underwool in the fleece from dual-coated sheep. In Norwegian the term is 'bunnull', which is ironic, as 'bunn' is also bottom.

Intangible cultural heritage includes traditions or living expressions inherited from our ancestors and passed on to our descendants, such as oral traditions, performing arts, social practices, rituals, festive events, knowledge and practices concerning nature and the universe or the knowledge and skills to produce traditional craft.

Kemp —hollow wool hairs.

Kofte is a sweater/cardigan or another type of clothing that covers the upper body, often with sleeves and either with or without an open solution for buttoning or zipping up. The kofte has particularly referred to the outer garment which may be made of leather, fur or heavy woollen fabrics (fulled or felted) such as the Sámi kofte (see under), both for women and men.

Kofte is also the designation of the Sámi folk costume. In North Sámi it is called 'gákti', in South Sámi 'gåptoe' or 'gapta' and in Lule Sámi 'gaping'. The cardigan is considered an important expression of Sámi culture and identity. The Sámi costumes are used across national borders in the North Calotte (Sápmi), in the same way as Sámi languages and other cultural features. The shape, colour and pattern of the cardigan and hat, and other elements such as the shawl, vary from district to district.

Life Cycle Assessment (LCA) is a methodology for assessing environmental impacts associated with all the stages of the life cycle of a product, process, or service. For a product like wool Environmental impacts are assessed from raw material extraction farming (cradle), and processing through the product's manufacture, distribution and use, to the recycling or final disposal of the materials composing it (grave). An LCA study involves an inventory of the energy and materials that are required across the value chain and calculates the corresponding emissions to the environment. If the aim is to document and improve the overall environmental footprint of the product this will be an attribunal LCA; which should not be used in comparisons. For comparisons between products (or fibres), only comparative LCAs using the exact same boundaries should be used.

Medullation —wool hairs with a mellow, i.e. hollow.

Merino sheep are a breed or group of breeds of domesticated long tailed sheep, that are characterised by soft, fine wool and bred for their wool rather than meat and/or milk. The wool has a long, even-length staple, is generally less than 24 microns in diameter. Merino wool represents around half of the world's wool production and is mainly used in apparel. Australia is by far the largest Merino wool producing country, followed by New Zealand, Argentina, South Africa and Uruguay.

Minga is a Spanish word used in South America which connotates expertise, learning and social interactions between women in close, trusted relationships.

Nordic Welfare Model is a concept designating how the Nordic states take responsibility for the welfare of their citizens. This is a specific form of the welfare state which to a large extent guarantees the members of society help if they should suffer from health failure, social distress or loss of income, for example in the event of unemployment or old age, and which ensures the individual right to education. Typical of the Nordic welfare state is that the state's benefits are general, i.e. not means-tested (as several European states do) and not dependent on payments and insurance as, for example, welfare in the USA is organised. The welfare state is largely financed through general taxation, i.e. taxes on income, consumption and wealth that is not directly linked to welfare benefits. Most public services are free or only require a small deductible in the Nordic countries.

Norwegian Old Spælsheep is the older of the short-tailed Spæl breed in Norway. It stems from the Old Norse breed, with the same short tail and pigmented, dual-coated wool.

Norwegian White Spælsheep is a more modern version of Spæl Sheep in Norway and is also the main breed in Iceland. After 1950, the breed was bred for more colour uniformity and polledness (lack of horns). The lustre of the wool has been important for textile art and tapestries. The Spæl sheep has been central to Norwegian textile arts, crafts and handicrafts. The special shine in the sheep's wool, together with the incredible strength that the smooth cover hairs give, made it sought after for textile art and handicraft production. It ensured that tapestries have both shine and duration. Several Norwegian spinning mills have delivered handicraft yarns in this wool for tapestry-weaving.

Nålebinding is a technique for making textiles from thread, using a needle. Loops are sewn together with over a hundred different types of stitches. The technique is very old and has been used both in and outside Europe. It is characterised by its flexibility and strength. Unlike knitting and other techniques with loops, it cannot unravel. The needle can be made from wood, bone and other materials.

Old Norse breed is descended from the sheep that once were common throughout all of Europe. Dual-coated, pigmented wool with a short tail. These are the sheep that are genetically closest to the Indigenous sheep breeds throughout Europe.

Pastoralism is a form of animal husbandry where livestock are released onto large vegetated outdoor lands (pastures).

Planetary boundaries is a concept involving Earth system processes that contain environmental boundaries. It was proposed in 2009 by a group of Earth system and environmental scientists, led by Johan Rockström, from the Stockholm Resilience Centre and Will Steffen from the Australian National University.

Pulk is a Sámi sledge that is pulled behind. This has become a popular way of transporting infants when cross-country skiing in the Nordic region.

Putting out is in German called 'kaufsystem', in Norwegian 'forlagsvirksomhet'. The system was based on merchants who supplied the raw material, also in some cases rental of machinery, and then bought the final products to resell.

Rangeland grazing is the utilisation of land supporting vegetation suitable for grazing such as shrublands, woodlands, wetlands and deserts. Types of rangelands include tallgrass and shortgrass prairies, desert grasslands and shrublands, woodlands, savannas, chaparrals, steppes and tundra. Rangelands do not include forests lacking grazable understory vegetation, barren desert, farmland. Livestock grazes extensive native vegetation. Rangelands are also managed principally with practices such as managed livestock grazing and prescribed fire rather than more intensive agricultural practices of seeding, irrigation and the use of fertilisers.

Rátnu —(see grene)

Regenerative agriculture is a conservation and rehabilitation approach to food and farming systems that focuses on topsoil regeneration, increasing biodiversity, improving the water cycle, enhancing ecosystem services, supporting bio-sequestration, increasing resilience to climate change and strengthening the health and vitality of farm soil. Practices include recycling as much farm waste as possible and adding composted material from sources outside the farm, with minimal chemical input.

Rooing is plucking the wool by hand, without shearing.

Scouring is the process of washing wool to remove grease and dirt.

Shearing is the process of removing the fleece from a sheep by a mechanical or electrically powered handpiece, such as a scissor or shaving apparatus.

Spindle whorl is a disc or spherical object fitted onto the spindle to increase and maintain the speed of the spin. It is one of the objects that prove textile activity when found in graves and excavation sites.

Spæl sheep are named for their short tail, and is a collective term for a group of sheep breeds. Spæl sheep are descended from the oldest sheep in Europe, which dominated in Norway until the import of crossbred from the eighteenthcentury onwards. They are distinguished by their dual-coated wool, and they also often have horns. They are also referred to as the older breeds and as a landrace.

Sustainable development is that which satisfies the needs of the present generations without compromising the abilities of future generations to satisfy their own needs.

Terroir is an era or terrain, usually rather small, whose soil and microclimate impart distinctive qualities to products.

Transhumance is a type of pastoralism or nomadism, a seasonal movement of livestock between fixed summer and winter pastures. In mountain regions ('vertical transhumance'), it implies movement between higher pastures in summer and lower valleys in winter.

Tufting is a textile technique where the yarn is stitched to a backing fabric so that a loop or cut pile is formed on one side of the surface. The technique is mostly used to produce rugs and carpets.

Value chain is a word that originates from business management and then denotes a set of activities that a company operating in a specific industry performs in order to deliver a valuable. The term is also used about the many different processes that follow one another from the extraction of raw materials to finished product, and in our perspective also the use of the product. The value chain for wool is long and complex and consists of farming, scouring, carding, spinning, weaving/knitting, sewing, dyeing, etc. Most of the projects in this book are based on a value chain perspective, in that they aim to develop collaboration and improvement throughout the whole value chain.

Vegetable matter is residue from plants, straw, etc. that remains in the wool fleece after shearing and which creates problems downstream, specifically when the yarns or fabrics are dyed.

Wardrobe studies is a research method for acquiring knowledge about clothing habits. The method has been developed over the last 20 years and is suitable for environmental research on textiles. The focus of a wardrobe study is on each individual garment, its history, use and possible future, as well as form, function and materials. Wardrobe studies have helped to anchor clothing research in the study of materials.

Warp is the longitudinal yarns that are held stationary in tension on a frame or loom.

Warp-weighted loom is the simple and ancient form of loom in which the warp yarns hang freely from a bar supported by upright poles. Bundles of warp threads are tied to hanging weights, called loom weights, which keep the threads taut.

Weft is the transverse yarn that is drawn through and inserted over and under the **warp.**

Wool station is the physical place where the wool is collected after shearing in Norway, mainly in connection with a slaughterhouse.

Worsted wool is wool that has been carded so that the fibres lie parallel, as opposed to woollen yarns; where the fibres are not parallel and therefore allow for more air to be trapped in the yarn.

Yarning is an expression used by Tyson Yunkaporta in his writing, connotating the spinning of words and thoughts, conversation and textile work together.

Index

I. G. Klepp and T. S. Tobiasson (eds.), *Local, Slow and Sustainable Fashion*, https://doi.org/10.1007/978-3-030-88300-3

The manufacturer's authorised representative in the EU is Springer
Nature Customer Service Centre GmbH, Europaplatz 3, 69115 Heidelberg,
Germany. If you have any concerns regarding our products, please
contact ProductSafety@springernature.com

Printed and bound by CPI Group (UK) Ltd, Croydon, CR0 4YY
30/09/2026
02225499-0003